M000275488

Charles Boyer

Charles Boyer
The French Lover

John Baxter

UNIVERSITY PRESS OF KENTUCKY

Scholarly publisher for the Commonwealth,
serving Bellarmine University, Berea College, Centre
College of Kentucky, Eastern Kentucky University,
The Filson Historical Society, Georgetown College,
Kentucky Historical Society, Kentucky State University,
Morehead State University, Murray State University,
Northern Kentucky University, Spalding University,
Transylvania University, University of Kentucky,
University of Louisville, and Western Kentucky University.
All rights reserved.

Editorial and Sales Offices: The University Press of Kentucky
663 South Limestone Street, Lexington, Kentucky 40508-4008
www.kentuckypress.com

Unless otherwise noted, photographs are from the author's collection.

Library of Congress Cataloging-in-Publication Data

Names: Baxter, John, 1939– author.
Title: Charles Boyer : the French lover / John Baxter.
Description: Lexington, Kentucky : The University Press of Kentucky, [2021]
  | Includes bibliographical references, filmography, and index.
Identifiers: LCCN 2021026151 | ISBN 9780813155524 (hardcover) |
  ISBN 9780813155562 (pdf) | ISBN 9780813155555 (epub)
Subjects: LCSH: Boyer, Charles, 1899–1978. | Actors—United States—
  Biography. | Actors—France—Biography.
Classification: LCC PN2287.B67 B39 2021 | DDC 791.4302/8092 [B]—dc23

This book is printed on acid-free paper meeting
the requirements of the American National Standard
for Permanence in Paper for Printed Library Materials.

Manufactured in the United States of America.

Member of the Association
of University Presses

Contents

Preface   vii

1. The Eyes of a Stranger   1
2. All Quiet on the Western Front   5
3. Paris   8
4. On the Road   14
5. To Be Famous and to Be Loved   17
6. Movies   21
7. Bernstein   25
8. On Trial   31
9. Ufa and After   34
10. Mid-Atlantic   40
11. A Ride on the Carousel   46
12. The Boyer Type   50
13. The Love of His Life   53
14. Japanese Sandman   60
15. Think American   65
16. Discord   68
17. The Sleeping Prince   71
18. "Only God and I Know What Is in My Heart"   75
19. The Best Headwaiter in Europe   81
20. Immortal Longings   85
21. Exiles   90
22. Lazy and Hot and Happy   96

Contents

23. "Come with Me to the Casbah" 99

24. Sex on the High Seas 103

25. The Gathering Storm 108

26. Blood, Toil, Sweat, and Tears 112

27. The World's Best-Dressed Governess 116

28. The War at Home 121

29. A Voice Singing in the Snow 128

30. The Golden Door 131

31. The Most Popular Frenchman in America 136

32. Love and Death 142

33. Not What It Looks Like 147

34. Love in a Cold Climate 150

35. Stranger in a Strange Land 156

36. "Why, This Is Hell, nor Am I out of It" 166

37. No Fixed Place of Abode 173

38. One Star Short 179

39. Superficially Superficial 184

40. Great Body, Lovely Soul 189

41. Sins of the Father 194

42. Men of Distinction 198

43. Calm before the Storm 202

44. Man and Boy 205

45. Fade to Black 209

46. The Role of a Lifetime 217

47. Envoi 219

Filmography 221

Notes 225

Bibliography 233

Index 237

Illustrations follow page 130

Preface

Early in Charles Boyer's Hollywood career, a director asked him, "Do you think in English or French?" Boyer replied that although he was acting in an American film, he still thought in his native language. "That's a problem," said the director. "Until you learn to both think and act in English, you'll never make it in pictures."

During a long, creative life during which he won honors in both Europe and the United States for his work on screen, stage, and television, Boyer often told this story. For a time, he tried to follow the director's advice, but he came to believe that, in whatever language he acted (and he was fluent in three), he would always remain, mentally and emotionally, French.

For generations of film and theater audiences, Boyer was the archetypal Frenchman—cultivated, courteous, and seductive, yet never quite at home in a culture not his own. The sense of loss conveyed in his murmuring baritone voice was the very essence of romance. Women longed to comfort him; men wanted to become his friend.

One would not have been surprised if, in real life, Boyer had been a playboy and serial seducer. But he married only once, and he so loved his wife that, two days after her death, he killed himself. It was the end of an often tragic life during which he lost his only son, also to suicide.

In fact, Boyer was intensely private, thoughtful, and both intellectually and politically astute. Nominated four times for Academy Awards, he was honored by the Academy of Motion Picture Arts and Sciences for his activities on behalf of France during World War II.

Boyer's refusal to commit himself completely to any one language or medium may have been the secret of his success. Having established himself as a *jeune premier* in the theater and cinema of France, he sailed confidently through the transition from silent film to sound, made his name as a romantic leading man in Hollywood during the 1930s and 1940s, adapted to postwar character roles in Europe and the United States, entered television in the 1950s as both a producer and a performer, and, one suspects, would have done even more had not personal tragedy intervened.

Far from clinging to the performances that made him famous, Boyer showed a readiness to break the mold. After playing the continental lover in *Algiers,* he was a credible Napoleon in *Conquest* opposite Greta Garbo; he reemerged in the sentimental romantic comedy *Love Affair,* only to remake himself once again as the malevolent manipulator of Ingrid Bergman in the Victorian thriller *Gaslight.*

His choice of roles during and after World War II showed a shrewd perception of his image. Realizing that his accent would always mark him as an outsider, he embraced that trope but also subverted it. In *Hold Back the Dawn,* he was a European gigolo loitering on the Mexican border, ready to seduce an American tourist and convince her to marry him. In *Arch of Triumph,* he played a principled Austrian doctor stranded in Paris, with little hope of evading the advancing Nazis.

At a time when actresses were expected to swoon in the arms of their male lovers, Boyer chose leading ladies who declined the submissive role in their relationship. Jean Arthur was his equal in *Love Affair,* Hedy Lamarr his nemesis in *Algiers,* and Ingrid Bergman a worthy adversary in *Arch of Triumph* and *Gaslight.* In *The Garden of Allah,* Boyer's character was in thrall to the supremely confident Marlene Dietrich.

Often ineptly parodied, Boyer never descended to parodying himself. He ended his career with the same respect for the craft that characterized his life. He was rewarded with the admiration of discriminating filmgoers everywhere. In Alain Resnais's *Stavisky . . .,* one of his last films, he embodied both his archetypal Frenchness and the universal tragedy of a man of principle betrayed by friendship. "I've often wished *Stavisky . . .* were an hour longer," wrote the film critic for the *Los Angeles Times,* "so we could see more of Boyer, whose poignancy, delicate mastery and supreme subtlety and grace easily steal the movie."[1]

1

The Eyes of a Stranger

Later in life, Charles Boyer imagined his mother sewing his baby clothing by hand while she awaited his birth. He often saw her engaged in this activity as he grew up, the work of a practical woman devoted to her only child. When the midwife put him in her arms, she noticed his eyes first. Dark and slightly slanted, they didn't resemble those of his father but belonged, she said, to a "stranger." Along with his baritone voice, his eyes would prove to be Boyer's most seductive characteristic. Women in particular would find themselves captivated by his gaze.

Boyer was born on August 28, 1899, in Figeac, a town in the valley of the River Célé in Lot, a hilly, forested region of southwestern France. Well away from the main north-south rail and road routes, Figeac was a backwater and content to be so. The last celebrity born there was Jean-François Champollion (1790–1832), the first to translate Egyptian hieroglyphics, sparking a vogue for all things having to do with ancient Egypt. Reticent people, the Figeacois regarded with suspicion anyone who looked for a life outside of Lot. Until 1986, when the French state built a museum in Figeac to celebrate Champollion's accomplishments, the only monument to him was the Collége Champollion, where Boyer attended secondary school. Not until 2000 would the town affix a plaque to the house where Boyer was born.

Charles was a small baby, only 2.2 kilograms—or about five pounds. His mother, eighteen-year-old Augustine Marie Louise Durand (known as Louise), had married Maurice Boyer when he was twenty-three. Almost immediately, Maurice opened his own bicycle shop, suggesting an injection of capital, perhaps from the traditional dowry Louise would have brought to the marriage. Within a few years, he added a workshop where he made farm machinery. It wasn't the career he had hoped for. Before he married, Maurice had intended to study law. His unread legal books were a feature of Boyer's childhood, perhaps inspiring his later love of reading and his passion for collecting books.

The earliest photograph of Charles shows him at age five or six in front of the shop on Figeac's Boulevard Labernade. The five men standing behind him are its employees. Ranged around them are samples of the plows, mowers, and harvesters Maurice produced. From the balcony above, decorated with the Boyer name in extravagant capitals, Charles's parents look out from the apartment where he was raised.

It would have been a precarious living for an outsider like Maurice, particularly since Figeac was mostly surrounded by forest, with a thin layer of topsoil over porous limestone, and the demand for plows and harrows was limited. Some accounts suggest that Maurice had tuberculosis, which was incurable at the time. This, plus the stress of running a struggling business, may explain why in 1909, at age thirty-five, Maurice died suddenly of apoplexy (a stroke). Charles was just ten years old.

Louise later remarried, but while her son lived at home, she lavished all her affection on him. "He was pampered and indulged as a youngster," noted a profile of Boyer, "and made himself very unpopular in the neighborhood."[1] Soon after Maurice's death, Louise sold the business but kept the apartment. Her plans for her son didn't include him taking over the workshop, as he might have felt obliged to do as an adult. That Charles would eventually leave Figeac was, to her, a foregone conclusion. She envisioned him becoming a success in Paris or perhaps further afield, lecturing at a university or arguing a case in court or even entering the church. She was never overawed by her son's later fame. It was no more than she expected.

As an actor, Boyer always played city dwellers, yet he remained nostalgic for country life. In August, French cities traditionally empty as people leave to spend a few weeks in the countryside, reconnecting with regions of significance to their families. Boyer's contracts always stipulated a two-month break each year, with the right to spend that time in France. According to friend and fellow actor Pierre Blanchar, "The Charles who returns often to Paris from triumphs all over the world is the same Charles who once came to Paris from Figeac. His attitudes were fixed then, and they have never changed. Wealth and culture came to him, but they did not make him a Parisian." Part of this background was his natural reticence and distrust of anything pompous or exaggerated. "There can never be any foolishness in him," said Blanchar, "and for that he holds Figeac responsible."[2]

As a child, Boyer was already displaying the reserve that characterized him in adulthood, sometimes attracting the criticism that he was a stick-in-the-mud. He agreed that he was not a typical child. "I was sociable but introverted;

shut off. I didn't seek out the company of others of my age. I was like an old man in the body of a little boy. The company of adults pleased me more."[3] Among the qualities that set him apart was an exceptional memory. At age two, he knew the names of his father's workmen and could identify all the implements they manufactured. He was reading at three, taught by his mother; by age nine, he had memorized poems by François Villon, speeches from classical authors such as Racine, and even passages from French translations of Shakespeare.

Figeac was still in many respects a medieval town, with narrow, crooked streets, stone bridges across the river, and more open markets than shops. It took little effort to imagine the Three Musketeers swaggering out of an inn or Cyrano de Bergerac blustering around the square, flinging taunts as sharp as the sword he wielded. The very atmosphere of the town urged one to dress up, and Boyer needed little encouragement. He improvised costumes from his mother's capes and scarves and whitened his face with her powder to suggest stage makeup. Louise let Charles's hair grow to his shoulders, which gave a flourish to his fantasies. In a British or American town, the other children might have mocked his appearance and behavior, but in Figeac they passed without comment. The revolution of 1789 had overturned the monarchy but not the respect for men with land and servants. Charles was simply acting out an item of faith for every Frenchman: somewhere in his past was a gentleman.

He attended the Jeanne d'Arc primary school and continued at Collége Champollion. Under Napoleon, church schools were replaced by the lycée system, which guaranteed every child a free education. Most girls left school at fifteen, but boys continued for two more years before graduating. Those who qualified could enter a university or one of the specialist technical schools, including, for the performing arts, the Conservatoire National Superieur de Musique et de Déclamation. Students were selected to continue their education based on merit alone. There were no fees, but competition was fierce, and students from regional schools were at a disadvantage

The cinema at the time was still dominated by knockabout farces and digest versions of literary classics. Boyer matured as it did, learning as it learned, but the theater taught him the most. It trained him to speak and move in harmony with a story and a text, while cinema's most famous actors still relied on pantomime.

The circumstances of Boyer's birth conferred additional advantages. He was middle class and well educated, whereas most actors grew up poor and seldom read a book. In 1937, at the height of his popularity, he admitted that he had never known hardship; "life has been very kind, and success has come easily."[4] Unlike his friend Maurice Chevalier, Boyer's rise to fame was not so much a struggle as a progression.

Figeac had a theater and, beginning in 1911, a cinema, but the former was too small to attract touring companies from Paris. Boyer saw his first live performance in the nearest large town, Toulouse, where Louise took him when he was about twelve. The play was *Samson,* starring Lucien Guitry and written by Henry Bernstein, both of whom would become important figures in Boyer's career. Guitry and Bernstein belonged to "boulevard theater," the Paris equivalent of New York's Broadway or London's Shaftesbury Avenue. These theaters presented new plays for large audiences, leaving the classics to the national theater, the Comédie-Française. *Samson,* a hit of the 1908 season, was one of Bernstein's early successes—an updating of the biblical story of Samson and Delilah: a young entrepreneur is destroyed by the daughter of an aristocratic family whose impoverished relations pressure her into marriage. Like most successful actor-managers of the time, Guitry had his own theater, the Renaissance, for which he commissioned plays from writers such as Bernstein. The plays opened in Paris and then toured throughout France and sometimes abroad.

In 1913 Louise took Charles to Paris. Reconstruction in the 1860s and a new network of wide boulevards had transformed the city. Social life, which had once taken place almost entirely in private, had moved into the streets. Cafés helped create a society where talk was the currency. Theaters went from being preserves of wealth and position to places of mass entertainment. They played to the crowds and attracted the most agile minds of the day, both writers and performers.

It didn't take long for Boyer to contract what poet, playwright, and artist Jean Cocteau called "the red and gold disease"—a passion for the theater. He imagined himself onstage, declaiming for an audience the boastful speeches of Cyrano de Bergerac or the stately alexandrines of Racine. (His taste would always run to drama rather than comedy.) Even then, he sensed his future would be as an actor, but before he could do anything about it, the whole world was put on hold when war broke out in 1914.

2

All Quiet on the Western Front

In August 1914, while an unsuspecting Europe was on holiday, the German army swept through Belgium, intent on seizing as much territory as possible in the west before turning to confront the vast Russian army in the east. Fortunately for the French, soldiers searching the body of a German officer found General von Kluck's plans. Commandeering hundreds of Paris taxis, General Gallieni, the city's military governor, ferried reinforcements to the front by night and halted the advance at the Marne River, only forty miles from the city. Within a few weeks, the two forces had dug in, facing off against each other from Belgium to Switzerland. With minor variations, this line remained static for the next four years. German American novelist Erich Maria Remarque immortalized the phenomenon in his 1929 novel *All Quiet on the Western Front.*

The declaration of war had an unanticipated effect on Boyer, introducing him to the attractions and complications of sex. His philosophy teacher was drafted in 1914, and a twenty-year-old woman took over the course and its four students. "I worshipped her with boyish adoration," Boyer recalled, "which I'm perfectly certain she was never conscious of." Too shy to approach her directly, he put his feelings into the essays he wrote as class work. Not long after, she asked him to stay after class. As Boyer recounted:

> Standing there by her desk, my hands and feet slightly chilled, my heart hammering as I considered the now somewhat terrifying prospect of clasping her to my adolescent breast, I began to feel a little sick.
>
> She said, in her grave sweet voice, tinged with just a little amusement, "Charles, one day you will be a very charming man, possibly you may even be a very great lover. But that day has not yet come. Why don't you wait for it?"

Somehow, with those cool, kind words, she brought me to my senses. She made me conscious of myself as a half-grown boy, rather ridiculous, rather more funny than tragic, certainly not devastating at all. And I had an actor's quick repulsion for a role he doesn't fit, for a part in which he cannot cut an impressive figure.[1]

More than fifty years later, Boyer added some details to this story, providing an intriguing new dimension. He confided to publisher Gerald Guégan that, as a boy, he had been in love with an older woman. "She had been the mistress, according to gossip, of the consul of a South American country and a British military attaché." When Guégan asked how it had ended, Boyer said, "She moved to Sussex, but told me to visit her when I was older."[2]

Could Boyer's teacher have been on intimate terms with international diplomats? The British maintained schools in many cities around the Mediterranean for the children of its consular and military personnel, and she might have taught in one of these before arriving in Figeac. For the moment, however, it remains a question mark in Boyer's *education sentimentale*.

Many young men volunteered to fight, including Boyer's school friend Yves Garand, who lied about his age to join the army. Fifteen-year-old Charles and others, including his closest friend, Philippe Gambon, remained in Figeac. The town saw no actual fighting, but it did witness a lengthening roster of young men *mort pour la patrie*. Injured servicemen were sent south, where it was hoped the fresh air and good food would help heal them, particularly the damage inflicted by poison gas. Châteaux and hotels, deprived of tourist revenue, become convalescent hospitals. One of them was located just outside Figeac.

Charles and Philippe rallied other students to volunteer as orderlies at the hospital. They pushed the invalids around in their cane wheelchairs, brought them books and games, and helped them write letters home. At most such establishments, theater troupes put on shows, and Boyer organized a Figeac version. They rehearsed in a barn next to his father's former factory and performed for an audience that might not be able to walk but could still applaud. The sound electrified him.

Boyer's school took over the town theater for a production of *L'Aiglon*, Rostand's play about Napoleon Bonaparte's short-lived son, known as *l'aiglon*—the young eagle. In a monocle and greasepaint mustache, Boyer played the statesman Count Metternich. Decades later, workers renovating the theater found some names written on the wall of a dressing room. One was Boyer's.

For the invalids at the hospital, Boyer also staged a version of *Macbeth*, thin on plot but well endowed with swordplay, mysticism, and rhetoric. Another boy played Macbeth; Boyer preferred the role of Lady Macbeth, since he already knew that his talent lay in speaking rather than action. He never learned to fence or fight nor even to run gracefully. It was the same with music. His mother had played the harp as a girl, and she often sang as she moved around the house, mostly songs from operettas. Unfortunately, she did so badly, and her son inherited her tin ear. He learned to play the piano and violin but never to sing in tune.

After appearing in *L'Aiglon*, an elated Boyer informed his mother that he had chosen his life's work: he would become an actor. He felt, he said, a "conviction" as powerful as any priest's vocation. "I remember so perfectly," he reminisced, "the little twilit parlor and the way my mother looked as she sat there, serene, in her high-backed chair, a bit of sewing in her hands. This was how she invariably spent the last daylight hours, dreaming no doubt about my future—which I was about to murder in front of her eyes."[3]

Louise assumed the acting bug would pass, like most adolescent enthusiasms. She was wise enough not to dismiss it but rather to insist that Charles complete his education first. He passed his exams in the nearby town of Cahors, then marked time in Figeac until the war ended with the armistice of November 1918. Further urging wore Louise down, and on one of the last days of 1918, she waved good-bye as her boy boarded the train for Paris.

3

Paris

The Paris of 1918 was a shadow of the vivacious city of the belle epoque. The deaths of 1.3 million young Frenchmen during four years of war left it largely a place of women and old men. Restrictions on electricity reduced to a brown gloom the street lighting that had once earned it the title *Ville Lumiere*—City of Light. Paris had suffered relatively little artillery or bomb damage, but when Boyer arrived, the facades of many great buildings were still hidden by walls of sandbags. Art galleries were closed, their paintings stored far from the city. Theaters remained dark most of the week, and performances ended at 10:00 p.m. to adhere to the curfew. By day, brown-uniformed doughboys of General Pershing's army still filled the streets, waiting to be shipped back home to America. Eavesdropping on them in the cafés gave Boyer a smattering of English and excited his dreams of going to the United States.

Early in 1919 he signed up to audition for the Conservatoire. Hundreds applied for its three-year theater course, out of which only thirty were admitted each year, equally divided between male and female. To placate his mother and justify the allowance she paid him, he also enrolled at Paris's oldest university, the Sorbonne. His exam scores were too poor to qualify for his first preference, history. Fortunately, his crush on his philosophy teacher must have encouraged him to pay more attention in her class, and he was accepted for a four-year diploma course in that subject.

Like most newcomers to Paris, Boyer gravitated to the bohemian southern part of the city on the left bank of the Seine. The cultural divide represented by the river was far wider than might appear on a map. The boulevard theaters were on the bourgeois right bank, as were the Comédie-Française, the Conservatoire, the Louvre, the presidential palace of the Elysée, and almost all the great hotels. Students and artists congregated on the left bank and in the so-called Latin quarter, where narrow streets and ancient houses clustered around the Luxembourg Gardens, and in the hilltop community of Montparnasse.

New friend and fellow actor Philippe Hériat shared a house with another actor, Pierre Brasseur, and they invited Boyer to move into their empty room. Both men would become distinguished performers and Boyer's lifelong friends. The house was on rue de Fleurus, a short walk from the Odéon theater (and, though Boyer never met them, not far from the home of Gertrude Stein and Alice B. Toklas).

As he awaited a summons from the Conservatoire, Boyer saw all the plays he could afford. This usually meant watching from a seat in the steeply raked upper circle called the *poulailler*, or henhouse, since the occupants had to perch there like poultry. In their more boastful moments, the called themselves *les enfants du Paradis* (children of paradise), since their seats placed them closer to God. Boyer was happy wherever he sat. Increasingly, it was only when the house lights dimmed and the curtain rose that he felt truly at home.

Social and cultural life ceased in August as Parisians abandoned the city. Boyer returned to Figeac in the summer of 1919 and had his first encounter with film production. At nearby Decazeville, director Henri Pouctal was filming *Travail* (Work), an ambitious eight-hour adaptation of Émile Zola's novel about the steel industry and a young engineer's efforts to revive a failing factory by forming a workers' cooperative. To Boyer's astonishment, a member of the film crew knocked on his door, looking for someone to play a small role. Word had got around that he could act. Boyer hurried to where Pouctal was shooting, but one look from the director was enough. "Far too young," he said, and Boyer was dismissed.

Undeterred, he returned to the set each day, sometimes filling in as an extra. He befriended some of the actors, including Raphael Duflos. A commanding figure, Duflos spent years with the Comédie-Française before becoming a professor at the Conservatoire. He had made his reputation in costume roles, for which he usually wore a short, pointed beard and mustache. For *Travail*, however, he had shaved both, signifying his commitment to a new acting method from Austria and Germany that producers were pioneering—a performing style closer to real life than pantomime. "He imposed slow, measured, expressive gestures on his troupe," wrote one critic, "and the quasi-immobility which he adopted at times contrasts with the agitation of the characters in Méliès."[1]

In the long breaks typical of film production, Duflos befriended Boyer, who shared his hope of entering the Conservatoire. Duflos immediately recognized that Boyer's voice, potentially his most attractive asset, lacked power and taught him a few exercises to strengthen it. It was clear to Duflos that the boy needed professional tutelage—and soon, before his bad habits became ingrained.

Meanwhile, Boyer, who was familiar with the quality of the food at the hotel where the cast was billeted, boldly invited Duflos home for Sunday lunch, the most important meal of the week. One can imagine the flustered Louise in her best dress serving the traditional roast leg of lamb with green peas, followed by local cheese. Inevitably, they would have discussed Boyer's ambitions. It would not have been Duflos's first such conversation, and he was no doubt diplomatic. He might have said: *Of course, Charles is young, and acting is a difficult profession. Many try, but few succeed. On the other hand, the boy shows flair.*

Once they were both back in Paris, Duflos returned the favor by inviting Boyer to dinner. Crossing the Seine, the young actor felt like he was making the journey for the first time. No longer a tourist, he was a true Parisian. They dined at one of the most stylish restaurants on the Champs-Elysées, the city's grandest boulevard. It was dominated by the massive Arc de Triomphe, a monument to the victories of Napoleon Bonaparte, whom Boyer would one day portray on film; the Arc itself would be featured in one of Boyer's most controversial productions. Feeling a satisfaction that was more than culinary, Boyer nevertheless recalled it as the best meal he had during his first year in Paris.

Duflos's friendship offered a key to the theater world, which Boyer did not hesitate to use—some might say abuse. "By chance," he recalled, "I met, a few days after my arrival in Paris, while I was walking on Boulevard Saint Michel, my compatriot Maurice Escande." Only a few years older than Boyer, Escande was not a "compatriot" at all; he had been born in Paris. He was, however, Duflos's student and had just joined the Comédie-Française, which made him a useful contact. "After the usual exclamations, I hastened to tell him of my secret ambitions. Escande was kind enough to listen to me and even offered to give me my first diction lessons."[2] With the help of men like Duflos and Escande, Boyer learned to use his voice theatrically, projecting it in a way that made him audible to those sitting in the highest circle of any theater.

The Comédie-Française made its home in an imposing right-bank building dating from 1680, close to the Louvre and the gardens of the Palais

Royale—both potent symbols of privilege. It took courage for the brash young actor to walk along the colonnade and request admittance at the stage door. He did so for the first time by introducing himself to another of Duflos's friends, Victor Francen. Ten years older than Boyer, the unsmiling, dignified Francen received the bumptious newcomer in his dressing room. Watchful and ominous even in repose, Francen contrasted in every way with the most glamorous *jeune premier* of the time, Lucien Guitry's son Sacha, whose popularity threatened to eclipse that of his father. A few people saw a hint of the young Guitry in Boyer, but he knew he would never achieve an easy command of the high style. But Francen—reserved, watchful, enigmatic—was someone Boyer could emulate. Their meeting began a long professional relationship that would be renewed decades later on the other side of the Atlantic.

Not long after that first meeting, and thanks in part to Duflos, the Conservatoire accepted Boyer, and he began studying his profession. Just before Christmas 1919, Duflos and Francen also helped Boyer get an audition to become a trainee at the Comédie-Française. Being accepted by the national company was the highest honor of the French theater. Auditions took place before a panel representing all its departments. Few applicants were accepted, since a single black ball meant automatic refusal.

Instead of returning home for the holidays, Boyer prepared for his audition. He recruited his new actor friends to help him polish his delivery and emerged from the interview confident that he had done well. He was devastated to learn a few weeks later that he had been blackballed. He spent Christmas in a self-pitying stupor induced by fizzy sweet red wine. A ferocious hangover turned him forever against it. Twenty years later, he still stigmatized sparkling burgundy as "slop."

Francen confided that the sole negative vote had been cast by a young actor named Pierre Jules Louis Laudenbach, who, as Pierre Fresnay, would soon become a household name in France. That he voted against Boyer on the grounds of his inexperience was particularly galling, since Fresnay was only three years his senior; he had debuted in movies at eighteen, then breezed through the Conservatoire and emerged as a model of elegance, with an expressively modulated voice to match. Fresnay would spend eleven years at the Comédie-Française before achieving both stage and screen stardom. Boyer particularly envied his effortless air of nobility, which made him perfect for roles as an aristocrat. He knew that such a quality would always elude him.

Boyer was now a familiar face around the theaters. When Lucien Guitry revived *Samson* at the Renaissance, Boyer attended ten performances in a row. After his tenth time, Guitry noticed the familiar face and invited him backstage. He gave Boyer some advice he never forgot: "The audience is always asleep, dozing, because all plays sound alike, really. You must come forward with such a striking reading that they're jarred, jolted awake. Above all, you must be original. You have no right to be an actor if you don't say even a line like 'Good night' differently each time."[3] Boyer recognized the truth of this. At heart, he knew himself to be individual—not necessarily superior to other actors, but unlike them. He would never be comfortable in a repertory company or as part of a team. Any success would come from those qualities that were uniquely his.

Working at the Moscow Art Theater through the 1920s, Konstantin Stanislavsky developed a system of mental exercises and games to help actors access feelings that paralleled the emotions of the characters they played. It never had a formal name; actors simply called it the Method. Long before this technique became popular, Boyer was tapping stored emotions and instincts to animate characters. No author or director could tell him how to play a role. Instead, often to their exasperation, he insisted on discovering a motivation within himself.

Philippe Hériat, who knew Boyer better than most people, was in awe of his friend's ability:

> He lets his whole being become permeated with the character he's
> playing. He lives in this somnambulistic state until the end of the
> first performance. This is not the time to disturb him, or to visit
> him in his dressing room between the acts. At such times he would
> throw the president of the republic out the door. He is nervous,
> worried, and remains like that until, as the curtain descends for the
> last time, the applause of the audience tells him the public has
> ratified his understanding of the role. Only then does Charles leave
> his dream, return to life and become again the exquisite friend he is
> always outside of these crises.[4]

His new familiarity with working actors made Boyer impatient to join them, but he faced two more years of study at the Conservatoire, including tedious courses in costume, movement, and theater history. Other young actors felt the same way. At the end of their second year, Boyer, Pierre

Blanchar, and Fernand Ledoux collaborated to present a scene in the school's annual competition. Despite the effort they put into it, they only won second prize and were so disappointed that all three resigned on the spot. Earlier than he expected, Boyer found himself adrift in the treacherous waters of professional acting.

4

On the Road

So many touring companies were on the road that a personable young actor who didn't mind traveling could usually find work, even if the parts had no lines and he was expected to help move scenery and manhandle the heavy costume baskets in and out of railway vans. In such plays, Boyer was frequently cast as a policeman, a sentry, or a doorman. The ill-fitting, shabby, and often malodorous costumes instilled a lifelong dislike of uniforms.

With no agents, no actors' union to provide hiring halls, and private telephones almost unknown, out-of-work performers gathered at certain Parisian cafés to gossip, exchange information, play dominos or cards, and wait for an opportunity to play a butler for a few nights or fill in on a tour. Some even arrived in costume or kept their tailcoats hanging in the toilet, ready to go at a moment's notice. Regardless of the language or the phrasing, "Have tux, will travel" was a concept understood by struggling actors everywhere.

The friendships Boyer formed in these cafés with such men as Marcel Dalio, Pierre Blanchar, Philippe Hériat, Pierre Brasseur, and, eventually, Pierre Fresnay were renewed at film studios and backstage at theaters all over the world, and they sustained Boyer for the rest of his life. He tried not to notice the older actors who frequented the cafés each day, looking up hopefully as each potential employer arrived and then returning to their coffee or *vin rouge*. All had stories of their great days, and some even carried a few dog-eared clippings of their good reviews. They were the specters at the feast, reminders of how few succeeded in this most competitive of pursuits.

Boyer also discovered gambling in the cafés, and it became a lifetime pleasure. "His all-consuming passion is gambling at cards," noted a 1938 profile. "*Chemin de fer,* poker, baccarat. He will gamble on the slightest provocation."[1] Games of chance gave him the same rush as acting. His remarkable memory gave him an edge, but Boyer's greatest advantage at the tables was his luck. Most gamblers die broke, but at the end of a lifetime playing for high stakes, Boyer would be a millionaire.

Winning at cards augmented his allowance, but occasional reverses forced him to take nonacting work. For a while, he played violin in a restaurant, strolling between the tables and enhancing the romantic atmosphere. He also shadowed erring husbands for a detective agency. Each job added to the stock of "sense memories" on which he drew to animate his performances.

As Duflos and Escande had realized, Boyer's voice was both his strength and his weakness. Initially he struggled to make himself heard. When he forced his vocal cords, what came out was a squawk. After begging for speaking roles, he got his chance in Orléans when another actor fell ill during a tour of the play *L'Arlésienne*. "I was so moved by this honor," he said, "that when I made my entrance at the first act, I had my first experience of stage fright. No sooner had I opened my mouth than a hoarse, almost inhuman cry came out, making me blush to the roots of my hair under my makeup. I remained speechless until the end of the performance."[2]

By the time he was cast in François Porché's *La Jeune Fille avec Joues des Roses* (The Young Girl with Roses in Her Cheeks), directed by and starring actress Simone de Bergy, he hoped he had overcome the problem. "I was given two roles," Boyer said. "But two roles with no more than five lines each. However, I had the great satisfaction of earning ten francs per evening— about twenty dollars." Now regretting that he had neglected voice classes at the Conservatoire, he disguised his nervousness with bluster. "I wanted to do well but I was so intimidated that I behaved very arrogantly. To make matters worse, my southern accent became even more audible." De Bergy quickly spotted his weakness. "As for you, Boyer," she suggested as she gave notes to the cast after rehearsal, "shout! Otherwise nobody will hear you." Later she took him aside. "I don't want to discourage you," she said, "but do you really feel that acting is the career for you? In your place, I'd look for another line of work."[3]

It was a low point—perhaps the lowest in Boyer's early years in the theater—and someone less determined might have given up. But his conviction never faltered. He took heart from the occasional scraps of good news. Returning to Figeac for the summer, he learned that the end of the war meant he would not be called to serve in the army. He could still be required to do three years' national service training, but his student exemption, reinforced by a series of medical certificates, kept him out of uniform. It was a concession that would rebound disastrously two decades later.

Boyer got his big break a few months into 1920. The play *Maria del Carmen,* a Spanish Romeo and Juliet story of the previous century, had been largely forgotten, but the management of the Théâtre des Champs-Elysées decided it was worth reviving, although they changed the title to *Aux Jardins de Murcie* (In the Gardens of Mercie). Disaster intervened at the final dress rehearsal when the leading man, Romauld Joubé, fell ill. He had no understudy, and sending someone onstage, book in hand, to read the text would have been hopelessly amateur. As word spread through the cafés, Philippe Hériat remembered Boyer's amazing memory and sent a hurried message to the Cirque d'Hiver, where his friend had signed on to play a small part. Thirty minutes later, Boyer presented himself breathlessly at the Théâtre des Champs-Elysées. The skeptical director showed him the script. Could he really learn his lines in time to go on that night?

"No problem," Boyer said, with a confidence he did not entirely feel. "Is there somewhere I can work?" The director installed him in a dressing room, leaving instructions that on no account was he to be disturbed. Occasional surreptitious glances showed the young actor casually paging through the play as if he were reading a detective story. Only a few hours before the curtain went up, he emerged. "So?" the director asked. In response, Boyer recited his first speech perfectly. The director listened in awe. The voice could be better, he thought, but the boy carried himself well and, with his slightly slanted eyes, looked even more Spanish than Joubé. "Better get to wardrobe and try on your costumes," the director said, making a decision. "They'll need altering. Which reminds me, there are a few changes to the script. I'll mark them in your copy."

Boyer looked stricken. "No, you mustn't!"

Actors! thought the director. "Don't worry," he said. "We haven't cut any of *your* lines."

"It's not that," Boyer said. "I learned all the parts, not just my own. I need it to be played exactly in the version you gave me."

Every role? For the first time that day, the director found himself looking forward to the evening's performance.

5

To Be Famous and to Be Loved

The unknown who becomes an overnight sensation is such a cliché that the simple surprise that greeted Boyer's last-minute rescue of *Aux Jardins de Murcie* seemed grudging. But despite his remarkable feat of memory, it remained an understudy's performance. His voice could barely be heard in the upper circle; nor did he carry himself with the confidence of a leading man. His recall, however, was everything he had claimed. A couple of times he even prompted other actors who forgot their lines.

The newspapers soon heard of this triumph by a newcomer from the countryside. It was exactly the sort of story they liked, and reporters jostled to interview him. Most young actors would have welcomed such attention, but Boyer evaded their efforts, as he would throughout his career. Even at the height of his fame, an editor noted bleakly, "Charles Boyer has difficulty hiding his disdain for interviewers."[1]

The warmth of Boyer's performance in *Aux Jardins de Murcie* was due in part to its female lead, Renée Falconetti. During the production they became lovers—Boyer's first adult relationship. Physically, she exemplified what people would come to recognize as the Boyer type—an oval face, large expressive eyes, and a quality of distance and hauteur. They made an attractive couple, as if Boyer had cast a leading lady who reflected well on him—not a companion but a consort. A decade older than Boyer, Falconetti had a sexual history that was as varied as his was uneventful. While still in her teens, she became the mistress of Henri Goldstuck, a millionaire old enough to be her father. They had a daughter, but she left them both to enter the Conservatoire.

After ten days, Joubé resumed his role, but word of Boyer's prodigious memory had spread, and he was besieged with offers. Some employers depended a little too much on this facility. During one tour, a manager who was unhappy with ticket sales ordered the troupe to replace the advertised play with a popular favorite, *Le Flibustier* (The Pirate), a period comedy by

Jean Richepin. "I didn't know the first word of the role," Boyer recalled, "but I had no difficulty learning it overnight. In the morning, another difficulty arose; Yvonne Ducos, star of our troupe, was urgently called back to Paris"— probably a ruse to avoid appearing onstage with an unknown. The manager found a local girl who looked the part. Meeting her for the first time in the wings at the matinee, Boyer and the other actors were already onstage when they discovered she didn't know any of her lines. The manager had told her not to open her mouth but to rely on the professionalism of the others and Boyer's now-famous memory to carry her through. "We took turns improvising or speaking her lines," said a furious Boyer, "and we got through the performance somehow."[2]

Boyer might have remained a second-rate touring actor, always in demand because of his remarkable memory, but for the intervention of someone who was in the audience the first night he performed in *Aux Jardins de Murcie*. Firmin Gémier would become Boyer's most important teacher and inspiration. Among actor-managers he stood out by virtue of his ordinariness. Short and bald, with an expressive, puckish face, he came from the country, like Boyer. Watching the young actor that night, Gémier saw not so much what he *was* but what he *might be*. A few months later, Gémier invited Boyer for an interview at his theater, the Antoine.

Boyer knew the imposing building on Boulevard de Strasbourg. He had often passed through its columned portico and admired the gilded interior, the three "golden horseshoe" balconies, and, above them all, the brilliantly lit cupola. To his surprise, the splendor did not make him apprehensive. To perform on that stage seemed no more than his right, the reason for living he had sensed almost since infancy.

Gémier had been keeping his eye on the young Boyer, and each performance only confirmed the special quality he had noted that first night. It was not Boyer's freakishly good memory. Gémier recognized that such a talent could become a crutch or even a burden, like the *jeune premier* who, recognizing that he looks good in tights, condemns himself to a career in period romances. What Gémier had noticed about Boyer was this: He acted with a special intensity when the scene involved a woman. His voice assumed an insinuating timbre, and his movements and gestures became subtly intimate. At first, Gémier had been afraid this quality materialized only when Boyer acted with Falconetti, but he had seen enough of his work to know it did not matter who his leading lady was. What he had seen was not a fluke. It would become the cornerstone of Boyer's career on stage and screen.

"I can offer you a contract for five years," Gémier said to Boyer. "Interested?"

To the disappointment of his mother, Boyer gave up his studies at the Sorbonne (from which, despite future claims by numerous publicists, he never graduated). Louise accepted at last that if her son were ever to appear in academic, religious, or legal attire, it would be onstage.

Théâtre Antoine paid him a salary, so Boyer was able to inform his mother, somewhat grandly, that he no longer needed her allowance. Her life was changing too. With her son established in his chosen career, she felt free to marry again. Her new husband, a Monsieur Rossignol, was an old family friend whom Boyer knew and liked. Louise traveled to Paris to help her son find a larger apartment, which she shared with him for a few months before, to his secret relief, she returned to Figeac and married life.

After *Aux Jardins de Murcie,* Falconetti appeared in Charles Méré's sensational *La Captive,* then left to join the Comédie-Française. From time to time, she and Boyer shared the stage at Théâtre Antoine. In 1923 it was with veteran actor Harry Baur that Boyer appeared in *Charly* and later in *Simili* by Claude Roger-Marx, who inscribed a copy of that text, "To Charles Boyer, without whom Simili would not be Simili."

In 1928 Falconetti starred in Carl Dreyer's film *The Passion of Joan of Arc,* a performance that would make her famous—some would say immortal. Her depiction of the young saint's anguish during her inquisition and execution set a benchmark for generations of actors. Her career and Boyer's had already diverged, but the young man she left behind would never again be uncomfortable with women—nor would they occupy a large part of his life. Paradoxically for an actor who became famous as a great lover, Boyer regarded women with something between indifference and hostility. His friend Anatole Litvak, a film director famous for his own sexual conquests, believed that Boyer "hated women [and] seldom had a satisfactory relationship" with one.[3] That judgment seems harsh, but there is much evidence to support it.

Fidelity is not a common attribute among people in the film industry, as the roster of show-business divorces attests. Love exposed to the limelight tends to curl up and die, and the ease with which stars exchange one existence for another in their working lives encourages them to do the same when the cameras are no longer running or the curtain comes down.

In *Rosencrantz and Guildenstern Are Dead,* playwright Tom Stoppard wrote that actors are "the opposite of people." To play a role demands a certain contempt for the reality of the character who inspires it, a capacity to step outside and see a personality as it appears to others. It follows that those who impersonate love must dispassionately observe its effect on both lover and loved, the better to illuminate the objective absurdity of those irrational urges that characterize what is thought of as the most perfect expression of our humanity. An actor who achieves that distance can effectively convey the outward effects of love, and few did so more successfully than Boyer. He was able to subdue those urges that Sophocles compared to being shackled to a wild beast. He could be charming if he chose to, but his most effective performances were men whom love had transformed into fools or villains, men who destroyed, or were destroyed by, those they loved.

After Falconetti, Boyer enjoyed many brief relationships. He established a friendly rivalry with Pierre Brasseur, another busy *tombeur*, or seducer of women. After Brasseur stole one of his girlfriends, acquaintances in the café greeted Boyer with, "Ah, here's the cuckold!" as if he were a deceived husband. He shrugged off their gibes: there would always be other willing women. As for marrying, he had seen the strain an actor's life imposed on relationships. What marriage could endure the repeated absences, the financial unreliability, the emotional slumps between acting engagements? He was determined not to inflict such a life on any woman or on himself.

But the more he avoided women, the more he was pursued, even by those who had once mocked him. While playing in Edouard Bourdet's *L'Homme Enchaîné*, Boyer was visited backstage by Simone de Bergy, the director who had once advised him to give up acting. She presented him with a specially bound copy of *La Jeune Fille avec Joues des Roses*, the play on which they had worked together. It was inscribed apologetically, "To my friend Charles Boyer, in admiration—and atonement."

6

Movies

The Paris theater season lasted from October to May. The rest of the year, most actors toured. Boyer appeared all over France, as well as in Beirut, Berlin, Copenhagen, and Cairo. Spending so much time on the road, he became a voracious reader. "He spoke often of what he had *not* read," said his friend André Daven. "There was so much he wanted to read. Fiction of every type; the classics, modern novelists. He was very fond of the Germans—Hans Fallada and Stefan Zweig. And history; history of all places and of all periods."[1] He became a collector of first editions, accumulating a library of 3,000 volumes.

Boyer also continued to gamble. A 1920 law forbade casinos in Paris and within 100 kilometers of the city, permitting them only in resorts and towns with a significant tourist industry. But Paris athletic and swimming clubs installed game rooms for members only, offering the usual table games as well as high-stakes poker and bridge. On tour, there was always a hotel or club-car game of poker or *belote,* and the towns where he appeared generally accommodated the serious gambler. "Everywhere I went," Boyer said, "there were casinos and I could never resist the temptation. Each time, I told myself it was the last. When I returned to Paris, I was completely broke. I began to hate our matinee days, for the afternoon performances kept me from the roulette table. I was a young actor and made little, and every penny of it I lost. There *are* systems by which you can beat roulette for small amounts of money but when you try to win a lot with a small investment you are sure to lose. I did."[2]

Movies offered the possibility of additional income, although film production in France was nothing like that in Hollywood. Aside from a few large enterprises such as Pathé and Gaumont, scores of small companies operated independently, generally centered around one man. They raised money film by film and often went bankrupt in the process.

Philippe Hériat was friendly with rising young director Marcel L'Herbier and had a role in a version of Honoré de Balzac's story *L'Homme du Large* (A Man of the High Seas). Shooting was about to begin, and L'Herbier needed a young actor to play Breton fisherman Guenne-la-Taupe (Guenne the Mole), a crony of the wayward son who prefers the city's fleshpots to his family's mystical partnership with the sea. Boyer, despite expressing his disgust with the low intellectual level of motion pictures, asked to be introduced to the director.

L'Herbier dispelled Boyer's doubts about the cinema. Poet, musician, dancer, architect, critic, and theorist, the tall, thin-faced, balding L'Herbier was only a decade older than Boyer. Nevertheless, he had already taken cinema far beyond the Harold Lloyd comedies and Pearl White cliffhanger serials Boyer had seen as a child. Nor was the location shooting near Morbihan and Finistère anything like Pouctal's rough-and-ready unit on *Travail*. A familiar figure around the salons of Paris, L'Herbier saw no reason to compromise his sartorial standards on the rocky and windswept Breton coast. His tailored three-piece suits remained uncreased even on the bleak heath where Boyer played his first movie scene among the Neolithic stone menhirs. Throughout the sequence, Boyer smoked a cigarette, a gesture that would become emblematic.

Along with his friend Hériat, L'Herbier's crew included a strikingly handsome young man named André Daven (a simplified version of his mother's family name, Davenport). Boyer and Daven were the same age and would be close friends and collaborators for the next thirty years.

Back in Paris, another independent producer-director, Jacques de Baroncelli, was about to film Balzac's *Le Pére Goriot* (Father Goriot) and offered Boyer the key role of Rastignac, an ambitious provincial who finds success in Paris society and whose name became a metaphor for any unscrupulous young man on the make. Boyer was eager to take the part, but Baroncelli's demand that he sign an exclusive contract with his company, Lumina, clashed with Boyer's agreement with Gémier. The experience turned him against long-term commitments, and it became his lifelong ambition, never fully realized, to be his own boss and have creative control over his own work.

Instead of playing Rastignasc, he appeared in three unremarkable films: *Chantelouve* (1921), a psychological drama about a husband's obsessive jealousy; *Le Grillon du Foyer,* a version of Charles Dickens's *The Cricket on the Hearth;* and a short film, *L'Esclave* (The Slave). The few reviews of these films that mentioned Boyer were brief but enthusiastic. One of these reviews was by André Daven, who moonlighted as a film journalist. His charm and good looks made him an instant success in this field. Sent to interview Rudolph Valentino in 1924, Daven dazzled the star, who fell under his spell. Valentino persuaded Daven to accompany him back to Hollywood and play his brother in *Monsieur Beaucaire* (1924), an overdecorated romance set in the court of Louis XIII. Handsome as he was, Daven did not see a future in acting, nor as part of a ménage à trois with Valentino and his wife, Natacha Rambova. After that one film role, Daven returned to Paris.

Gloria Swanson, Hollywood's biggest female star, had just arrived to make Léonce Perret's *Madame Sans Gene* (Madame without Manners), the story of a laundress who befriends the young Napoleon, marries one of his marshals, but scandalizes society with her uninhibited behavior. Daven charmed her, just as he had Valentino. He became the film's publicist and, as the first of many favors for Boyer, arranged for him to audition for the part of Napoleon. (Swanson, at only five foot one, decided he was too tall.) Asked to hire a translator, Daven recruited an impoverished young marquis, Henri de la Falaise de Coudraye, who also became Swanson's lover. Daven allegedly arranged for Swanson's abortion when she became pregnant. He was also a witness at the couple's discreet wedding in January 1925. When Swanson returned to Hollywood with her trophy husband, her sixth, mobs of delirious admirers greeted her.

Impatient with his progress in the movies, Boyer returned to the theater, where Gémier offered him an attractive new role. Indochina was far from France, but the French colonies in what is now Vietnam were of vital interest. The French navy patrolled the China Sea, as did ships from Britain, Germany, and the United States. Claude Farrère, a naval lieutenant, had published a number of books and plays about life on the China station, among them *La Bataille* (The Battle), a novel inspired by Japan's 1905 defeat of Russia in the Battle of Tsushima during the Russo-Japanese War. In Farrère's story, Yorisaka, a young Japanese marquis and lieutenant in the Japanese navy, persuades his beautiful wife, Mitsouko, to seduce Fergan, a British commodore, and feed him misleading information. The plan goes awry when she falls in love with Fergan and Yorisaka, disgraced, commits ritual suicide.

Pierre Frondaie's play minimized the novel's military elements to concentrate on the romantic triangle. Gémier decided that Boyer's slightly slanted eyes would make him particularly credible in the lead. His production of *La Bataille* at the Comédie-Montaigne and later at the Odéon, with Boyer as Yorisaka and Gémier as Admiral Hirata, was a popular success. As

Gémier had anticipated, Boyer was completely convincing as the fanatical young marquis.

In *La Bataille*, Boyer emerged as a charismatic leading man. Audiences spontaneously applauded the scene in which, to convince the dying Fergan he had been tricked, Yorisaka whispers to him a few words from the love song the Englishman had shared with Mitsouko. The climax that followed had them cheering. "The excitement of the whole theatre at the conclusion," wrote critic Gabriel Boissy, "while the Japanese sailors acclaimed their victory over the corpses of Fergan and the Marquis Yorisaka, was no longer emotion but fervor; no longer applause but an ovation, and a collective excitement that went beyond dramatic pleasure."[3]

7

Bernstein

E very theatrical era has its lightning rods: writers who address controversial topics and attract both hostile attention and queues at the box office.
In 1920s Paris, Henry Bernstein trod the same path as Ibsen, Strindberg, and
O'Neill, but even more sensationally, since his plays dissected the world
of privilege into which he had been born. A critic synopsized Bernstein's
themes:

> The hero of *La Rafale* (*The Whirlwind*, 1905) cheats his friends and
> kills himself, despite the love of his mistress who wants to save him.
> In *La Griffe* (The Claw, 1906), a politician uses his influence to
> seduce a wealthy woman. The hero of *The Secret* (1913) is a kind of
> maniac who destroys the happiness of his family and, finally
> admitting his gratuitous wickedness, destroys himself. All these
> dramas are played behind closed doors, and frantic beings move
> there under the effect of forced contrasts; a financier *must* ruin
> himself, a mistress *must* sell herself, a lover *must* lose the game, a
> politician *must* be hunted down by his enemies.[1]

Boyer never missed a Bernstein production, and after the premiere of *Judith*,
he went backstage to congratulate the playwright. Bernstein repaid the compliment when Boyer opened in *L'Homme Enchaîné*. It was only a matter of
time before the two collaborated. The opportunity came in August 1924
when Boyer's friends, including Hériat, Dalio, Brasseur, Duflos, and Francen,
threw him a twenty-fifth birthday party to coincide with the closing of his
run in *Le Voyageur*.

Bernstein came to the party and toasted Boyer as "the crown prince of
the Parisian theater." A few weeks later, he sent Boyer his newest play, *La Galerie des Glaces* (The Hall of Mirrors), which was due to open in the fall. It

reflected the playwright's interest in Freud and psychoanalysis but also in Luigi Pirandello's deconstruction of narrative and character. With Gémier's agreement, Boyer accepted the starring role in the production, which would be a triumph for both playwright and actor. Novelist François Mauriac, after praising the play's examination of consciousness, concluded, "M. Bernstein might never have achieved this miracle without the existence of his star, M. Charles Boyer. With a look, an inflexion of the voice, with silence, this artist reveals how he is torn. His walk, his hair, his clothing; nothing else in his appearance betrays his secret wound."[2]

In 1926 Bernstein took over the Théâtre du Gymnase, which would become the showcase for his greatest successes. Every performer in the country was eager to work with him, and he took full advantage of that situation, particularly with actresses. One young actress confessed to Jean-Pierre Aumont that, during an audition, Bernstein had invited her to perform oral sex on him. "Shocking!" said Aumont. "No role, even in a Bernstein play, is worth degrading yourself."

"You're probably right," said the actress. "So you think I shouldn't have done it?"[3]

Boyer signed a contract with Bernstein, despite some absurdly restrictive terms. No actor under contract to him could appear in a film while he was being considered for a part, even if the play was not yet written. To do so would incur a penalty of 300,000 francs. But the deal was a turning point in Boyer's career, given the prestige of the Gymnase and his appearance in plays both written and directed by Bernstein.

Bernstein wrote to his new star's strengths and skirted his weaknesses. Boyer disliked uniforms, so he was never cast as a military man; more often, he played someone involved in business or politics. His voice and manner were those of a person well born and well educated, so he could not play common people; his innate superiority would always surface. Boyer was also unconvincing as anyone indecisive; he was most effective as a man who applied his intelligence to a problem and dealt with it, no matter who got hurt. Had he acted in Shakespeare, he would have been a poor Hamlet or Macbeth but a good Henry V. Not that Boyer was ever an obvious choice to do Shakespeare. As he had intuited as a boy (when he chose not to play Macbeth), he was too short to carry off historical costumes. At five feet nine inches tall, he was of average height, but his compact build made him appear shorter, even when matched with someone of similar stature. Given the cinematic convention that a screen actor should always appear taller than his leading lady, Boyer often wore lifts in his shoes, and if the cinematographer couldn't "cheat" the shot, sometimes he even stood on a box.

During his eight-year association with Bernstein, Boyer appeared in only four plays. However, each had a long run in Paris, followed by a tour, often overseas, so he had no time for cinema, even if Bernstein had been willing to release him. Late in 1927 he did play the second lead in *La Ronde Infernale*. Written by Henri Decoin and directed by Luitz-Morat, the *nom de film* of Maurice Radiguet, the film is set in the Vel d'Hiver, Paris's indoor cycling stadium. Six-day bicycle races were among the city's most popular sporting events. Ernest Hemingway was a regular attendee, often taking a picnic and watching the riders for hours. Most of the film's action takes place in the mind of one of the cyclists, Jean Angelo, who is convinced his wife is cheating on him with Boyer. His fantasies and hallucinations about the imagined affair drive him into a jealous frenzy during which he wins the race, only to find that his suspicions were unfounded.

Boyer's next film—the last he would make in France for some time—took him to the desolate Landes region in the southeast corner of the country, named for the heath (*landes*) covering it. *Captain Fracasse,* by Brazilian director Alberto Cavalcanti, was adapted from Théophile Gautier's swashbuckling novel set in the seventeenth century. Boyer's close friend Pierre Blanchar played Baron de Sigognac, an impoverished young nobleman who joins a traveling theater troupe, mainly because he is infatuated with its ingenue, Isabelle (Line Deyers). She also attracts the attention of the villainous Duc de Vallombreuse (Boyer), who kidnaps her and spirits her away to his château, from which she is eventually rescued by Sigognac and the other actors in the troupe.

In the troupe's rowdy plays, Sigognac's role was that of Captain Fracasse (literally, Captain Crash), a comic swashbuckler. This was ideal casting for Blanchar, who looked the part of an awkward young romantic. As the evil duke, Boyer was less effective. Cavalcanti encouraged him to display his natural seductiveness, fastidiously applying pomade to his mustache while eyeing Isabelle and bribing the troupe's doyenne (Marguerite Moreno) to deliver her into his clutches. Not until *Gaslight* would he again combine sex and villainy. But Boyer was overdressed in a broad plumed hat and long wig, and he was so obviously inept at swordplay (having skipped those classes at the Conservatoire) that Blanchar had to fake their final duel, thrusting his sword into him from the other side of a door. Boyer compensated for these deficiencies with the sexual magnetism Gémier had identified as his most valuable attribute. The first time the duke glimpses Isabelle, she is rehearsing a scene with Sigognac. Looking away from him briefly, she meets Vallombreuse's eyes for a few seconds. Deyers was not a good enough actress to fully convey her guilty attraction, but the moment provides a glimpse of Boyer's sexual magnetism.

In 1929, immediately after *Captain Fracasse,* Boyer appeared in Bernstein's *Mélo.* Exploiting the actor's skill with the violin, not to mention his ambivalence about marriage, Bernstein cast him as one of two musician friends who are competing for the same woman. In *Mélo,* Boyer enjoyed his greatest theatrical success. It was also one of his last appearances on the French stage for quite some time.

Just before the play closed for the summer, Boyer was visited in his dressing room by American movie executive Paul Bern (born Paul Levy in Germany). The short, balding Bern spoke softly and in good French—not characteristics Boyer associated with Americans. As right-hand man to Irving Thalberg, the innovative head of production at Metro-Goldwyn-Mayer (MGM), Bern had wide authority to scout for new talent. He asked whether Boyer's contract permitted him to accept work in Hollywood.

The inquiry puzzled Boyer. During the silent era, American studios imported a few French actors, but once sound revealed their accents, they were demoted to roles as headwaiters and gigolos. (An exception was Maurice Chevalier, who signed with Paramount specifically to appear in musicals.) European actresses continued to be offered Hollywood contracts because an accent made a woman more exotic, but in 1929 the only European actors being hired were British.

Bern explained that he didn't want Boyer for American films but for French remakes to be screened outside the States. Such bi- or trilingual productions were a feature of early sound cinema. Each version used the same sets and crews, and sometimes the same director as the original in English, but the films were reshot with French, German, or Spanish performers. Bern thought Boyer would be ideal for the French version of Greta Garbo's next film, *The Kiss,* which would also be her sound debut. Conrad Nagel would star, but Bern visualized Boyer as the second lead, replacing Lew Ayres. Bern proposed the standard starting salary of $400 a week for a thirteen-week contract, plus all expenses. Boyer didn't need to think very long. Once *Mélo* closed, he would be free until the fall. And no other offer was likely to improve on spending the summer in Hollywood making love to Greta Garbo at $8,000 a week (in today's dollars).

Boyer probably owed Bern's offer to Belgian director Jacques Feyder, who was set to direct the French version of *The Kiss*. They were friends, and Feyder's wife, actress Françoise Rosay, was one of Boyer's most enthusiastic supporters. Sailing from Le Havre, Boyer found both of them on board, headed for MGM, where Rosay had been cast opposite Buster Keaton in *Buster Se Marie*, the French version of *Parlor, Bedroom, and Bath*. Boyer and Rosay were probably never lovers—she was older than Boyer, and her mannish look and manner were nothing like his usual type—but he often professed his admiration and affection for her. "I had vowed never to marry," he said, "but I would have married Françoise in a moment if she hadn't been taken."

After arriving in New York, they made the three-day transcontinental rail journey, first on the Twentieth Century Limited to Chicago, and then on the Chief to Los Angeles. Boyer was an experienced traveler, but he had never seen anything like Los Angeles. After Paris's busy street life, with its cafés and theaters, the empty sidewalks of a city that relied on the automobile disoriented him. He was rescued by Maurice Chevalier, who had been only a nodding acquaintance in France. Superficially, the two men had little in common. Boyer, well read and thoughtful, was a star of boulevard theater, while the streetwise but uneducated Chevalier had started as a hoofer in variety shows, partnering first with the drug-addicted, bisexual singer Fréhel and then with the glamorous queen of the Folies, Mistinguett.

"I never got to know him well there," Chevalier said of their early years in Paris. "He had seemed to belong to a different world from mine." But exile drew them together, and they became best friends for life. Chevalier confessed that he found Los Angeles no less hostile and alien than Boyer did. "At a time when I was lonely and shaken," he wrote, "Charles offered me his friendship." He continued: "I liked him more every time I saw him and found I could talk with him on subjects that usually found me speechless. Finally we were together almost every evening. He had all the education I had missed. Charles made lists of books for me and I read everything he suggested. When we travelled, we wrote long letters to each other and I told him about my intellectual progress. Reading brought me joys I never knew before, and I will always be grateful for the friendship of this man."[4]

When Feyder introduced Boyer to Garbo, it was not the electric experience he had expected. For the rest of his life, people would ask him what Garbo was really like. His best response was, "She was really like Garbo." However hypnotic she appeared onscreen, in the flesh she was monosyllabic, formal, and remote. Boyer was pondering how he was going to work with this monument when he learned, to his secret relief, that she had changed her mind about making her sound debut in *The Kiss*, so he wouldn't be needed after all. Instead, Bern cast him in the French version of a courtroom melodrama, *The Trial of Mary Dugan*. It was the first setback in a Hollywood career that would get worse before it got better.

8

On Trial

Bayard Veiller's *The Trial of Mary Dugan* had been a stage success in New York, London, and Paris. The popularity of the 1929 film, amateurishly directed by Veiller himself, encouraged MGM to remake it in other languages and with better directors. For the German version, MGM imported American-born Artur Robison; for the Spanish and French versions, the studio turned to Marcel de Sano, a young Romanian who was already in Los Angeles and was married to French actress Arlette Marchal.

Some studios shot the domestic and foreign versions concurrently, having the different casts take turns on the set. Others accelerated the process by shooting one version during the day and another at night. Universal used this method for a Spanish-language *Dracula*. Josef von Sternberg filmed *The Blue Angel* with two cameras, doing a scene in English and then switching to the second camera to do it in German.

For *The Trial of Mary Dugan*, MGM chose to keep the courtroom set standing while filming the German, French, and Spanish versions consecutively. This avoided the need to keep the foreign performers under contract for long periods, but it took time. The English version began shooting on December 1, 1928, and premiered in April 1929. The French version, *Le Procès de Mary Dugan*, took ten weeks to shoot and did not open in Paris until more than two years later, in November 1931.

The play was a straightforward courtroom drama. Mary Dugan, a Broadway star, is found beside the murdered body of her wealthy lover. At the trial, she listens, too shocked to speak, as the prosecutor systematically demolishes her character, revealing that she has lived with many different "protectors." These men provided her with money, most of which she handed over to a mysterious person named Jimmy, assumed to be another lover. The testimony of the dead man's widow (Françoise Rosay)—a figure in impenetrable black veils, the very embodiment of grief—convinces the jury of Mary's guilt.

She is saved by the appearance of Jimmy, who is actually her younger brother, whom she has put through law school. He takes over the defense and clears her in a startling denouement.

The American version of the film featured Irving Thalberg's wife, Norma Shearer, as Mary and Lewis Stone and H. B. Warner as the rival attorneys who defend and prosecute her. For the French remake, Hughuette Duflos, wife of Boyer's friend Rafael Duflos, played Mary. Boyer's youth might have suggested him for the role of Jimmy, but that went to André Burgère, who had appeared in the Paris production of the play and was being groomed for stardom. Instead, Boyer was miscast as the district attorney, a part better played by someone older. (H. B. Warner, the original film's DA, was fifty-two.) It was a long way from making love to Garbo, but Boyer did his best, fearing that his voice would be insufficiently resonant for the General Electric recording system, which favored a booming, theatrical delivery.

Away from the studio, he didn't lack diversions. Poker was popular in the movie community, and it required no knowledge of English. Also, beginning in 1928, a flotilla of gambling ships was anchored just outside the three-mile limit, where international waters began. Women too blossomed in the California heat. "It is lovely to sit under the moon at midnight," wrote British novelist Hugh Walpole, "and watch these beautiful creatures with practically nothing on play tennis under artificial light."[1] Young, single, and handsome, Boyer learned the truth of the witticism that there is little to do after the workday in Hollywood but lie on the beach and look at the stars—or vice versa.

Through Maurice Chevalier, Boyer met Claudette Colbert, who was about to raise eyebrows with her scenes as the dissolute empress Poppaea, naked in a bath of milk, in Cecil B. DeMille's *The Sign of the Cross.* Though technically French—her parents had brought her to America as a toddler—she spoke both languages and was soon intimate with the charismatic young actor. "I had a mad crush on Charles," she confessed years later, "even though I couldn't understand a goddamn word he said. He asked me to marry him several times and I told him to go back to France and get a grip on himself."[2] Isolation may have made Boyer look more favorably on marriage than he had in Paris—or perhaps Colbert failed to understand that he had something less permanent than wedlock in mind.

Shortly before shooting ended on *Le Procès de Mary Dugan,* Boyer was surprised to receive a cable from Berlin. News of the young Frenchman had reached Germany's largest company, Universum Film A.G., also known as

Ufa, which needed an actor for *Barcarolle de l'Amour,* the French version of *Brand in der Oper* (Fire in the Opera House). Boyer's MGM contract allowed him to take work in Europe, so he crossed the continent once more; visited Chevalier in New York, where he was shooting *The Love Parade* with Ernst Lubitsch at the Astoria studios; and boarded a ship for Europe. He was leaving the United States in the midst of a financial boom, but when he returned, he would find it reeling from the 1929 stock market crash and about to slide into the Great Depression.

9

Ufa and After

Only a few weeks later, Boyer was driven to the Ufa studios at Neubabels-berg in Potsdam, a leafy satellite of Berlin. Mansions, some of them hous-ing foreign embassies, lined the shores of the lake known as the Wansee; the water was busy with pleasure boats, and its shores hosted family picnics. There were few signs of the financial and political turmoil that was about to ravage the world economy and bring Hitler to power; nor could anyone anticipate that, a few years later, in one of these lakeside residences, the Nazi hierarchy would meet to refine the details of the "final solution" to the Jewish question.

Boyer was learning firsthand that each country took a different approach to making movies. Hollywood directors affected costumes and threw tan-trums, while a hierarchy of key technicians jealously guarded their fiefdoms. By contrast, at Pathé/Natan and other Paris studios, the atmosphere was relaxed. Distinctions blurred between director, crew, and cast. Out of consid-eration for those who might have been partying the night before, filming began at noon. Ufa's sound stages were as hushed as hospital wards. The floors gleamed black with polish. Equipment operated with oiled efficiency. Directors wore white gloves, signifying that they never soiled their hands with technical matters, reserving their expertise for performances alone. Work began at 6:00 a.m., and directors were required to advise the producer in advance and in writing of what they intended to shoot that day and how long it would take to do so.

Like many films made in multiple languages, *Brand in der Oper* made maximum use of a single spectacular sequence—in this case, an opera house in flames. Henry Roussell was directing the French version with Simone Cer-dan and Suzanne Charpentier (aka Annabella), whom Boyer met for the first time while working on this film. His life would often intersect with that of Charpentier, an open-faced and frankly sexual actress who became a lifelong friend and, probably, lover.

34

The sharpness of the film's photography by Fritz Arno Wagner and the sensitivity of the Tobis sound system surpassed anything Boyer had seen or heard in Hollywood. American cinema owed much of its famed technical mastery to Germany's techniques and technicians, but the Americans had not yet caught up with its latest innovations.

Boyer had barely returned to Paris when he was called back to MGM. Far from being disappointed with *Le Procès de Mary Dugan*, the studio wanted him for another production—a prison film called *The Big House*. MGM even offered to buy up the balance of his Ufa contract—a paper transaction only, since MGM and Paramount were majority stockholders in Ufa under the so-called ParUfaMet agreement. The offer was, once again, probably initiated by director Jacques Feyder, so Boyer took the boat train to Le Havre and boarded yet another liner bound for New York.

That summer, every boat from Europe carried new talent to Hollywood, and many of the travelers were headed for MGM. After protests that the actors used in Spanish-language versions were Mexican or South American and spoke different dialects, the studio imported ten actors from Spain to revoice films in classic Castilian. They arrived on the same ship as Spanish-born Luis Buñuel, codirector with Salvador Dali of the surrealist *L'Age d'Or*. With him was that film's star, Lya Lys, and two young French directors, Pierre Weill and Claude Autant-Lara. Françoise Rosay had suggested the latter to direct her and Buster Keaton in *Buster Se Marie*.

The Big House would be MGM's most ambitious multilanguage production. For the next half century, directors reused the walled yard and three-story cell block built for the film. It also broke new ground in depicting prison conditions. Frances Marion had persuaded Irving Thalberg to let her tour penal institutions to ensure authenticity, but the mass of faceless prisoners trudging into the prison yard or seated silently in the dining hall—their every movement dictated by the shrill of a whistle—owed more to the regimented workers of Ufa's *Metropolis*. The film's realism contrasted with such contemporary productions as Josef von Sternberg's *Thunderbolt*, in which a barbershop quartet of death-row inmates serenades each condemned man on his way to the electric chair.

George Hill directed the English version; Ward Wing the Spanish, called *El Presidio*; and Pál Fejös the German, *Menschen hinter Gittern*. Feyder began work on a French version, *Révolte dans la Prison*, but Fejös took that over as well. In the English version, Lon Chaney was supposed to play Butch, a brutish career criminal who instigates the film's climactic breakout and riot, but he was too ill and died before the film wrapped. Frances Marion was walking through the MGM restaurant when she noticed burly contract player Wallace Beery, who generally played good-natured oafs but had not worked in a year, as he delayed his sound debut. Casting him against type as Butch revived his career and earned him an Academy Award nomination.

Lumbering and ignorant but cunning, Butch shares a cell in the overcrowded prison with white-collar offender Morgan. They are unlikely friends, and Morgan helps the big man control his periodic rages. The attacks worsen when Butch and Morgan are joined by a new inmate, Kent, a playboy who killed two people while driving drunk. Unable to endure the prison regime, Kent survives by turning informer. Robert Montgomery played Kent in the American version, and Chester Morris played Morgan, but the film belonged to Beery's Butch. In the French version, André Berley made Butch more blubbery, mingling charm and brutality. Hangdog André Burgère, sallow and hollow-eyed, more busboy than playboy, was poorly cast as Kent. In contrast, Boyer was quietly effective as Morgan, the film's moral hero.

Following *The Big House*, Boyer lingered in Los Angeles, waiting to hear MGM's plans for his future. From time to time he tried to see Paul Bern, who was invariably busy. Otherwise, life fell into a routine. Each Saturday he visited the studio to collect his salary. He got a shoeshine and a haircut and ate lunch in the commissary. Most Saturday evenings, the Feyders had a party at their Beverly Hills home. For the rest of the week, except for occasional poker parties and dates, Boyer sat in his room reading and waiting for the phone to ring. His smoking increased to four packs a day, and a cigarette became integral to his screen persona. It would soon be rare to see him, on screen or off, without one in his hand.

Boyer did not know that *The Big House* would be MGM's last parallel production. Most had been expensive failures, and early in 1931 the studio decided to discontinue them. Henceforth, new dialogue in other languages would be dubbed over the original. A consortium of American studios was already building a facility in the Parisian suburb of Joinville to turn out such copies en masse. Rather than explain the change to its foreign employees and risk resentment, poor performances, and perhaps even walkouts, MGM simply let their contracts expire. Those who were regarded as expendable were assigned demeaning tasks until they became disgusted and quit. This was Luis Buñuel's fate. Following months of inactivity, he was asked to approve some Spanish dialogue spoken by Lili Damita in *The Bridge of San Luis Rey*. "I'm not here as a Spaniard," he snapped, "but as a Frenchman—and what's more, go tell Thalberg that I don't waste my time listening to whores."[1] Within weeks, he was on his way back to France.

After being bumped from the French version of *The Big House,* Jacques Feyder moved on to an adaptation of Arthur Schnitzler's *Daybreak,* set among young military officers in Hapsburg Vienna. Once again nudged by his wife, he offered a small role to Boyer, who was being fitted for a uniform in the costume department when the front office, anxious that he not be given any reason to stay in Hollywood, overruled his casting. Instead, he was given a few days' uncredited work as a doctor in Edgar Selwyn's *War Nurse,* about American girls who volunteer as nurses in France during the war and experience the worst horrors of trench warfare.

Françoise Rosay, who was moving to Paramount for her next film—*The Magnificent Lie,* starring Ruth Chatterton—found a place in the cast for Boyer, and MGM was more than happy to lend him. Boyer recognized this as a milestone. It was not a parallel production. For the first time, he would be acting for Americans alone. He already knew the director, Viennese producer Berthold Viertel, who had seen him in the Berlin production of a Bernstein play. The Viertels had arrived in Hollywood in 1928, after the failure of their theater company. They hoped to learn the film business and then return to Germany and become producers. Instead, Salka Viertel joined MGM and found a niche as Greta Garbo's confidante and script adviser, while Berthold was given one-film contracts and shunted from Fox to Paramount to Warner Brothers. To the few Americans who noticed him, he was just "Bert Vertel," another incomprehensible foreigner.

MGM had made a fortune with *The Big Parade,* in which a wounded American soldier falls in love with a French woman, so any similar property became instantly valuable. The hero of Paramount's *The Magnificent Lie,* Bill Childers (played by newcomer Ralph Bellamy), is a victim of post-traumatic stress who suffers periods of blindness. He is a patient at a field hospital when it is visited by actress Rosa Duchene (Rosay). While she is there, the hospital is bombed, and she nurses Bill through the raid, a kindness he never forgets. Years later, in New Orleans, Bill sees Rosa playing *La Dame aux Camellias,* but he goes blind before they can renew their acquaintance. As a joke, two actors in her company (one of them played by Boyer) persuade café singer Poll (Chatterton) to impersonate Rosa and fool the blind Childers. A relationship begins, based on this complicated lie. Then, just when it seems the plot cannot become any more confusing, a car accident restores Bill's sight.

Chatterton never hid her disgust with the film, convinced she had been cast as punishment for intending to desert the faltering studio. Boyer's heavy accent, slicked-down hair, and continental good looks made him the perfect choice as one of the actors behind the cruel trick. But the film labored under Viertel's difficulties with English. Mostly he communicated with the actors through his assistant, the young Fred Zinnemann.

Boyer finished the film with his self-confidence at a new low. Word had spread of MGM's policy on foreign versions. Clearly, he had no future in Hollywood. Without telling Bern he was leaving, he took the train to New York and was back in Paris before *The Magnificent Lie* opened there, permitting him to dub his role (unenthusiastically) for its French release. He looked back on the last two years as "a period of my life I would rather forget. I spoke painfully little English and could not seem to learn very quickly. Everyone knew me on the boulevards of Paris but there I was just another foreign actor. My bitterness with Hollywood was so intense that my ears rang with it."[2]

At Ufa in Berlin, Boyer's friend André Daven had a job supervising parallel versions under Erich Pommer, the studio's head of production. An executive possessing vision and flair, Pommer was responsible for such masterpieces as Fritz Lang's *Metropolis* and the international career of Germany's biggest male star, Emil Jannings, who was then working in Hollywood as part of a deal Pommer had engineered. Once Jannings won the first Academy Award for best actor, Pommer would bring him back in a cunningly stage-managed coup to appear in Germany's first sound film, *The Blue Angel*. Under Pommer, Ufa became one of the world's most innovative studios, although, as a Jew, he was fatally vulnerable to the increasing power of Adolf Hitler and his propaganda chief Joseph Goebbels.

Daven was producing *Tumultes* (Uproar), a French-language version of Robert Siodmak's *Sturm der Leidenschaft*, which starred Jannings and Russian actress Anna Sten. Instead of reshooting the entire film in French, Pommer and Daven saved money by importing only a handful of French performers, including Boyer and Odette Rousseau (aka Florelle), to replicate only the Jannings-Sten dialogue scenes. They left the rest unchanged, reasoning that French audiences wouldn't mind policemen in German uniforms or a few obese, bald-headed extras in bowler hats who could have stepped straight out of *Der Dreigroschenoper*.

Erich Kettelhut's sets—consisting of a bank, its vault doors secured with gleaming locks and wheels, and the prison kitchen, with cauldrons and serving hatches more substantial than anything in *The Big House*—were impressive, indicative of Ufa's high technical standards. Siodmak also made effective use of Ufa's standing sets of tenements and courtyards, which were better constructed and more authentic than anything Boyer had seen in Hollywood.

Typical of the style that would become known as film noir—of which Siodmak was a pioneer—most of the story unfolds at night, with key scenes set in a cheap Berlin amusement park and cabaret. The decision to retain much of the original for the French version pays off in a showdown between the rival lovers that takes place during a fireworks display. Cinematographer Gunther Rittau, in a series of flashing, high-angle tracking shots, follows Boyer as he pursues his victim across a crowded dance floor. Then, in silhouette, the chase continues through a yard and up a wooden staircase, at the top of which Boyer smashes his rival through a closed window above the river, right into a whirlpool of light reflected from the spinning Catherine wheel overhead.

Boyer was never comfortable with violence, but in the Jannings role, he stepped into the shoes of an actor for whom it was second nature. His boyish grin has none of Jannings's threat. Nor does Florelle rival the beauty of Anna Sten, who would soon be recruited by Hollywood producer Sam Goldwyn. But it was the best sort of film to rinse the taste of Hollywood from Boyer's mouth, and his performance is more complex than anything demanded of him there. "That face," wrote Joseph Kessel, "brutal and sensitive at the same time, the lips that display from instant to instant lust, shame, boldness and vengeance, the brow that little by little clears or frowns under the weight of conflicting passions, is unforgettable."[3] Boyer considered *Tumultes* the sole film of value in his early career.

10

Mid-Atlantic

Disappointed European artists were straggling back from Hollywood, among them Jacques Feyder and Françoise Rosay. Although Feyder had finally directed Greta Garbo in her French sound debut, a version of *Anna Christie*, MGM offered him no more work. "You should not feel so bad," he consoled Boyer. "It even happened to us." Some took rejection worse than others. Marcel de Sano, who directed *Le Procès de Mary Dugan*, killed himself in Paris in 1936.

Given this dispiriting situation, Boyer was surprised to be invited back to Hollywood for another film—this time not a French version of an American film, and not for MGM but for Paramount. He owed the offer to Claudette Colbert, who still carried a torch for him. She had suggested that Paramount cast him in her next film, *The Man from Yesterday*. The character was French, so his accent would be appropriate, and if he had language problems, she could help. The salary was a fraction of what MGM paid, but Boyer welcomed the chance to redeem his earlier dismal showing.

Once again, his director was Berthold Viertel, whose career had slumped even further since *The Magnificent Lie*. This would be his last American film. The original title was *Wound Stripes,* another story following in the wake of *The Big Parade.* Clive Brook plays a British officer, and Colbert is the French nurse he marries while on leave in Paris. During the hour between the ceremony and their return to the front, he manages to impregnate her, apparently in the back of a cab while driving through the Bois de Boulogne during a blackout—a feat deserving of a medal. A victim of poison gas, Brook ends the war in a Swiss hospital, and Colbert, believing him dead, takes up with surgeon Boyer. The chance reunion of husband, wife, and lover concludes with scenes of self-sacrifice and renunciation, a tearful Colbert, and Brook the very embodiment of the British stiff upper lip. Any acting honors, however, belong to Boyer, who underplays with assurance and compassion. He comes

40

to terms with Colbert's decision on the train returning to Paris, his face eloquent with despair as the landscape slides by unseen.

The Man from Yesterday excels in evoking wartime Paris. Working with cinematographer Karl Struss, whose credits include F. W. Murnau's *Sunrise*, Viertel demonstrates the theatrical flair that brought him to Hollywood. One striking sequence shows crowded cafés emptying as an air-raid warning sounds. Once the bombs cease falling, the trumpets of the all-clear, blown by firemen racing through the city, resonate with shots of the megaphone through which a nightclub singer croons "St. Louis Blues."

Boyer finally caught up with Paul Bern and the Thalbergs at a Santa Monica beach party thrown by actress Marion Davies, mistress of newspaper magnate William Randolph Hearst. Thalberg shrugged off *The Trial of Mary Dugan* and *The Big House* as failed experiments, but he had the grace to be embarrassed at how badly the studio had treated its imported talent. He suggested that as long as Boyer was back in Hollywood, he might do another film at MGM. Although the offer seemed to be spontaneous, the idea probably originated with Bern. He was planning the first feature starring brazen blonde Jean Harlow and thought they could move past the whole sorry episode by giving Boyer a part.

Red-Headed Woman was based on a Katherine Brush novel in which a gold digger (Harlow) seduces her way to a fortune. F. Scott Fitzgerald attempted an adaptation but lacked the common touch needed for what *Time* magazine called "the quick, caustic biography of an alert, successful strumpet."[1] The project was passed along to fashionable novelist Anita Loos, who gave Harlow's character a Russian wolfhound, a 1932 Packard De Luxe, and a French chauffeur named Albert—the role proposed for Boyer. At any other time, the offer of such a small part would have been an insult, but Bern added some financial sweetening. Since Boyer had returned to France without advising MGM of his departure, Bern proposed that they regard his contract as still being in force and pretend that Boyer had merely been "on leave," so he would immediately go back on the payroll at $400 a week.

"I liked all the people involved," Boyer explained later, "but the reason I agreed to play the chauffeur was simply that it was an MGM picture. In France and everywhere else, MGM pictures seemed more important than those of any other company. I intended to do well in the Harlow picture, and then get larger roles at MGM. And perhaps more money. There was some talk of putting me in a picture opposite Helen Hayes. Once Irving [Thalberg] promised that *Red-Headed Woman* would not be shown in France, I said, 'Yes. I'll do it.'"[2]

41

Fitted with a uniform, a peaked cap, and a mustache, he had little to do but carry Harlow's packages, drive the Packard, and deliver a few monosyllabic lines. Staff writers had polished the script and slightly improved his part with a scene in which one of Harlow's protectors exposes him as her lover and fires him. Even so, his character was so insignificant that Boyer's name did not even appear among the major credits.

Red-Headed Woman was released in June 1932. Boyer remained in Los Angeles for the summer, but no one at MGM admitted to having any knowledge of the promise of additional work. Nor were any other studios interested in a has-been Frenchman with poor English. Fox offered some hope that Boyer might be cast in *Adorable,* a German comedy rewritten by, among others, Billy Wilder and starring Janet Gaynor, but the role went to the younger Henri Garat, fresh off the boat from Paris and able to sing and dance. Bern was preoccupied with Harlow, whom he would marry that July. A defeated Boyer asked MGM to pay for his voyage back to France. The accounting office, however, did not share Thalberg's generous view of his contract and regarded him as being in default. Boyer went home in disgrace, and he had to pay his own fare.

In September, Bern was found shot dead, an apparent suicide (but probably murdered by a jilted ex-mistress). The following month, Boyer revoiced his part for the French release of *The Man from Yesterday* (as *Le Revenant*). When *Red-Headed Woman* arrived, MGM's Paris office professed ignorance of any promise not to release it in France (as *La Femme aux Cheveux Rouges*). Boyer realized, belatedly, that he had been naïve to expect MGM to forgo the income from such a commercial film. Appeals to Hollywood were useless. Thalberg was supposedly in seclusion following Bern's death. On principle, Boyer refused to dub his scenes as Albert, so he had to stand by while another actor did so. His humiliation at the hands of Hollywood was complete.

Hollywood might be winding up its multilanguage program, but parallel productions remained important in both Germany and France. An estimated 15 percent of all French films made between the arrival of sound and the outbreak of World War II were coproduced with other countries. So many people in the film industry traveled between Berlin and Paris that the trade magazine *Cinématographie Française,* in the style of *Variety*'s column "From the Coast/To the Coast," published details of who was in which city and where they were staying. Behind the scenes, Nazi infiltration of Germany's film industry continued under Joseph Goebbels, who understood better than anyone its value in advancing Nazism. "For us," he said, "cinema is the most important art."

Tumultes was released in France in April 1932. Soon after, Ufa invited Boyer back for the technological thriller *F.P. 1 Antwortet Nicht* (F.P. 1 Fails to Reply), known in England as *Secrets of F.P. 1* and in France as *I.F. 1 Ne Répond Plus*. Boyer appeared only in the last, but all three were directed by Austrian Karl Hartl.

Ufa's specialty was *utopischefilme*—futuristic stories in which German technology makes life more efficient. *F.P. 1 Antwortet Nicht* imagines a floating airport stationed permanently in the mid-Atlantic. By refueling there, aircraft could link Europe, the Americas, and Africa, making ocean liners obsolete. When sinister interests—Cunard or some other cruise line?—sabotage the project, the adventurous aviator Ellisen foils their plot.

Arriving in Berlin to make the French version, Boyer found himself among friends. His costar Daniele Parola was married to André Daven, and second lead Jean Murat was engaged to Annabella. Hans Albers played Ellisen in the German version, with Sybille Schmitz and Paul Hartmann. The lead in the British version went to another German, Conrad Veidt, who, unlike Albers, spoke good English. Efficient as always, Ufa drew up a roster to ensure that the three casts received equal treatment, taking turns being the first on the set or the last to leave.

All three leading men detested the role of Ellisen. Not only does he fail to get the girl; he almost disappears for the last two-thirds of the film, supplanted by sequences of the platform under construction, some mediocre model work, and a couple of musical interludes. Boyer disliked having his hair bleached to make it easier for the editor to match him in long shots of the blond Albers. Producer Pommer also required Albers, Veidt, and Boyer to record, each in his own language, an inspirational theme song, "March of the Aviators," which was released as a recording. Boyer did his version in an apologetic half sung–half spoken *spechgesang*.

In August and September, filming moved to Greifswalder Oie, a tiny island in the Baltic where Ufa had constructed its "floating platform" with unobstructed background views of the sea. Cast and crew stayed nearby on the larger island of Rügen, at a *gasthaus* occupied by each national contingent in turn. During the French shoot, Boyer, Parola, and Murat were joined by assistant director Marcel Vallée, an accomplished chef who prepared meals from the local seafood and game. In the evenings, hunters and fishermen joined the film people to eat and dance. Afterwards there was poker. "I don't have the instinct," Vallée said. "Charles, though; he had the gift, and the taste for it too. I always admired the calm and patience with which he played, no matter how much the rest of us joked."[3]

Boyer had hardly settled in after returning to Paris when Daven invited him back to Berlin for something entirely different: a costume musical called *Ich und die Kaiserin* (Me and the Empress). Conrad Veidt starred in the German version, Boyer in the English and French. German cinema had few artists as popular as Veidt. Tall (about six feet two inches) and with a wolfish grin, he enjoyed a long European film career before international audiences rediscovered him as Major Heinrich Strasser in *Casablanca*. The female lead, Lilian Harvey, of British and German parentage, was the undisputed queen of film operetta, confirmed by her appearance in the 1931 film of Erik Charell's *Der Kongress Tanzt* (Congress Dances), the most lavish film of its type at the time.

Boyer had not been considered for the French version of *Der Kongress Tantz* because he couldn't sing. Once again, Henri Garat got the role. In *Ich und die Kaiserin*, however, Harvey did the singing, helped by second lead Heinz Ruehmann. The Veidt/Boyer part—as the Duke of Campo Formio or Marquis de Pontignac, depending on the version—called for comedy and romance, which Boyer could handle with ease. Paul Martin, Harvey's lover, directed all three versions, with an additional directing credit going to Friedrich Hollander, the composer who wrote the music for numerous films, notably *The Blue Angel*. Hollander enjoyed the challenge of composing new music in the midst of filming. To do this, he retired to the calm of the lavatory, where he worked on music paper pinned to the inside of the door.

Berlin social life was so agreeable that Boyer was in no hurry to get back to Paris. Erich Maria Remarque, author of *All Quiet on the Western Front*, was a regular in its fashionable bars and cabarets, and he and Boyer became friends. Boyer also saw Berthold Viertel, who mentioned their meeting in a nostalgic letter to Salka, who was still in Hollywood: "The S&M prostitutes still gather on the corner of *Tauentzien* and *Kurfurstendamm*, complaining aloud to passers-by that the police will not let them wear their high boots anymore. Despite the new morality, their numbers have increased. They look younger, prettier, rather middle class, and beg more than solicit. The Eden Bar and other night spots are ultra-chic and full of foreigners and film people. There you can see Conny Veidt, Charles Boyer, prominent stage actors and financiers. Berlin is still more elegant than New York."[4]

Nobody who witnessed the widening gap between Germany's rich and poor believed the party could continue. As Viertel hinted, gangs of Nazi Brownshirts of the *Sturmabteilung* took it upon themselves to police its "decadent" society. Erich Pommer, Fritz Lang, and André Daven were already planning to leave. Other Jewish artists foresaw disaster but perversely relished it. Max Reinhardt, the most innovative stage producer of the day and director of the Salzburg Festival, hosted his customary party at the conclusion of the 1932 festival. As the elite of the Austrian and German theater, many of them Jewish and socialist, speculated nervously about what 1933 would bring, Reinhardt refused to worry. "The nicest thing about these festival summers is that each one may be the last," he said. "You can feel the taste of transitoriness on your tongue."[5]

II

A Ride on the Carousel

The end came more swiftly than anyone expected. In January 1933 the Nazis seized power. Joseph Goebbels became *Reichminister* of Public Enlightenment and Propaganda, in absolute control of the theater and film industries. On March 18 he summoned filmmakers to Berlin's Kaiserhof Hotel to announce that, beginning on March 31 (designated Jewish Boycott Day), all contracts with Jewish artists would be dissolved. The day after the meeting, Ufa's board met to implement the law. Among those immediately affected were Erich Pommer and chief *dramaturg* Robert Liebmann. Others notified of their imminent dismissal included Elizabeth Bergner, Conrad Veidt, Fritz Kortner, Peter Lorre, and Friedrich Hollander.

I.F. 1 Ne Répond Plus opened in Paris in February 1933. By May, only a handful of the artists and technicians Boyer had worked with at Ufa remained in Germany. The same day as the Kaiserhof meeting, Pommer left for Paris; Fritz Lang, André Daven, Max Ophuls, and hundreds of other artists would soon follow. Kortner, Lorre, and Bergner and her husband, Paul Czinner, went to London. Lilian Harvey and Paul Martin were already in America. Veidt, completing work on *Secrets of F.P. 1* in London, was unable to return to Berlin. His Jewish wife joined him in England, and both became British citizens. He would complete the English version of *Ich und die Kaiserin,* retitled *The Only Girl,* before continuing his career in the British cinema and Hollywood.

With most of their competition fleeing the country or unable to work, Germany's gentile artists flourished. Emil Jannings, Hans Albers, Willy Forst, Gustav Frohlich, and other Aryan leading men, even those privately opposed to Hitler, never stopped working. Once the dust of the Kaiserhof announcement had settled, some reappeared in Paris and London. They were not shunned. Business was business.

Among the new arrivals in Paris, Lida Baarová stood out. Only nineteen, the slim Czech actress with a wide mouth, high cheekbones, and fathomless blue eyes made an instant impression. Already fluent in three languages when she arrived early in 1934, she quickly picked up French, speaking it without an accent after only a month. Her affair with Boyer began just as speedily. Though fifteen years her senior, he still trailed wisps of Hollywood glory, and the glamorous couple became a feature of the gossip columns.

As Lida had hoped, her proficiency in languages attracted the attention of Ufa, which called her back to Berlin to appear in *Barcarole,* opposite Gustav Frohlich, the blond hero of *Metropolis.* Like Boyer, he was more than ten years older but had better connections in German cinema. Lida never returned to Paris and moved in with Frohlich. Boyer mourned her loss but was philosophical about their stormy relationship. He recognized that, for "Lidushka," as he called her, all men were just stepping-stones on the route to international fame.

The subsequent scandal that erupted around Lida during the shooting of *Barcarole* came as no surprise. While showing Hitler around Ufa, Goebbels met Lida and instantly fell in love. Always alert for the smart career move, she encouraged the affections of the dwarfish, limping *Reichminister.* They were soon meeting secretly, sometimes at the home she shared with Frohlich, who surprised them together one day and punched Goebbels. The incident was hushed up, and Frohlich continued to work. Ufa paid Lida off with a long-term contract; she would appear in twelve films before war broke out. Hearing news of Lida's involvement with Goebbels, Boyer congratulated himself on dodging a bullet. It could have been him in Frohlich's situation. Years later, when she reappeared on Boyer's horizon, he would describe her ruefully as his "biggest casting error."

Pommer had contracted with Fox to open a studio in Paris called Fox-Europe. At the time, this seemed to be a shrewd move. Instead of bringing actors to America to make films for the European market, Pommer could produce them in France, using artists exiled from Germany and Austria. And as long as France and Great Britain continued to appease Hitler, that market could only flourish.

Pommer leased space at Joinville, where Pathé/Natan had recently operated. For Fox-Europe's first (and, as it turned out, only) productions, he selected a crime story, *On a Volé un Homme* (Man Stolen), and Ferenc Molnar's fantasy *Liliom.* He hired Liebmann and Hollander to adapt *Liliom* and assigned Lang to direct, while Daven handled production design. Ophuls protested: surely Lang, having shown his mastery of the crime melodrama with his *Doktor Mabuse* films, was the logical choice to direct *On a Volé un*

Homme. But Pommer stood by his decision. Boyer didn't care which film he appeared in. To work with a German refugee director was, he said, a political decision—a gesture, however insignificant, against the Hitler regime. His rival Henri Garat replaced him in *On a Volé un Homme* opposite Lily Damita, and Boyer took the role of Liliom.

Arguably, Pommer did err in giving *Liliom* to Lang and Boyer. Ophuls would have treated the play more lightly and perhaps made the film into an international success, as Rogers and Hammerstein did when they adapted it into the musical *Carousel.* As for thirty-five-year-old Boyer, who was thickening around the waist and going bald, he was hardly the obvious choice to play a young carnival roustabout. After a few days' shooting, production had to be halted while he was fitted with a wig. To his distaste, he was given black curls. After *Liliom,* he swapped it for a conventional toupee and wore a variety of hairpieces for the rest of his career.

Liliom Zadowski works the carousel in the carnival of Madam Muscat (Florelle, from *Tumultes*). His brash patter—half boasting, half flirting—makes it one of her most popular attractions, at the expense of the other concessionaires. Muscat lets him get away with it until he takes up with Julie, a girl he met on the carousel. Jealous, she fires Liliom, who moves in with Julie and her aunt. Julie's pregnancy tempts Liliom into committing a robbery, but when it goes wrong, he kills himself rather than go to jail. Following a stretch in Limbo, he is allowed to return to earth for one day to make amends to his now grown-up daughter.

Lang's concept of the afterlife has more in common with the street than the church. The couriers who escort Liliom's spirit lack wings or haloes; they wear identical suits and hats and identify themselves as "God's police." Liliom's sluggish reception in the next world replicates the hours he spent cooling his heels in the waiting rooms of earthly prefectures.

The film shifts impatiently between fantasy and realism. One moment, Liliom is a brash charmer; the next, he is an arrogant lout. Some backgrounds are detailed; others are barely sketched in. A few scenes are played without sound. Some are falsely ostentatious, redolent of the carnival, while others use the classic editing and camera work that distinguished such films as *M.* One scene shows the carnies' numbed reaction to the news of Liliom's death. The carousel falls silent; men in a bar stare into the middle distance as a clock ticks; a girl in a caravan weeps, her hands filled with photographs.

Neither the French film industry nor its audience welcomed *Liliom.* The influx of German refugees had already triggered an endemic anti-Semitism and xenophobia. Critic François Vinneuil called the film "a French-Jewish-Hungarian collaboration" and suggested that its alien atmosphere "stifled the audience." The church condemned its irreverent depiction of the afterlife.

For Boyer, working with a director of Lang's inventiveness was an education. Staging the scene in which Liliom's soul is lifted out of his body, Lang had the actor remove his shoes and socks. Sitting just out of the shot, he said, "Charles, when I pinch your toe, close your eyes. Then, when I pinch your toe again, open your eyes." It was demeaning for an actor so concerned with motivation to surrender control of his performance in this way. "I don't want to be told when to close my eyes and when to open them," Boyer complained, "but I must admit it is effective on the screen."[1]

12

The Boyer Type

As sound recording improved, more women became familiar with Boyer's insinuating baritone, attractively roughened by the inevitable cigarette. Until then, it had not been obvious that women played only a minor role in his life, eclipsed by his books, his gambling, and his work. Once his misogyny became common knowledge, a profile in the magazine *Ciné-Miroir* broke the news to his female fans: "It's crazy what havoc he can wreak on women's hearts! He receives boxes of chocolates by the crate; ties, scarves, cigarette cases, enough to set up a shop. He sends it all away, with a word so cold that he would discourage Messalina herself. He loves only solitude, to be alone with his books and paintings, and beautiful music of any kind. This man, who is animated by a burning and hidden flame, is externally cold and even discouraging; a volcano under a glacier."[1]

One woman he did admit into his affections was an actress he had known since they were students at the Conservatoire. Pierre Blanchar reintroduced them. Alice Fille was four years younger than Boyer; born in Algiers, she was a rangy ash blonde with an oval face and expressive eyes, reminiscent of Marlene Dietrich and Annabella. Since French audiences liked a hint of the English milord, she had changed her surname to Field. Unlike most women in Boyer's life, Field was well read, politically aware, and confident in her opinions. It may have been surprising that they got along, as Boyer disliked being contradicted, particularly by a woman. But they were increasingly seen as a couple, and friends thought they might have considered marriage. (Blanchar conjectured that Boyer did propose, but Alice turned him down.) Just two years later, Boyer would meet a complete stranger in another country and make his home there with her for the rest of his life, suggesting he was no longer so sure that actors should remain single. Acting could be a lonely business.

There was a certain appropriateness to the title of Boyer's next film. Based on a play called *L'Eprevier* (The Hawk), it was renamed *Les Amoureux*

(The Lovers). In it, Boyer would star with the woman who became his next and, as chance would have it, last mistress. A near look-alike for Greta Garbo, Nathalie Paley had deep-set gray eyes and pale blonde hair—two elements of the so-called Boyer type, according to people who noticed such things. These women were slim with an oval face, pointed chin, high forehead, and large expressive eyes. They wore clothes well. Discreet, with a hint of hauteur or even aristocracy, they probably weren't French, or at least didn't look it. There was nothing vulgar, voluptuous, or openly sexual about them. They epitomized that indefinable term *chic*.

Nathalie Paley was in fact Princess Natalia Pavlovna Paley, daughter of Grand Duke Paul Alexandrovich, uncle of Tsar Nicholas II. Her family had fled the 1917 revolution with enough money to live well in France, where her flair for fashion caught the attention of couturier Lucien Lelong, who left his wife to marry her. Nathalie became his hostess and model, a regular in the glossy magazines, but marriage bored her. So did physical sex, reflected in her lifelong preference for gay male companions.

Ambitious to be more than a mannequin, Paley studied singing and acting, then decided to try movies. Conveniently, Lelong's cousin was Marcel L'Herbier, who chose *Les Amoureux* as a vehicle for her debut. The "Hawk" of the title is Georges de Dasetta, a count of dubious credentials who, along with his wife, Marina, preys on the rich as a card cheat. The two are thriving until Marina falls for a young diplomat. In despair, Georges attempts suicide, which has the effect of reuniting the couple, and they continue their depredations at the card tables.

With an unknown quantity like Paley, L'Herbier needed a reliable leading man. After considering Blanchar, he decided on Boyer, who was more at home in the world of high-stakes gambling. But while *Les Amoureux*'s locales were ideal for showing off Lelong's clothes, the film never overcame the stiffness of an *haute couture défilé;* nor did Paley lose the cold asexuality of a shop-window mannequin. After small roles in French, British, and American films, she abandoned cinema for a life of parties and serious drinking, but not before she and Boyer enjoyed a brief liaison. They were seen dining and dancing, at the races or a premiere, and if Boyer sometimes went home not to her bed but to a cigarette, a cognac, and a good book, well, so what?

Boyer used his time with L'Herbier to interest the director in a play being written specifically for him by Henry Bernstein. *Le Bonheur* (Happiness) had all the ingredients of a hit: a crime story with a show-business background, including a spectacular trial, a romance, and a surprise ending. If it succeeded onstage, coaxed Boyer, a film version would be the next step—with, naturally, L'Herbier directing. Cautiously, the director agreed.

While he waited for *Le Bonheur,* Boyer returned to one of his earlier successes. As Japanese, Chinese, and Russian navies clashed off the China coast, Russian director Viktor Tourjansky recalled Boyer's success in *La Bataille.* Tourjansky had settled in Berlin following the 1917 revolution, but Goebbels had forced him to relocate to Paris. With cinematographer Nicolas Farkas, he adapted *La Bataille* for the screen and invited Boyer to reprise the role of Yorisaka. Boyer persuaded Bernstein to release him from his contract for a single film.

Bernard Natan contributed the cost of filming at Pathé. For the rest of the budget, Farkas approached fellow Hungarian Alexander Korda in London. Their deal called for French and English versions, with Boyer starring in both but with different leading ladies: Annabella for the French version, to be called *La Bataille,* and Korda's wife, Merle Oberon, for the English version, retitled *Thunder in the East.* Korda relied on Farkas to show off Oberon's velvety skin and exotic eyes while disguising the fact that, contrary to publicists' claims that she had been born in remote but Anglo-Saxon Tasmania, she was the illegitimate daughter of a Scots infantryman and a teenage Sri Lankan prostitute.

Oberon arrived in Paris and was whirled through a succession of receptions, dinners, and cocktail parties. Aware of how easily the good life could be snatched from them, Russian exiles partied hard. In tsarist restaurants, they wept to the sound of the balalaika and drowned their despair in vodka. Merle, who ate lightly and seldom drank, was miserable. Her misery only increased once shooting started, when each day began with hours having makeup applied to make her look Asian. For the ocean battle scenes, Farkas moved to Normandy, where a shipboard set was mounted on rockers to simulate the high seas. Both Oberon and Boyer became seasick.

La Bataille/Thunder in the East enjoyed some success, but only as a curiosity. However, Boyer's performance smoothed his eventual acceptance by American audiences, who admired actors who physically transformed themselves for a role. Oberon also came out a winner. Her appearance in this film persuaded Sam Goldwyn to sign her for *The Dark Angel,* her Hollywood debut. The film's most durable souvenir, ironically, was the name of Yorisaka's wife. "Mitsouko" caught the attention of *parfumier* Jacques Guerlain, who chose it for his newest fragrance. It survives to this day.

13

The Love of His Life

*L*a Bataille changed the lives of both Boyer and Annabella, but for sentimental rather than artistic reasons. It brought the actress to America,
where she met and married Tyrone Power. It was also in America that Boyer
would find the love of his life.

For all his doubts about Hollywood, Boyer could see that his future lay
there. European cinema was too unreliable. Even while they shot *La Bataille*
at Pathé, rumors were rife about Bernard Natan. In 1935 he would declare
bankruptcy and be jailed for fraud. Boyer could have made films in Germany,
but he refused to support the Hitler regime. That left Britain, where Alexander Korda kept London Films alive largely by sleight of hand. "The art of
film-making," he declared, "is to come to the brink of bankruptcy and stare it
in the face." Boyer had no desire to follow the wily Hungarian into a financial
abyss.

Prospects in Hollywood were better. MGM, Paramount, and Warner
Brothers weathered the stock market crash, although others were struggling.
William Fox lost control of his studio in 1929. (In 1936, he would serve a six-
month jail sentence for trying to bribe the judge in his bankruptcy hearing.)
Still bearing Fox's name, the studio stayed afloat with cheap serials, news-
reels, westerns, and mysteries. In lieu of male action stars or glamorous leading ladies, its biggest names were popular moppet Shirley Temple and folksy,
wisecracking Will Rogers, a favorite with rural audiences.

Fox bought an occasional European film, including *Secrets of F.P. 1,* if it
could do so cheaply. It also imported some of the talent stranded in Paris.
This included producer Erik Charell, known as "the Ziegfeld of the German
musical." Outside of Germany, only the United States had an industry and an
audience sufficiently large to support Charell's lavish productions. Pommer
lacked the resources to produce one of these extravaganzas in Paris, so Fox
put Charell under contract. A series of émigré screenwriters, old hands at

molding marzipan, were put to work confecting a script. Melchior Lengyel conceived the idea, Hans Kraly adapted it, and Robert Liebmann added dialogue. The result was *Gypsy Melody*, which became *Caravan*, destined to be one of Hollywood's last bilingual productions.

In Paris, another new arrival from Berlin was Russian-born director Anatole Litvak, and he wanted Boyer for his film *Cette Vielle Canaille* (That Old Rogue). Boyer did not know Litvak but was familiar with the play on which the film was based: a young acrobat seduces the mistress of a famous surgeon, only to find that, following an accident, his life depends on the surgeon's skill. Boyer was not particularly tempted by the play or by this unknown director, until he heard that Harry Baur, the elder statesman of French theater, would play the doctor. Boyer took Alice Field with him to his first meeting with Litvak. Though surprised and a little offended that the actor had arrived at the audition with his girlfriend, Litvak liked Boyer immediately, and vice versa. Field was also attracted to the director, who had a reputation as a ladies' man. However, the meeting did not turn out as any of them expected.

Boyer was almost ready to sign a contract for *Cette Vielle Canaille* when Fox cabled an offer for him to star in the French and American versions of *Caravan*—both to be produced in Hollywood by André Daven. Boyer's friend had gone out of his way to make the offer attractive. His leading ladies would be Loretta Young and Annabella, and the second lead in the French version, called *Caravane*, would be another old pal, Pierre Brasseur. Boyer needed little persuading. He relinquished his role in *Cette Vielle Canaille* to Pierre Blanchar and left for Hollywood, abandoning Field in the process. Fortunately, Litvak was there to console her. He not only cast her opposite Blanchar and Baur in *Cette Vielle Canaille* but also made her his mistress.

The *Caravan* party sailed on the *Ile de France*, the French Line's newest and most fashionable ship, admired for its Art Deco interiors. It was a convivial voyage. Along with Boyer, Daven, Brasseur, and Annabella, the group included Daven's wife Daniele Parola, Annabella's fiancé Jean Murat, and Marcel Vallée, all veterans of *I.F. 1 Ne Répond Plus*. Erik Charell was also on board, as was British actor Sir Cedric Hardwicke, with whom Boyer would appear both on stage and in film.

The group arrived in Los Angeles by train and checked into the Hollywood Hotel. There was a lunch party at Fox on January 23, 1934, to celebrate the wrapping of *David Harum*, Will Rogers's latest film. Production head Winfield Sheehan insisted that Boyer and some of the others make an appearance—in Boyer's case, to meet his *Caravan* costars Phillips Holmes and Loretta Young. Boyer recognized a few of the guests, among them Spencer Tracy, with whom he shared the same rung on the career ladder. Tracy was winding up his last film for Fox, the comedy *Bottoms Up.* Also at the party was that film's female lead: Pat Paterson, a young English actress making her Hollywood debut.

From the first moment, Boyer could not take his eyes off her, nor she from him. It was a *coup de foudre,* the classic thunderclap. In hindsight, those who were familiar with the Boyer type conceded that she ticked all the boxes. Her oval face and pointed chin, high forehead, and large eyes all conformed to his ideal. She dressed well, was foreign (although she played a Canadian in *Bottoms Up,* she actually came from Bradford, in the English midlands), was ten years younger than Boyer, and, at five feet two inches, was much shorter, all of which added to her appeal. That night, he called and asked her for a date.

For the next three weeks, they were seldom apart. One evening toward the end of that time, they arrived at the premiere of Garbo's *Queen Christina* at Grauman's Chinese Cinema on Hollywood Boulevard, only to find that the film had already started. Rather than fumble to their seats in the dark, Pat asked, "What shall we do now?"

Boyer said impulsively, "Well, we could get married."

They both laughed, but three days later, on Valentine's Day, they drove to Yuma, Arizona, a state that allowed quickie weddings. A justice of the peace conducted the ceremony, and Boyer discovered that his new wife's real name was not Patricia Elizabeth but Eliza Cissie. They spent their wedding night in a motel—a first for both. Despite the abbreviated courtship—or perhaps because of it (any awkward discoveries took place after the ceremony, too late for second thoughts)—the marriage endured. They would remain together for the rest of their lives and die within days of each other in Phoenix, less than 200 miles from where they were married.

The news astonished everyone who knew Boyer and his antipathy to matrimony. "I couldn't believe it of Charles," Maurice Chevalier said. "Why, he could have had any woman in France. Women were mad over him, but he was never intrigued."[1] He threw a party for the newlyweds, and Boyer moved into Pat's apartment. Plans to return to France after shooting *Caravan/Caravane* were put on hold. When he did go, he wanted Pat on his arm. Their honeymoon coincided with the release of *Bottoms Up* in April 1934. The *New York Times* called Pat "a clever and charming actress. She sings agreeably and plays this particular part ingratiatingly."[2]

Those close to Boyer sensed that Pat suited him in more ways than just her appearance. André Daven was among those who recognized their complementary natures. "Charles couldn't help it that he was such a moody person but Pat understood his moods perfectly. She reads a lot too, but not the same things. She read *Gone with the Wind* and, I suppose, *Forever Amber*. She wasn't deep, and he loved her because she didn't pretend to be."

Meanwhile, Boyer was discovering that he had much to learn about succeeding in Hollywood. First of all, he needed an agent. In Europe, theatrical agents were rare; most actors worked from film to film, relying on their personal relationships with producers. But in Hollywood, an aggressive agent was essential. Leland Hayward represented Pat, but her stop-and-start career was no recommendation for his services. A new friend, actor Adolphe Menjou, suggested Myron Selznick, but Boyer disliked his hard-drinking reputation and feared that if he signed with the Selznick-Joyce agency, he would also be committing to Myron's hustling, hands-on producer brother, David.

Boyer wanted someone who shared his values and culture—or at least knew what they were. He found such a person in Charles K. Feldman. Trained as a lawyer, Feldman had just formed his Famous Artists agency. Boyer liked him immediately. With his dapper manner and Errol Flynn mustache, Feldman could have passed for an actor. His wife, the former Jean Howard, had been a member of the troupe of glamorous eye candy known as the Goldwyn Girls, before she retired from the movies to become a successful portrait photographer. Feldman was well read, sociable, and a tireless party-giver. He was also, in the opinion of producer Robert Lord, "the master bullshitter of all time," with a reputation for creative deals that enriched his clients.[3] Ambitious to produce films himself, Feldman pioneered the practice of buying the rights to books or plays and matching them with one or more of his clients in packages that yielded much more than he would have earned from simply representing an individual.

Feldman was happy to accept Boyer as a client. As his first task, he negotiated terms for *Caravan*. Fox wanted Boyer to sign for three more films, but there were rumors of hard times ahead for the studio. Feldman settled on $40,000 for the two versions of *Caravan* alone and began to look for other opportunities, while Boyer applied himself to the role of a Romani fiddler.

The plot of *Caravan* was vintage Charell. Countess Wilma, heiress to Hungary's biggest estate, arrives at the family vineyards on the eve of her twenty-first birthday and discovers that she can inherit only if she marries by midnight. Her dishonest neighbor—played, in a rare departure, by that symbol of British rectitude C. Aubrey Smith—urges her to marry his playboy son, thus surrendering control of her lands to him. Instead, Wilma impulsively decides to marry Latzi, the Romani violinist whose tribe has been hired to tread her family's grapes.

First seen reclining, violin in hand, on a huge cushion like some indolent lapdog, Boyer's Latzi, in snug breeches, high boots, embroidered jacket, and a mop of black curls, looks both ridiculous and oddly at ease. Perhaps this contentment mirrored the real-life love story he was enjoying with his new wife. Phillips Holmes is less comfortable as the lieutenant of hussars who falls in love with a Romani girl, not realizing that she is, in disguise, the countess he was supposed to marry in the first place. When all the plot strands are untangled, aristocrat is united with aristocrat, Wilma's vineyards are saved, and Latzi, along with the rest of his Romani tribe, heads back to deepest Hungary. His consolation prize is the adoring girlfriend (Jean Parker) who loved him all along.

Charell believed that if a spoonful was good, the whole bottle was better. Seldom does the camera focus on just one couple. Instead, hordes of people pour through the frame. The army, sent to put down a supposed revolution, advances on a mob of Romani. At the order "Hands up!" they don't lay down their arms but pick up their instruments and, in a burst of music, let loose dozens of girls, who soon have the soldiers subdued. Boyer has little to do but mime ecstasy or resentment. His big moment comes when Wilma offers him money to marry her. "I may be a gypsy, but I'm not for sale," he responds. "You may be a lady—you may be the richest lady in Hungary—but you haven't got enough money to pay for my love."

"I cringed to see myself wearing black curls," Boyer wrote, "and playing haunting melodies in the moonlight. I have never looked more ridiculous nor felt more uncomfortable in a part."[4] Even so, the New York Times awarded him the film's meager acting honors, while highlighting his special appeal as a sex object. Boyer, the paper observed, "who has a reputation on the Gallic screen, plays the gypsy lover with liquid-eyed ardor, and his voice has the vibrant tenderness of accent which makes the ladies suspire."[5]

So much middle European talent was arriving in Hollywood that a sign appeared in the writers' room at Paramount warning, "Here you must work. It is not enough just to be Hungarian." Yet despite being set in Hungary, not a single character in Caravan is played by a native of that country. Instead, British imports Dudley Digges, Lionel Belmore, and Billy Bevan struggle to project eastern European abandon. Taking the prize for deracination, however, is

Eugene Pallette, born in Winfield, Kansas; as the tribal chieftain, he is required to improvise a speech in gobbledygook Romani.

While Boyer completed *Caravan/Caravane,* Pat served out the remainder of her Fox contract beginning with *Lottery Lover,* a romantic comedy about military students in Paris competing to seduce the star of the Folies Bergère. Next, *Call It Luck* paired her again with Herbert Mundin of *Bottoms Up,* this time as the niece of a London cab driver fleeced of a windfall fortune by some New York sharpies. She got to sing a couple of songs but otherwise made little impression. *Love Time* followed, a low-budget biopic of composer Franz Schubert, played by Danish actor Nils Asther. Once a major star, Asther was now kicking around the studios at the frayed end of his career. For him, this travesty was the last straw. Ignoring Fox's option on his services, he left for Europe. Pat shared his detestation of the film, but she was not ready to tear up her contract and accompany Boyer to France, at the risk of suffering the same fate as Asther—a general blacklisting.

Feldman initially had no luck finding more work for Boyer. Darryl Zanuck at Twentieth Century considered him for the musical *Folies Bergère de Paris,* until he discovered the actor could neither sing nor dance. Chevalier got that part, but such musicals were disappearing, and Chevalier's Hollywood career along with them. Nor were there any takers for the two Frenchmen as a comedy duo. American audiences were weary of Chevalier's moues, leers, and winks, and in 1934 he went back to France, not to return until 1947.

Boyer was ready to leave too when Feldman came through with a last-minute offer, and an attractive one. The loss of Chevalier left Ernst Lubitsch, now head of production at Paramount, without a leading man for Marlene Dietrich in the romantic comedy *I Loved a Soldier.* Feldman persuaded him that Boyer was perfect for the part.

I Loved a Soldier began as Lajos Biro's 1927 play *Hotel Imperial.* The hotel of the title sits in a no-man's-land in central Europe, between two armies. The officers occupy the hotel in turn, as the front shifts back and forth. After a hotel maid is jilted and kills herself, her sister takes a job there, determined to unmask the culprit.

Henry Hathaway began preproduction with Boyer and Dietrich, who told everyone she had broken with her mentor, Josef von Sternberg. In fact, he had secretly traveled to Berlin, intending to start his own production company with Dietrich as his star. Unfortunately, he arrived on the eve of the Kaiserhof pronouncement. It was clear that Dietrich, a favorite of the Führer, would be welcome, but not von Sternberg. Their plan in ruins, Dietrich changed her mind about *I Loved a Soldier*. She agreed to star—but only if von Sternberg directed. Her bluff failed. Paramount, having rid itself of the autocratic director, was not about to take him back. "I was liquidated by Lubitsch," von Sternberg said bitterly. The film was shelved.

Both versions of *Caravan* were critical and box-office disasters. With notably poor timing, it opened in the United States within a few months of *Flying Down to Rio*, avatar of the new musical and a showcase for Fred Astaire, Ginger Rogers, and Busby Berkeley. When Darryl Zanuck's Twentieth Century swallowed Fox, jazz, showgirls, and Broadway supplanted Romani violins, princesses, and old Vienna. Operettas and bilingual productions disappeared into cinema history.

But Boyer was philosophical. "Everyone should have a flop, to know what it's like," he said. "I suppose they believed they might make capital of a man whose eyes looked as if they could mirror all the sorrow of the world, but really I wasn't the type to play mad music in cinema moonlight. But had I not come to Hollywood to make *Caravan* I should not have met Pat."[6] Pat was no luckier with her career. About to be taken over by Zanuck, Fox did not renew her contract. On the bright side, both she and Boyer were now free to make their delayed honeymoon trip to France.

14

Japanese Sandman

Boyer found France in worse turmoil than when he had left. In the wake of the stock market crash, the 1932 elections had given power to the Left, but factional squabbling led to a succession of short-lived coalitions marked by riots, strikes, and even assassinations. In October 1934 King Alexander of Yugoslavia and French foreign minister Louis Barthou were murdered as they rode in an open carriage through Marseilles.

Henry Bernstein wrote an attempted assassination into the play he and Boyer had been discussing during the production of *Les Amoureux. Le Bonheur* (Happiness) mirrored the prevailing political disorder by juxtaposing two people from radically opposed ways of life. Philippe Lutcher is an anarchist who scratches out a living drawing political cartoons, and Clara Stuart is an adored stage and screen star. Disgusted by the frenzy surrounding Clara's recent return from Hollywood, Philippe decides to commit a symbolic act of protest and kill her. The shot only wounds her, however, and he is arrested and put on trial, with unexpected results for both: they fall in love. What could have been a chalk-and-cheese romance becomes an inquiry into how deeply they embody their respective values. Even the title is ambivalent. "Le Bonheur" is also the name of Clara's dreamy theme song, as redolent of synthetic sentiment as Judy Garland's "Over the Rainbow."

Assuming that Boyer was lost to Hollywood, Bernstein offered *Le Bonheur* to Pierre Fresnay and his partner, Yvonne Printemps, but Fresnay turned him down. The actor argued that it was essentially Clara's story, and Philippe didn't even appear until the second act. Boyer had no such reservations. To be on the Paris stage again, and in a Bernstein play, would be a breath of fresh air after the frustrations of Hollywood. Fresnay withdrew, leaving the play to Boyer and Printemps. If Boyer felt any satisfaction at supplanting the man who had blackballed him at the Comédie-Française, he did his best to disguise it.

Le Bonheur was a hit in its limited stage run, and L'Herbier had no trouble persuading Bernard Natan to produce a film version at Pathé/Natan, with Boyer in the lead but experienced screen actress Gaby Morlay replacing Printemps. Knowing that film audiences would expect it, Bernstein rewrote the first act to introduce Boyer earlier, when Philippe's editor sends him to cover Clara's return from Hollywood.

There is more than a hint of Gloria Swanson in the self-regarding Clara, for whom every action is a performance. Bernstein even gave her an aristocratic trophy husband, played by Jaque Catelain with the ingratiating servility of a Pekinese lapdog. As Philippe, Boyer embodies truculence, bluster, and sarcasm but little romance, and Morlay is too self-absorbed to be a credible love object. As Fresnay intuited, it is really Clara's story, leaving Philippe, at the end of their affair, a slightly pathetic figure as he watches Clara onstage, hoping she will sing "Le Bonheur" to show she still thinks of him.

Filming *Le Bonheur* involved some drama of its own when a camera fell on L'Herbier, causing him to lose the sight in one eye. (A shot from a jealous woman had already deprived him of the use of a finger.) He took Pathé to court, claiming that his creative contribution to the film entitled him to compensation beyond that earned as a hired hand. The court's acceptance of this argument established in law the special role of creative artists and the principle of ownership of their work.

After *Le Bonheur*, L'Herbier planned his next film as a crowd pleaser aimed at mass audiences. *Le Route Imperiale* (The Imperial Road) would be an action story exploiting the success of Rudyard Kipling's novels and poems celebrating the British army in India and a 1930 autobiography, *Lives of a Bengal Lancer*, that glamorized Britain's military achievements and would itself be made into a successful Hollywood film. The heroes would be British soldiers suppressing an Iraqi revolution that threatens the caravan route to India.

L'Herbier offered a starring role to Boyer, who was tempted. Feldman had so far failed to find a project that would justify a return to Hollywood. Moreover, he enjoyed the relaxed atmosphere of L'Herbier's sets. On the downside, the film would be shot on location in Algeria, which meant many weeks of separation from Pat. While he made up his mind, the newlyweds took a driving holiday through Britain—research, Boyer told everyone, for his possible role as a British officer. In London, he gave interviews and tried his best to distract attention from *Caravan*. Pat dutifully stayed in the background. No longer "British star Pat Paterson," she was simply "Mrs. Charles Boyer," something that would never cease to rankle.

Meanwhile, in Hollywood, Paul Bern's place as Irving Thalberg's right-hand man had been taken by the personable and dynamic New Yorker Walter Wanger, a contrast in every way to his mild and self-effacing predecessor. Following Thalberg's death, Wanger was put in charge of MGM's East Coast operation until the company moved all its activities to California. This was his cue to leave the studio and strike out as an independent. As a first step, Wanger went talent shopping in Europe, and one actor on his wish list was Boyer. Broadway husband-and-wife team Alfred Lunt and Lynn Fontanne had seen *La Bataille* and recommended Boyer to Wanger as someone with promise. After seeing *Liliom,* Wanger understood why. Boyer exhibited a quality almost unknown among actors trained in Hollywood. "He always seems to be hiding something," said an admirer. "There's a restraint in his *amour* which suggests a dam holding back passion that would like to break loose. Women are captivated by such men because they feel that no matter how madly they love, there is still more in reserve."[1]

Boyer might never be a man of action to rival Clark Gable or Gary Cooper, but Wanger sensed that he was uniquely suited to play the moody outcast, the charmer, the tragic hero, the man of principle. With his almond-shaped eyes and seductive voice, Boyer had all the makings of a great screen lover, with enormous appeal to the female audience. As a young executive at Paramount, Wanger had persuaded the studio to buy E. Mayne Hull's novel *The Sheik* as a vehicle for Rudolph Valentino. That coup sparked a lifelong search for another actor with Valentino's onscreen sexuality. Wanger believed he had found him in Boyer. "I knew what he could do," Wanger said, "and I knew that he had something no one else had on the American screen."[2]

Marriage had softened Boyer's hostility toward women. His new manner was gentler, amused, provocative. Janet Flanner of the *New Yorker* defined his sleepy, languid gaze through half-lowered eyelids as *le regard de Venus:* the Venus look—in other words, bedroom eyes. But resentful rivals would label him the Japanese sandman, after a popular song of 1920.

He and Wanger met for the first time in Paris when Boyer returned from Britain. The producer offered him a five-year contract with $50,000 for the first film. (That sum reflected Wanger's caution. He had already offered $75,000 per film to his other hire, English actress Madeleine Carroll, and he had lured Henry Fonda from Broadway with a guarantee of $100,000 per film.) After that, collaborations would be by mutual agreement, with Boyer retaining the right to work with other producers and to visit France and work there in either theater or film. He was also guaranteed two months' vacation each summer, which he could spend in Europe.

Boyer remained suspicious of long-term commitments, but this one was less restrictive than most. Wanger was an independent producer, not a studio executive, so he would always be available to discuss a problem, and his decisions would be final. Boyer promised to think it over and recommended that Wanger speak to Feldman. The agent thought the deal was a perfect means to launch Boyer's career in American films, and he urged the actor to agree.

Meanwhile, Wanger's plans ran into trouble. His principal investor pulled out, and he was forced to look for another partner. This task was made easier when Ernst Lubitsch offered him a home at Paramount. Wanger would continue to choose and develop projects, which Paramount would fund and distribute in return for 15 percent of the profits.

Returning to America on the *Ile de France,* Wanger noticed some female passengers reading *Private Worlds,* a new novel by British author Phyllis Bottome. Trained as a psychiatrist, Bottome worked at a Swiss clinic for patients with schizophrenia, a little-understood disorder at the time. In the novel, two doctors—one of them a woman—favor compassion and conversation over padded cells and straitjackets in treating mental patients. They clash with a new administrator who is unsympathetic to their ideas and to female doctors. The trio are soon embroiled in a complex relationship involving the doctor's new wife and the administrator's disturbed, possibly homicidal sister.

His interest piqued by the prospect of making the first film set in a mental hospital, Wanger bought the film rights and had Lynn Starling write a screenplay. Joel McCrea and Claudette Colbert agreed to play the doctors, Alex MacGregor and Jane Everest, but the role of Charles Monet, the administrator, had not been cast. Coincidentally, Colbert recommended Boyer, unaware that he was already in Wanger's sights. She hadn't seen him since *The Man from Yesterday* but still thought about his marriage proposals. In 1934, as she reminisced later, "I went to New York for a sinus operation and was so lonely I started to have second thoughts." Her marriage to director Norman Foster was failing, which may have suggested Boyer as a replacement. She phoned him in California but found he was "on location, Poland or someplace. Four days later I wasn't feeling so bad, so I let it pass. It's just as well."[3]

"Poland or someplace" was the ersatz Hungary of *Caravan,* no less remote than the real thing. Once they caught up and she learned of his whirlwind marriage, Colbert revised her expectations. In December 1935 she married Dr. Joel Pressman, who remained her husband until his death in

1968. In true Hollywood fashion, the Boyers and Pressmans, indifferent to their complicated history and mutual knowledge of one another's idiosyncrasies, forged an enduring friendship. Pressman even became one of the Boyers' physicians, sharing those duties with Dr. Francis Griffin, the husband of Irene Dunne.

As soon as Boyer arrived back in Hollywood, he received the screenplay for *Private Worlds*. On his first reading, he disliked Monet's negativity. Moreover, in a fault shared with the stage version of *Le Bonheur*, the character didn't appear until twenty minutes into the story. Dining with the Wangers at Perino's, one of the few restaurants in Los Angeles that could approximate the cuisine of Paris, he tried to explain his misgivings. The discussion continued at Wanger's house. Boyer's inability, as an intuitive actor, to articulate his doubts made him testy. When Pat weighed in on Wanger's side, Boyer snapped at her. For the first time, she saw a different aspect of her new husband, angry and resentful at being contradicted, particularly by his own wife. Jumping in, Wanger asked, "Would it help if we did a read-through?"

Boyer reluctantly agreed, taking the Monet part, while Pat played all the female roles and Wanger the male. And gradually, the power of the writing convinced him. Shadings and nuances suggested themselves, and differences in emphasis emerged as Boyer intuited where his own misogyny and that of Monet coincided. Before they finished, he had changed his mind and agreed to the deal negotiated by Feldman. For the first time, he and Pat could settle down and become Americans.

15

Think American

Because it was not part of Paramount's official output, *Private Worlds* was shot at the independent General Services Studios. The cramped sets and sense of confinement contributed to the friction between Boyer and director Gregory La Cava. Most of the better directors were under contract to studios, and La Cava, a former comic-strip artist and veteran of two-reel comedies, seemed an improbable choice to handle a story as sensitive as *Private Worlds*. However, Wanger's faith in him was not misplaced, and La Cava would go on to direct *Stage Door* and the classic comedy *My Man Godfrey*.

La Cava and Boyer first locked horns on the pronunciation of Boyer's name. Having seen how Berthold Viertel became "Bert Vertel," the actor insisted that he was *Sharl Bwoy-ay*. The next difficulty was not so easy to correct. La Cava asked, "In what language do you think?"

"As I am French," Boyer replied, puzzled, "I think in French."

"That's a problem," said La Cava. "Until you learn to think in English, you will never reach American audiences."[1]

Later, Boyer credited this as a key insight, drawing his attention to the fact that acting in two different cultures demanded psychological as well as linguistic changes.

As a film about mental illness, *Private Worlds* is realistic for its time. The patients appear credibly disturbed. Notably, Guinn Williams—who, as "Big Boy" Williams, usually played a comic cowpoke—is believable as a homicidally violent inmate. There are none of the miracle cures found in other films such as *Spellbound*, which *Private Worlds* otherwise resembles. As in Alfred Hitchcock's film, the therapists' often irrational actions give weight to the message that, as Dr. MacGregor remarks, there is less difference between sanity and insanity than one might imagine. Boyer holds his own with the experienced American cast, though there is no disguising that he is not the film's star; he is a slightly marginal character enmeshed in a sometimes overcomplicated plot.

The Boyers rented a house in Beverly Hills, acquired dogs—Pat loved them and always kept at least one—and bought a secondhand Duesenberg touring car and a smaller Dodge coupe for Pat to drive to work. Boyer never enjoyed driving and hired a chauffeur as soon as it seemed appropriate. They also bought a boat and leased a Malibu beach house, though there was little time to enjoy either. Thanks to Feldman, they were soon on first-name terms with movie aristocracy. The agent liked to gamble, so he and Boyer had something else in common. Adolphe Menjou also introduced the Boyers to bridge. The couple thought about starting a family, but early attempts ended in a miscarriage. Many actresses found motherhood inconsistent with a movie career, and Pat seemed to be one of them. While she continued to work, any plans for a child were put on hold.

Paramount rushed to release *Private Worlds* to fill a gap in its schedule. Reviewers praised it, but there was no time to prepare audiences for its challenging themes, and it made only $10,000 profit. Even so, Wanger was up and running as an independent producer, with the nucleus of the team that would remain with him for years. As a bonus, Colbert was nominated for an Academy Award. She lost to Bette Davis for *Dangerous,* but her year would come in 1936, when *It Happened One Night* swept the board.

Throughout his career as an independent, Wanger strove to assemble a team of actors and technicians similar to those surrounding directors like John Ford. In this, Boyer recognized the impulse that motivated Henry Bernstein to place his actors under such absurdly restrictive contracts. To work freely, one needed to be supported by others who shared one's aesthetic and were ready to drop everything and start work on any project.

Whenever gifted professionals came on the market, Wanger tried to acquire their exclusive services. Henry Fonda, Madeleine Carroll, and Boyer were the cornerstones of an acting stock company, augmented by secondary performers such as Sylvia Sidney. Designer Alexander Toluboff, director Tay Garnett, Arthur Ripley (one-time director for silent comedian Harry Langdon), and screenwriters Graham Baker and Gene Towne provided strong creative support. (To show their gratitude for a regular paycheck, the boisterous Baker and Towne had dustcoats embroidered with "Walter Wanger Productions" and roll-neck sweaters sporting the letter *W*.)

Given Boyer's Japanese character in *Thunder in the East* and the success of other non-Asian actors in Asian roles, such as Nils Asther, Warner Oland, and Akim Tamiroff, Towne and Baker suggested casting Boyer as a Eurasian. The result was *Shanghai.* Boyer plays Dmitri Koslov, son of a Russian who took refuge in Shanghai after the 1917 revolution and married a Chinese aristocrat. Despite the large portrait of his Chinese mother hanging on his wall, nobody in Shanghai's American community suspects Dmitri's ancestry. He also hides his background when he falls for socialite Barbara Howard. Despite warnings that "coming out" would mean social and business disaster, he holds a costume party, at the height of which—"with rather less tact and judgment than one might have expected," in the apt words of a *New York Times* reviewer—he reveals his parentage.[2] Everyone, including Barbara, shuns him, so he flees to the mountains, where a repentant Barbara tracks him down. Whether they stay together is left vague, a sop to those audiences for whom any mixing of the races was anathema.

Lynn Starling, who wrote *Private Worlds,* was brought in to expand the female lead, initially intended for the wisecracking Carole Lombard but eventually given to a tremulous Loretta Young. After reading the script, Boyer warmed to the film. In *Private Worlds* he had taken a backseat to two well-established American performers. In *Shanghai* he would be the unchallenged star in a role that allowed him to show his versatility.

From the opening scene of a tourist boat gliding into the nighttime chaos of dockside Shanghai (actually Catalina Island), director James Flood makes his best points visually. Nobody associated with the film had ever been to China, which freed their imaginations. This is particularly evident in the last half of the film, as Barbara plunges into the country's interior in search of Dmitri. Her passage upriver is strikingly staged. Gangs of anonymous Chinese laborers drag a junk deeper into the mountains, where Boyer broods in a cliffside palace, presumably part of his noble inheritance.

Flood's habit of framing characters full length sometimes draws attention to Boyer's shortness, but he otherwise dominates the film. The tearful and wide-eyed Young is overdressed and hampered by a succession of unfortunate hats. "Against the weeping and fluttering anguish of Loretta Young," the *New York Times* wrote, Boyer's "mournful, almost inscrutable expression and evenly modulated voice are not merely in character but doubly potent in highlighting his scenes."[3]

Young's distraction was understandable. While making her previous film, *Call of the Wild,* she became pregnant by her leading man, Clark Gable. She claimed he raped her on an overnight train while they were returning from location. Shortly after *Shanghai,* she disappeared to Europe, returning with an "adopted" baby girl whose true parentage she hid from everyone— including her daughter—for twenty years.

16

Discord

Shanghai made a respectable $142,000 profit, confirming Lubitsch's judgment in giving Wanger a home at Paramount, but Boyer was less pleased. A film intended as a showcase for him had emerged as a novelettish melodrama. In the opinion of the *New York Times, Shanghai* was a "handsomely mounted photoplay that conceals the decrepitude of its plot beneath a multicolored cloak of setting, incident and characterization."[1] All the same, it indirectly helped his career. On the strength of his performance as a Eurasian, *Thunder in the East* was reissued in America. *Liliom* was also belatedly shown in art houses, and one distributor even exhumed *The Only Girl,* the English version of his German musical with Lilian Harvey, now retitled *Heart Song.*

Unexpectedly, Fox chose to exercise its option on Pat's services one more time and cast her as an archaeologist's daughter in *Charlie Chan in Egypt,* where she was upstaged by a mummy. Invitations for Boyer to film in Europe had increased, but he refused to work there unless Pat could accompany him. Wanger had no film in the works, so he was happy to agree when RKO producer Pandro Berman asked to borrow Boyer for *Break of Hearts.*

The film had a rocky history. It had been written specifically for the aging, alcoholic John Barrymore and RKO's newest recruit from the stage, Katharine Hepburn, in the hope of repeating their success in *A Bill of Divorcement.* The advertising promised "the star of a million moods together with the new idol of the screen," but Hepburn rebelled when—if legend can be believed—Barrymore invited her to his dressing room and received her while reclining naked on a couch. Francis Lederer replaced him, only to clash with director Philip Moeller, whose Broadway career had not prepared him to deal with the irascible Czech. After they collided over which side of his face constituted his "best" profile, Berman, with Hepburn's approval, fired Lederer and hired Boyer.

The character of conductor Franz Roberti was modeled on Arturo Toscanini and Leopold Stokowski, both media heroes because of their flamboyant style on the podium and their equally newsworthy appearances in the society pages (Stokowski reportedly had an affair with Greta Garbo). In the film, Roberti marries young composer Constance Dane. His womanizing and drinking drive her away, but she eventually abandons her career to nurse him back to health. Graham Greene praised both performers as "talented enough to keep some of our interest even in a story of this kind," but Boyer disliked the film.[2] He has a few histrionic scenes—abusing the orchestra with heavy sarcasm and driving it through some breakneck excerpts from the classical repertoire—but essentially, this is Hepburn's film.

For the first time in Boyer's Hollywood career, but by no means the last, rumors circulated of a love affair with his costar. Like many other leading men, Boyer could have enjoyed a busy sex life off camera, and it was widely assumed that he did. However, the women with whom he acted often sensed his disdain, even hostility. Given the widespread use of the casting couch and the plethora of wandering hands actresses had to fend off, a costar who didn't grope them was likely a welcome change. "Women are comfortable with him," said one, "because they sense right away that their bodies are safe; he isn't hell-bent on screwing them. Women become his friends because they trust him, and because of that trust, women play well with him. Whether he's being informal on the set or acting for the camera, Charles does know how to handle women."[3] Did he, when he encountered a consenting partner, go to bed with her? It remains an open question.

Break of Hearts made only a modest $16,000 profit. Meanwhile, Lubitsch moved to MGM as its new head of production. Wanger had no wish to remain at Paramount without Lubitsch's protection and negotiated an agreement with United Artists. He would produce some of his most memorable films for that company, two of them with Boyer.

Wanger's last film for Paramount was *Spendthrift,* a piece of fluff with Henry Fonda as Towny Middleton, a tapped-out former millionaire who recoups his fortune by becoming a sports commentator. Pat's association with the moribund Fox had ended with *Charlie Chan in Egypt,* and no other studio was in a hurry to sign her; nor was Feldman optimistic about finding her work. He did, however, have some ideas about a new contract for Boyer with Wanger at United Artists. It envisaged four pictures at a salary of about $100,000 each, which would put him on the same level as Fonda. Boyer, a quick study, was learning how things were done in Hollywood. While assuring Wanger that he was interested in the deal, he appeared to hesitate—if only Wanger could also find something for Pat. Recognizing the squeeze,

Wanger gave in and cast her in *Spendthrift* as the daughter of J. M. Kerrigan, Fonda's stableman.

Pat clashed with Raoul Walsh, the film's writer and director. She had experimented with dialect in *Bottoms Up* and sought to make an impression in *Spendthrift* by adopting, perhaps too enthusiastically, an Irish accent. "Miss Paterson, the stableman's daughter, is presumed to have grown up with young Towny Middleton," wrote Frank Nugent in the *New York Times*, "but she speaks as though she had just arrived from the Ould Sod the week before."[4] Asked to assess Pat's future as a comedienne, Walsh reportedly growled, "Well, she's no Carole Lombard." Boyer protested that she never set out to be a wisecracking comic like Lombard but rather a soubrette in the style of Ruby Keeler. Labels stick, however, and Pat would carry this one for the brief remainder of her career.

17

The Sleeping Prince

The Boyers sailed for Paris after the release of *Spendthrift* in July 1936 but arrived to find France paralyzed by a national strike. The Popular Front, a left-wing coalition, was in control, inaugurating two years of civil unrest before it was overturned.

Boyer knew from Philippe Hériat that Anatole Litvak and Joseph Kessel had written a screenplay with him in mind. It dramatized the 1889 deaths of Crown Prince Rudolf, the thirty-year-old heir to the throne of the Austro-Hungarian empire, and his teenage mistress, Baroness Marie Vetsera. They died at a hunting lodge in the Vienna woods called Mayerling.

Litvak hoped *Mayerling* would be the project that took him to Hollywood, particularly if Boyer agreed to star. But Boyer doubted his ability to play a nobleman. Why not get Pierre Fresnay, for whom the necessary hauteur was second nature? "Fresnay could play Rudolf," agreed Litvak, "if there were no Charles Boyer. But for Charles Boyer there is no substitute. I will not make the film without you."[1] Litvak may have been thinking of Boyer's Hollywood connections, something Fresnay did not possess, but Boyer was flattered and gave in, even though the financing company, Concordia, demanded an option on his next two films.

With the political Left gaining power in France, it was a propitious time to expose the excesses of monarchy. Also, it seemed the public could not get enough of this Hapsburg Romeo and Juliet, with Rudolf the idealistic reformer stifled by protocol, and Marie willing to join him on a journey to "the land of no return." Litvak and Kessel smoothed some of the real-life story's rougher edges, mentioning that Rudolf was married and had a daughter but not that he suffered from syphilis. Vetsera was actually somewhat beefy, with a sullen stare, but the film made her a waif. It also ignored rumors that Rudolf had already proposed a suicide pact with another lover, that Marie's death may have been caused by a botched abortion, or that both were murdered by the emperor's secret police. Not until 2015, when Marie's suicide note came to light, was the most romantic of these scenarios confirmed. "Dear Mother," she wrote. "Please forgive me for what I've done. I could not resist love. I want to be buried next to Him in the Cemetery of Alland. I am happier in death than life." Few writers could have improved on such simplicity.

By the mid-1930s, Hollywood's practice of importing the best continental talent had accelerated a process already evident in architecture: the evolution of an international style. Even so, some differences persisted. Robert Kane, in charge of the dubbing factory at Joinville, admitted that American puritanism stifled any depiction of extremes in behavior. "In some pictures," he said, "the Germans, like the French and Italians, go the limit. I have seen films that could not pass a blind censor in any Anglo-Saxon country. They are the last things in the *risqué.*" But America needed what Europe offered in the way of style. "Artistic Europe has eyes," Kane continued. "Europe is all color, scenery, variety, a clash of cultures. She is theatrical—she is always looking for 'effects.' We need more of the bizarre, the grotesque, the exotic."[2]

As the sets went up for *Mayerling,* Litvak and Boyer began to spend their weekends together at the casinos in Dinard and Deauville, on the coast of the English Channel. While Boyer indulged himself at the tables, Litvak exercised his flair for seduction among the gamblers' neglected wives. In anticipation of an eventual move to California, he asked Boyer to coach him in the ways of Hollywood and began to apply those lessons immediately. For instance, he skirmished with producer Seymour Nebenzal, who insisted that the extras playing a theater audience need not be in costume unless they were seen on camera. Litvak overruled that decision. Without costumes, how could they applaud with authentic vigor?

Mayerling illustrates Kane's point about the differences between American and European treatments of filmed history. Its cinematography, décor, and costumes were world class, and in evoking Europe's social, political, and cultural life, it outshone contemporary Hollywood productions such as Henry King's *Lloyds of London* and Alfred Werker's *The House of Rothschild.* American historical dramas would always smell of waxworks. Instead of speaking, their characters made speeches.

Litvak set out to subvert the sentimental vision of Rudolf and Marie as star-crossed lovers and the prince as a political visionary. In the film, Rudolf's few chats with Szeps (René Bergeron), editor of a radical journal, suggest that the prince is less interested in reform than in tweaking the nose of the father who ignores him. He lets himself be arrested after a demonstration and does not reveal his identity until he gets to the police station, where it will cause the greatest embarrassment to the palace. His motives are further illuminated in a scene where, as the scandal with Marie approaches a showdown, Rudolf is refused permission to see Franz Josef. "A father won't see *his own son*?" he asks incredulously.

To play Marie, Litvak chose nineteen-year-old Danielle Darrieux. She had already signed to do another film but was so keen to play the part that she bought herself out of the contract, her salary barely covering the penalties for canceling. She plays Marie, in Graham Greene's words, as someone "lovely and lost and childlike."[3] She is dreamily indifferent to the fate bearing down on her like an express train. When Rudolf asks if she is ready to die, she pauses for only a moment before assuring him, "I am—with you."

The film implies that Marie's greatest appeal to Rudolf is the distress their affair will cause his father. Otherwise, it depicts him as a political naïf. In a key scene, he and Szeps meet in a cabaret where Tyrolean dancers in lederhosen stomp rhythmically onstage. "I'm only happy in places like this," Rudolf tells a bemused Szeps as the burly Teutons indulge in a frenzy of stylized punches and face-slapping—hardly the most appropriate setting to discuss matters affecting the empire. Even so, Szeps tries to talk politics, but Rudolf speaks only of sex, even taunting the journalist by asking how he would react if Rudolf seduced his daughter. We sense Szeps's dawning realization of Rudolf's true nature—shallow and childish. When Marie appears in the doorway and Rudolf sees her for the first time, the conversation ends abruptly. As the couple wanders away together, the dancing continues onstage. Szeps is not seen again.

Graham Greene singled out this scene as a key to understanding the film and Darrieux's future stardom. In that moment, when Marie pauses at the edge of the dance floor, intrigued by the lights and the music, she conveys all we need to know about this impressionable young woman. "She was sentenced to death by the world as soon as she appeared in the pleasure-garden," he wrote, "lost in the boisterous darkness."[4]

Litvak seldom films Boyer in long shot, partly to avoid drawing attention to his shortness. Shown only in head and shoulder shots, and often with the camera angled down, Rudolf appears crushed, an effect amplified by Boyer's skilled acting. Watching him grow into his role, Litvak congratulated himself on his choice. "It is a sublime tragedy," he said of Rudolf's story, "and Charles is, in essence, a tragic artist."[5]

Mayerling opened in France in January 1936 and was an instant success. As there were no immediate plans for a US release, Boyer took a print back to Los Angeles and screened it for studio executives. Its visual qualities had the desired effect on Irving Thalberg, who invited Litvak and Kessel to Hollywood to discuss making a film with Boyer. Darrieux was offered a single-film contract with Universal.

But hopes that *Mayerling* would serve as a calling card for its creators and a confirmation of Boyer's new status were premature. Darrieux's film, *The Rage of Paris,* flopped. Litvak and Kessel accepted Thalberg's invitation but, hampered by their inability to speak English, made a poor impression. Harry Cohn at Columbia opened the conversation by asking Litvak why, in *Mayerling,* he dissolved between scenes rather than cutting. Litvak's terse response—that he liked it that way—was not designed to charm.

When it came right down to it, Thalberg had nothing specific for Litvak and Kessel either. The closest they came to a deal was with Walter Wanger, who offered them *Sahara,* a French Foreign Legion story planned for Boyer and Madeleine Carroll. He promised a more authentic film than von Sternberg's *Morocco,* but Litvak found the treatment banal and was about to turn it down when David Selznick announced his intention to produce Robert Hichens's florid novel *The Garden of Allah,* kicking every other desert film into the weeds.

Charles Feldman agreed to represent Litvak but warned that it would take time to establish his name. Crestfallen, he and Kessel returned to Paris. Boyer too experienced a setback when Concordia, the company that had financed *Mayerling,* insisted on exercising its option on his next two films. After lengthy negotiations, he got himself out of the deal for half a million francs (about $100,000 at 1937 rates).

Both Boyer and Wanger were disappointed that the actor's reputation still rested on *Private Worlds, Shanghai,* and *Break of Hearts*—none of them breakout films. They showed his versatility, but Hollywood was full of versatile actors who never graduated from the second panel of the credits. Wanger's goal of making Boyer one of the screen's great lovers seemed as remote as ever. Paradoxically, the film that would achieve this result was made not by Wanger but by some improbable collaborators and under the least propitious of circumstances.

18

"Only God and I Know What Is in My Heart"

A mong Hollywood's independent producers, none rivaled David O. Selz-nick. In 1936 the burly, blustering former wunderkind of MGM had just launched Selznick International Pictures. Although designed to put some distance between himself and his former employer (and father-in-law) Louis B. Mayer, Selznick's first effort, a version of the sentimental *Little Lord Fauntle-roy*, was an MGM film in all but name. It turned a profit but excited nobody. "There is a benign aura about the photoplay," yawned the *New York Times*, "a mellow haze of things long past which should lull even the most adamant anti-Fauntlerite into a state of restful receptivity."[1]

Selznick knew he had to be more adventurous, and he needed to justify the claim that his productions were international. (Almost the entire cast of *Fauntleroy* had come from Hollywood's British colony.) In the hopes of doing so, he acquired another MGM property, *The Garden of Allah*. Robert Hichens's novel had been filmed twice before, the last time in 1927 by Rex Ingram, the renegade director who had relocated with his wife, actress Alice Terry, to the Victorine studios in Nice. While still at MGM, Selznick had con-templated making the film with Greta Garbo but could not clear the dialogue rights. (Authors who sold their work for silent films often wanted more money if it was remade in sound.) Now he decided that a new version with an international cast, shot on location and in Technicolor, could justify his company's grandiose motto: "In the Tradition of Quality."

In 1936 few advances in cinematic technique excited more interest than three-color Technicolor. An earlier two-color process could depict only shades of blue-green cyan and pink-purple magenta. Used inexpertly, it ren-dered white skin brick red and skies a bilious chartreuse. The three-color process offered far greater realism but demanded some fundamental adjustments in lighting and design.

Like T. E. Lawrence—Lawrence of Arabia—novelist Hichens, who lived part-time in Egypt, was attracted to the epicene sensuality of the Arab world and the lure of the desert. The same readers who doted on Edward FitzGerald's translation of the *Rubáiyát of Omar Khayyám* admired Hichens's florid language and ersatz Eastern wisdom, a nugget of which provided the book's title: "The Arabs have a saying; the desert is the garden of Allah." But the book was not natural movie material. It had almost no story, was grossly overwritten, and was inhabited by the kind of people one seldom encountered in real life.

One such character is Domini Enfilden, a young Englishwoman who has just nursed her father through his final illness. She drifts to North Africa in search of "nothingness." In an oasis at the edge of the Sahara, she meets two men: Count Anteoni (Basil Rathbone), an Italian in a turban and cape who has "gone Arab," and the reticent, unworldly Boris Androvsky (Boyer), a fugitive from some crisis of faith that he is reluctant to discuss. "A man who fears to acknowledge his god is unwise to set foot in the desert," Anteoni observes darkly.

After a romance during which Boris and Domini wander into the desert, expressing high-flown sentiments about Love, God, Life, and Fate, they marry and have a child. Only then does Boris reveal that he is a Trappist monk who fled his monastery with the recipe for a liqueur on which the monks' livelihood depends. Once their child is born, he can no longer resist the call of duty and returns to a life of meditation, privation, and distillation.

Garbo was not available to play Domini, so Selznick signed Merle Oberon at the urging of his brother Myron, who was her agent. Their relationship got off to a bad start when Selznick asked her to shoot a screen test. She took this as an insult and was only partly mollified when he explained that he needed to see how she looked in the new Technicolor process. Filmed in a tent under blazing lights, and with Latin lover Gilbert Roland as Boris, Hichens's dialogue sounded ridiculous. Selznick was brooding over the disappointing results when he heard that Marlene Dietrich was about to end a seven-year residency at Paramount. Deciding that, on reflection, Oberon lacked the necessary box-office appeal, he signed Dietrich in April 1936, just in time to begin shooting. Oberon immediately filed suit for breach of contract.

Creating a screenplay for *Garden of Allah* was complicated by protests from the Catholic-dominated Production Code Administration, headed by

Joseph L. Breen. The Production Code specifically forbade any film that brought priests or ministers into disrepute, let alone one in which a renegade monk conceives a child with a woman in the grip of suicidal despair. Some new scenes, hurriedly written by Lynn Riggs, explain that Domini has returned to the Sahara not out of existential ennui but to visit the convent where she was raised.

The character of Boris was harder to repair. Edward S. Schwegler of the Buffalo, New York, Legion of Decency wrote to Breen, "The idea of a priest, a monk, having intimate carnal relations with a woman just grates against the grain. . . . You and I know that such sort of relationships have existed and do exist; we know that in the past priests have married and had concubines almost with impunity . . . but all that does not alter the fact that here, to the ordinary, simple Catholic, the thought of a priest having carnal relations with a woman is sacrilegious."[2] He was particularly troubled by a speech in which Boris thanks God for sending him Domini, appearing to assign divine approval to their liaison.

As high summer approached, when shooting in the desert would be intolerable, the film still lacked a leading man. Selznick, aware of Wanger's ambitions for Boyer, sent Feldman the latest draft of the screenplay and suggested that Boyer play Boris. It was not quite the compliment it seemed. Selznick had already considered and, in many cases, been turned down by Robert Donat, Ivor Novello, John Gielgud, Jean Gabin, Herbert Marshall, Brian Aherne, Robert Taylor, Vincent Price, Noël Coward, Maurice Evans, George Brent, Fredric March, and Laurence Olivier. All of them recognized that it is really Domini's story. Boris does not emerge as a character until halfway through the film, and when he does, he is indecisive—one of the most difficult states of mind to convey, as any actor who has ever played Hamlet knows.

Boyer was preoccupied with domestic matters. He and Pat had set up housekeeping at 2003 La Brea Terrace. Furniture had to be bought and staff hired. They had also initiated the process of becoming American citizens, a signal that Boyer now regarded himself as based in the United States. Never much of an athlete but determined to cut a better figure and fight a tendency toward flab, Boyer took up golf. He later joined the Beverly Hills Tennis Club and started taking lessons, though with little enthusiasm.

If any leisure activity, aside from omnivorous reading, set his blood racing, it was gambling. Through Feldman, he met mobster "Bugsy" Siegel, who would be instrumental in creating Las Vegas, the high rollers' mecca that

Boyer would visit frequently. The Boyers became enthusiastic bridge players, though at home, they preferred gin rummy. The business manager hired by Feldman recognized the potential for disaster in Boyer's passion for gambling and put him on a monthly allowance. Boyer, however, generally left the tables a winner.

With a start date for *The Garden of Allah* looming, Selznick pressed Boyer to make a decision. Numerous rewrites had not improved the role. Boyer was at his best when his character was taking charge and acting decisively—not prominent elements in the behavior of a tormented monk. But the names Dietrich and Selznick made it difficult to decline, as did the generous deal negotiated by Feldman. Reluctantly, Boyer signed the contract.

There was no chance of shooting the film in the Sahara, so Selznick compromised on Arizona. To direct, he chose Richard Boleslavski. There was nothing in particular that qualified the burly former Polish lancer for such a project, and "Boley" was soon struggling. Hopes that his Polish-Russian background would be useful in dealing with a multinational cast proved optimistic. Almost from the moment the unit pitched its tents at Castle Dome Peak, twenty-three miles outside of Yuma, the cast rebelled, mainly about the screenplay. In temperatures as high as 135 degrees, lines like "Only God and I know what is in my heart" sounded silly. An exasperated Selznick urged Boleslavski to get tough:

> Marlene's pictures have been notorious for their ghastly writing.
> Charles has yet to have an outstanding American picture, and
> neither of them has ever had a single picture comparable with any
> one of fifteen I have made in the last years. Tell them very brutally
> that this comes from me. It is high time for a showdown, and I am
> perfectly prepared for it because I am not going to face, or have you
> face, six or seven weeks of this nonsense. I wish you would lose
> your temper with them. I will have a lot more respect for you if you
> turn into a von Sternberg who tolerates no interference.[3]

This was easier said than done. The unit was 250 miles away, linked to home base only by Teletype and shortwave radio. Tempers flared in the heat, which was exacerbated by the powerful lights demanded by Technicolor. Boyer's face went tomato red, requiring makeup repairs between takes. Dietrich fussed with her hair, demanding retakes if even a few strands escaped from an elaborately wound scarf. Not to be outdone by Boyer's insistence on being photographed from his "good" side, she had a full-length mirror placed by the camera and directed the cinematographer how best to light her, as she had been taught by von Sternberg. Bullied at long distance by Selznick and helpless to control his recalcitrant cast, Boleslavski collapsed. The press office's hastily improvised explanation was that he had become ill from drinking polluted water.

During the hottest part of the day, Boyer and Dietrich took refuge in her deluxe tent, insulated from the worst of the heat by an inner lining of silk. Basil Rathbone sometimes joined them. It still rankled that Selznick had passed him over for the role of Boris. After Rathbone repeatedly refused to leave the comfort of Dietrich's tent to play a scene, Selznick, taking his behavior as a personal affront, threatened to write him out of the film entirely. When the unit returned to Los Angeles in June, the two men came to blows. "You'll never work for me again!" the producer reportedly snarled after Rathbone knocked him down. And he was as good as his word.

Clashes with the cast, particularly Dietrich, continued. After a visit to the set, Selznick implored Boleslavski: "Would you *please* speak to Marlene about the fact that her hair is getting so much attention, and is being coifed to such a degree that all reality is lost. . . . Even today, on the set, having the hairdresser rush in between takes to put each last strand of hair in place looked so nonsensical, when you could see the palms blowing in the background. Surely a *little* reality can't do a great beauty any harm."[4]

Among the scenes shot in Hollywood, one attracted the lion's share of comments, including another protest from Schwegler, who called it "barbarically sensual." To play an Arab dancer who arouses lustful yearnings in Boris, Selznick hired Tilly Losch. The Austrian-born Losch was well known on the European stage and on Broadway, and she was a favorite of choreographer George Balanchine. She possessed the ugly-beautiful face the French call *jolie laide*. The wordless byplay between Losch and Boyer as she writhes around a crowded bar is a high point of the film. *Variety* wrote, "The dance is the most erotic and at the same time fascinatingly artistic thing of this kind the screen has seen, and the emotional quality of the intimate play between the nautch terper and the runaway monk is of intense pitch."[5]

To further complicate the production, all the dialogue recorded on location proved unusable, so every scene had to be revoiced in the studio. Selznick saw a first cut in August and demanded additional editing that coincidentally removed the scenes Boyer regarded as his best work. The film opened in October, too long after the peak filmgoing months to recoup its $2 million cost. Reviews were mixed, most banishing it to the ghetto of "women's pictures." *Variety* moaned about its emphasis on photographic prettiness: "shots and more shots of the desert, silhouettes against sunsets. Bivouacked Bedouins *et al.* do not make for cinematurgy. It's good incidental by-play, but that's all. Nor is Boyer's struggle between worldly pursuits and his return to Trappist celibacy any great stirring premise, save for the femmes. *Garden of Allah* as matinee fodder thus impresses favorably, which in one aspect augurs well for its box office."[6]

In a somewhat backhanded tribute to the film, actress Alla Nazimova, who had converted her Sunset Boulevard estate into a bungalow hotel, took advantage of the free publicity and called it The Garden of Alla. For many decades it was a home away from home for European visitors.

The film took its toll on director Boleslavski. Not long after *The Garden of Allah*, he died of a heart attack at age forty-seven.

Whatever their reservations, most reviewers concurred with the *New York Times* that "Charles Boyer, an important player abroad and one who has been rather badly treated here by casting departments, has a role in keeping with his talents."[7] At last Boyer had the momentum needed to assume the mantle of a romantic leading man. In whatever role he played, his character would be sui generis. He had joined the company of actors who always, essentially, play themselves. Studios might describe such films as a Gable, a Crawford, a de Havilland, or an Astaire. Filmgoers no longer needed to ask of a Boyer film, "What's it about?" It would be about Boyer.

19

The Best Headwaiter in Europe

For some time, Selznick had been negotiating to import young Swedish actress Ingrid Bergman for a remake of *Intermezzo*, about a violinist romantically involved with her teacher. After William Powell and Ronald Colman turned down the male lead, Selznick became convinced that no major star would consent to playing second fiddle (literally) to an ingenue, so he considered forgetting about Bergman and casting the film in Hollywood. "The best I have been able to think of," he wrote in October 1936, "is the combination of Boyer and Loretta Young. This combination will cost us somewhere in the neighborhood of $150,000, which is a good deal more than it's worth . . . Boyer has already approved the role."[1] But by Christmas, Selznick had decided to take a chance on Bergman, matching her with Leslie Howard.

This freed Boyer to work for Wanger, who was considering a new version of Emily Brontë's *Wuthering Heights,* the story of the doomed love between a foundling and the daughter of the wealthy landowner who rescues him from the streets. The script by veterans Ben Hecht and Charles MacArthur streamlined the novel and updated it from the eighteenth to the nineteenth century, giving new emphasis to the bitter and violent Heathcliff's love for Catherine Earnshaw. Unsuccessful in persuading Paramount to back them, they offered the script to Wanger, who saw it as a vehicle for Sylvia Sidney as Catherine and Boyer as Heathcliff.

Sidney was eager to escape the urban dreariness of her recent films and agreed immediately, but Boyer had his doubts. Approaching forty, he was too old for the part. Nor did his appearance fit the popular image of Heathcliff as a Byronic hero, black hair wildly blowing. Then there was his accent, but Wanger shrugged that off. Heathcliff came from the streets, so who was to say his mother hadn't been foreign? Nevertheless, he looked around for a voice coach to make the Frenchman's accent more mid-Atlantic. Boyer suggested Joshua Logan, who had worked with him on his Russian accent for *The Garden of Allah*. Wanger called Logan. "Boyer says you're a dialog director," he stated with typical directness. "Might be able to use you to coach him for *Wuthering Heights*—if I do it and if he does."[2] Logan retorted that he had plenty of work and hung up. But shortly thereafter, he joined the other misfits on Wanger's payroll.

Wanger announced *Wuthering Heights*—and immediately regretted it. Accountants warned that due to recent failures, there was no money for weeks of location shooting. And Boyer's success in *The Garden of Allah* had revived Wanger's belief in his potential as a screen lover. So *Wuthering Heights* reverted to its writers. They sold it to Goldwyn, who produced it with Laurence Olivier as Heathcliff and Merle Oberon as Cathy. Meanwhile, Wanger called Baker and Towne and set them to work on an original screenplay to showcase Boyer as a romantic hero. The result was *History Is Made at Night*, a film as ambiguous as its title.

They began the story in a Paris hotel, where a pathologically jealous husband (played by Colin Clive) has sent his gigolo-like chauffeur to compromise his estranged wife (Jean Arthur). The husband lurks in the hallway with a witness, ready to burst in and catch them in flagrante. Unsure whether to continue in the spirit of comedy or suspense, Towne and Baker consulted Arthur Ripley, Wanger's resident gag writer, assistant director, and dramaturge. As this was supposed to be a vehicle for Boyer as a lover, he advised them to emphasize excitement and romance and employ humor only where it propelled the narrative. Accordingly, they angled the next scene toward drama. While putting a drunk to bed in the suite next door, Boyer (playing waiter Paul Dumond) hears the wife fighting off the chauffeur and being menaced by her husband. He steps in from the terrace and, pretending to be a burglar, knocks down the chauffeur, locks the husband in a closet, grabs the wife's jewels to justify his pose as a thief, and spirits her away, apparently as a hostage.

Baker and Towne could barely contain their glee as they described this episode to Wanger and Logan. "Here's the great scene, boss," they explained (according to Logan). "The big handsome prick charges into this beautiful cunt's bedroom, grabs her by the tit, then throws a fuck into her. Ha ha ha. When she grabs him by the balls, the door opens and Mr. Soft Cock Husband enters, yelling 'Shit! Shit! Shit!' Some scene, eh, boss?"[3] Naturally, the wife and her rescuer fall in love. A little champagne to calm her nerves leads to a night of tipsy tangos and intimate revelations. "Through these expository scenes," writes Wanger biographer Matthew Bernstein, "Boyer excelled as a romantic sophisticate who charms the gal from Kansas and, presumably, the women in the audience."[4] Neither is aware that the husband has bludgeoned the chauffeur to death and accused Boyer of the crime.

Baker and Towne made Boyer's character a waiter, but in line with Wanger's ambitions for a classier persona, they labeled him the best head-waiter in Europe. The choice of Jean Arthur as the wife, Irene Vail, was shrewd, since she suffered from a nervous disability that belied her wise-cracking self-confidence. Described as "intensely private, high-strung and insecure, beset with a pathological shyness born of fear and self-doubt," she made a natural foil for Boyer, her cracked, husky voice harmonizing with his soothing baritone.[5]

Having included all the ingredients of a chase thriller, Towne and Baker redirected the script toward comedy with the introduction of Leo Carrillo as Boyer's sidekick. His appearances in the Cisco Kid films made the actor everybody's favorite Hispanic. Once Frank Borzage came on board as direc-tor, he exploited Carrillo's ability to improvise speeches in fractured Spang-lish. Boyer and Carrillo make a good comedy duo, particularly during a set piece in which they enter a restaurant pretending to be dissatisfied diners and conclude by taking over as the chef and maître d'.

When anyone drew the director's attention to the film's improbabilities and its changes in tone, he shrugged them off. He was not in the reality busi-ness. Most of Borzage's films scorned narrative, the better to exemplify that simplest of exhortations: make love, not war. His lovers are buffeted by vast events—the Great War, the Depression, fascism—which they invariably weather. Eminent American critic Andrew Sarris called *History Is Made at Night* "not only the most romantic title in the history of the cinema but also a profound expression of Borzage's commitment to love over probability."[6]

A week before shooting ended, Wanger still could not see how the lovers would be satisfactorily reunited. Sensing that love born of violence should reach its apotheosis in violence, he decided that Paul and Irene would be pas-sengers on a ship that her madly jealous husband crashes into an iceberg. Borzage hurriedly improvised such a climax, disguising its ragged edges by staging it in thick fog. Certain that they are doomed, but indifferent to their fate, Paul and Irene amble around the ice-strewn deck, reveling in their love. Augmented by a foghorn's mournful blare and faint voices singing "Nearer My God to Thee," the sequence plays like a *Liebestod* (the Wagnerian concept of love celebrated at the moment of death). Gregg Toland, future cinematog-rapher of *Citizen Kane,* was called in to light it.

The film received puzzled but generally favorable notices. "It's hard to believe this one for a minute," wrote a perplexed *Variety* reviewer.[7] Even its most enthusiastic admirers conceded that credibility was not its most prominent characteristic. What sustained the film was the paradoxical rapport between these two people; as is often the case in real life, there was no rational explanation for their love. The film cost $821,000 to make, which was substantial for the time, and it returned only a modest $17,000 profit on its first release. More important to Wanger and Boyer, it confirmed Boyer's new status as a romantic hero.

While awaiting its release, Wanger offered Boyer the lead in *Vogues of 1938,* a color musical about a fashion designer who produces a Broadway show. To please Boyer, he also offered to cast Pat, but she was nervous about shouldering a starring role and unsure of her rusty dancing technique. Once she declined *Vogues,* so did Boyer.

In 1937 the Boyers moved into the home they would occupy throughout the war. The house at 9955 Beverly Grove Drive in Beverly Hills had been built in 1934; it stood on 2.72 acres and was shaded by palm trees. There were five bedrooms, plus accommodations for the butler, cook, housemaid, and chauffeur—all French. At a time when stars routinely supported a retinue of attendants, Boyer lived in relative simplicity, with only one other permanent staff member: his double and stand-in Irving "Fig" Newton, whom he kept on retainer. A part-time secretary handled business correspondence and fan mail—which, as an independent, Boyer had to respond to himself, rather than leaving it to a studio press office. He subscribed to no clippings service and did not employ a press agent. Requests for interviews were politely declined.

The house featured a patio with a retractable glass roof and a small screening room, but Boyer largely kept to his study, which replicated the library from his apartment in Paris, complete with a well-stocked bar. Instead of the customary gallery of shots taken with fellow celebrities, he displayed only two photographs—one of his mother, the other of Maurice Chevalier. The circular room, paneled in beech and lined with his book collection and leather-bound copies of the screenplay for every movie in which he had appeared, was reached via a spiral staircase as narrow as that in a lighthouse. Secure in his aerie—book, glass, and cigarette close at hand—he could watch the world go by but take no part in its events.

20

Immortal Longings

Early in 1935 Irving Thalberg authorized a production of *Marie Antoi-nette*, with Robert Morley as the ill-fated Louis XVI and Norma Shearer as his queen. On hearing this, Greta Garbo's adviser and friend Salka Viertel requested an appointment. "Thalberg's office was a long wood-panelled room," she recalled, "with a huge desk near the windows. One had to cross the full length of the room to reach the frail, small figure behind the desk, usually holding the telephone receiver in one hand while the other was jingling coins in his trouser pocket." She outlined her idea for a film (starring Garbo) about a little-known incident in the life of Napoleon: his affair with a teenage Polish countess, Marie Walewska, who bore him an illegitimate son. "He thought the political background too complicated for American audiences," said Viertel, "but became interested after I had suggested Charles Boyer to play Napoleon."[1]

Few actors who were short enough to play Napoleon could also convey the necessary imperial gravitas, but Thalberg thought Boyer might do so. Also, he was French, a proven romantic lead, and almost exactly Napoleon's age when he met Marie, although an inch and a half taller. Undeterred, MGM's research department measured the emperor's death mask and announced that his head and Boyer's were exactly the same size.

Thalberg asked Feldman about Boyer's availability. In doing so, he defied a standing directive from Louis B. Mayer, who had ordered executives not to do business with the agent. Some years before, Mayer had asked Feldman to make inquiries about Jean Howard, one of the Goldwyn Girls. Feldman married her instead, and the angry Mayer barred him from the studio. But when Thalberg inquired about Boyer's availability, Feldman made it clear that if MGM wanted the actor, it would have to deal with him.

The Thalbergs and Boyers had remained friends, and Irving offered Charles the role over dinner at the Thalbergs' home. Being proposed for such a prestigious part by the studio head himself was an offer no actor, least of all a French one, could refuse. It also would have amused Boyer to recall that just ten years earlier, Gloria Swanson had rejected him for the same part in *Madame Sans Gene.* Revenge is a dish the connoisseur prefers to eat cold.

Feldman gave no quarter in the negotiations. Half the film's budget would be spent on its two stars, and half of that would be Boyer's. His contract called for a fee of $125,000, with a similar amount for repeating his performance in French. With overtime and reshoots, he would likely bank $450,000. Thalberg had anticipated the size of the payout and was alarmed at the prospect of such serious money leaving the company. He suggested that when Boyer's commitment to Wanger ended, he should join MGM as one of its "charter" players, on a par with, if not Spencer Tracy and Clark Gable, at least with Robert Montgomery, William Powell, and Robert Taylor. Mayer vetoed this arrangement, but given Boyer's dislike of long-term commitments, he almost certainly would have turned it down anyway. He valued the independence he enjoyed with Wanger, who permitted him to work in France and to spend time there each summer, visiting his mother in the Paris apartment he had bought for her and his stepfather, complete with housekeeper and maid.

Many American businessmen found Napoleon an inspiring figure. Short, bald, plump, and, by reason of his Corsican birth, an outsider who nevertheless rose to become one of history's most powerful men, he furnished an obvious role model for the foreign-born moguls of Hollywood. Playwright Sam Behrman, one of the principal writers for *Marie Walewska,* which eventually became *Conquest,* regarded Bonaparte as "a disaster for the human race" but conceded, "it was not easy to get sympathy for this point of view from a group of men who had busts of Napoleon in their offices."[2]

Despite this affinity, Hollywood struggled when it came to putting Bonaparte on film, particularly at a time when Mussolini and Hitler were aspiring to world domination. Could a film celebrate one dictator without appearing to extol them all? A more troubling question was whether this ambiguous, slightly comic, but larger-than-life historical figure could be rebranded as a lover to rival those played by John Gilbert, Robert Taylor, and Garbo's other leading men. Behrman, for one, doubted it. "One may study even the final shooting script," he wrote, "and see that the emperor is not fully or satisfactorily developed."[3] It was up to Boyer to bring him to life.

Once Thalberg gave the project the green light, Salka Viertel led a team of writers in scouring more than 200 novels, plays, and histories for a filmable version of the story. The script that emerged six months later included contributions by Behrman, Robert E. Sherwood, Zoë Akins, David Boehm, and Samuel Hoffenstein. Donald Ogden Stewart polished the dialogue, and Talbot Jennings added some military details, but only Behrman, Hoffenstein, Viertel, and Helen Jerome, author of the earliest biography of Walewska, received screen credit. Even then, they had invented so much that a slightly shamefaced preliminary title assured the audience that "the imaginative detail supplied by the dramatist has not violated the spirit of this immortal romance."

Viertel was sent to negotiate with the Breen office, which disapproved in principle of a story that romanticized an illicit relationship and its offspring. But even the censors hesitated to tamper with Napoleon. "Since the characters and events are all historical fact," grumbled one, "and this illegitimate child survived and became a rather important person in France, it's not possible to 'clean this story up' under the [Production] Code." They reluctantly approved the screenplay, slightly mollified that both lovers ended up miserable and alone.

Conquest director Clarence Brown later admitted that "everything that could go wrong on a picture went wrong."[4] This was Garbo's tenth romantic role in seven years and, at $500,000, the highest paid. However, her acting technique, which had never been particularly accomplished, was wearing thin. Languishing wanly and laughing through tears could carry one only so far. Though barely thirty, she was weary of the movie treadmill. Except when publicists mandated some show of enthusiasm to placate the gossip columnists and fan magazines, she shunned the society of the studio, insisting on closed sets and retreating to her dressing room between takes. She emerged only to watch the dailies. A shrewd critic of her screen persona, she was quick to spot bad shots or dud lines. On these occasions, she always referred to her screen self in the third person as "she." "Greta Garbo" was a synthetic creation, not to be confused with Greta Lovisa Gustafsson from Stockholm.

Preproduction was well advanced when Thalberg died suddenly in September 1936, leaving the film in the less sure hands of producer Bernie Hyman. Hyman had never disguised his misgivings about the screenplay and insisted that it be made both sadder and more uplifting. Thalberg's choice to direct, George Cukor, pulled out after his death, so *Conquest* was assigned to Clarence Brown, who had planned to shoot Emlyn Williams's contemporary murder mystery *Night Must Fall*. Brown resented being forced to direct yet another Garbo vehicle—his seventh—and Salka Viertel called his handling of the film "disgruntled obstructionism."[5]

An old hand at historical subjects, Brown knew how to cut costs. Like all astute directors of spectacle, he was unwilling to be held hostage to the weather, so he shot the entire film indoors. MGM boasted that it had "more stars than there are in the heavens," and it had almost as many standing sets, which Brown put to good use. For example, the ballroom where the great of Poland congregate to meet the emperor was built for the Jeanette MacDonald–Nelson Eddy operetta *Maytime*. Battle scenes are montages of stock footage, and exteriors appear only in back projection. Faced with re-creating the Russian winter in sunny California, Brown resourcefully staged those scenes in the refrigerated warehouse of the Los Angeles Ice and Cold-Storage Company.

Conquest opens with a band of Russian Cossacks (led by veteran stuntman Yakima Canutt) riding out of the snowy Polish night and invading the palace of eighty-year-old Count Walewski and his teenage wife. They gallop through its reception rooms, heap works of art on the fire, and fill a grand piano with feed for their mounts. They threaten to do worse until Marie's brother arrives at the head of a troop of lancers to scare them off. This is the cue for brother and sister to voice their admiration for Napoleon, whom they hope will step in and protect Poland from Russia. Incongruously, Garbo plays the young Marie as the emperor's besotted fan. Hearing that he will be passing near her estate, she is seized by an impulse of hero worship and races to a nearby village where she can spy on him. To audiences who were used to Garbo's characters being shy and reticent, such behavior verged on the ridiculous.

Boyer plays Bonaparte as socially inept. The Polish aristocrats patronize him, and although his own courtiers defer to him, they do so tongue in cheek; they treat him like a brilliant but wayward child inclined to throw tantrums when he doesn't get his way. He even indulges in a petulant shouting match with Walewski's muddled old sister over a game of cards. When the Poles, anxious to enlist him as their savior, hold a ball in his honor, Napoleon has eyes only for Marie, whom he subsequently pesters with love letters. She resists until a delegation visits Count Walewski and begs him to relinquish her to Napoleon for the national good. He orders them out of his house, only to find that Marie is more than willing to share the imperial bed. We are never convinced that she surrenders out of patriotism. On the contrary, when one visitor suggests that Napoleon might not demand sex but "may be moved, as men often are, to give without asking anything in return," she looks disappointed.

Graham Greene considered *Conquest* "one of the dullest films of the year." He described as "crazy comedy" the moment when the delegation departs: "they embrace Count Walewski—'Good-bye, old friend'—and retire reverently on tiptoe from the awkward domestic impasse they have created."[6] A few years later, Judy Garland would play a similar situation for laughs in *The Pirate*. Gene Kelly, impersonating a buccaneer, holds a Caribbean town for ransom until Garland surrenders her virtue. Heavily veiled, she spurns a friend's offer to take her place with a frosty, "He asked for *me*." It can't be a coincidence that Sam Behrman also wrote the play on which *The Pirate* is based.

Napoleon is convinced that only by marrying into the Hapsburgs and producing a legitimate heir can he ensure the future of his empire. This drives the final stake into his romance with Marie. She rails against the "thin weak old blood" of royalty, ignoring the fact that her own is just as blue. Her visit to an exiled Napoleon on Elba is a failure. Marie, in the best tradition of melodrama, chokes back the tears as he ignores their child, pining instead for his legitimate son who has been kept from him by his wife, Marie Louise of Austria.

Anxious to show Napoleon foremost as a lover, *Conquest* downplays his ambition, presenting him, paradoxically, as a liberal who is committed to "a new idea in the world—democracy" and eager to form "a United States of Europe." These sentiments are belied by a shot of his shadow falling ominously across a map of the Continent. The film never hints at Napoleon's military genius. Instead, we get the slightly comic Bonaparte of his portraits, uncomfortable in tight white knee breeches, silk stockings, and a tricorn hat. The MGM press office photographed Boyer surrounded by paintings and sculptures of the emperor, apparently unsure which, if any, to imitate. He made no secret of his frustration with the role. Playing Bonaparte, he said, was like portraying Jesus Christ. No matter how nuanced his performance, some people would be dissatisfied, not least himself.

Critical reaction to *Conquest* was tepid. Garbo sensed correctly that audiences were getting tired of costume films. One exhibitor wrote to the trade paper *Wid's Daily*, "Don't send me any more of them films where the hero writes his name with a feather." *Variety* was supportive but found Garbo less than charismatic, noting that the "part calls for intense feminine feeling, for coquetry and renunciation. It is not due to any shortcomings on her part, however, that the audience interest is more closely held by Boyer's Napoleon." Discussing her leading man, the reviewer's language brightened: "Boyer plays the love scenes with brusque tenderness, and makes the character understood as a blazing individualist acting under reckless urges for power."[7]

21

Exiles

Even Clarence Brown's economies couldn't prevent *Conquest* from costing $2.7 million, only half of which it recouped at the box office. No MGM film since the coming of sound had shown so much red ink. In the recriminations that followed, the greater share of the blame was laid at the feet of Garbo. The criticism evidently stung. *Conquest* would be her last period drama. Her final films, *Ninotchka* and *Two-Faced Woman,* were comedies set in the present.

The French were never as numerous in Hollywood as the British, Germans, or Austro-Hungarians. Even during World War II, those working in film, music, art, and related disciplines seldom numbered more than a hundred. But they made up in vivacity what they lacked in numbers. Director Robert Florey had lived there since the 1920s and served as unofficial French consul to the film industry. He recalled:

> Many French lived at hotels like the Garden of Alla, and formed
> separate groups, gathering together in the evenings at dinners and
> parties where no one spoke English and everyone complained
> about the life in California. They went on Sundays to Santa Barbara,
> Arrowhead or Big Bear, below the border to Tijuana for the
> bullfights or the Jai Alai games. While working at the studio—any
> studio—the French ladies would bring baskets of food and bottles
> of wine and organize picnic luncheons, drinking and laughing,
> speaking loudly in French at noon time to the amazement of the
> Americans not accustomed to this kind of behavior.[1]

Among those arriving from Europe in 1937 was Anatole Litvak. His visit coincided with the release of *Mayerling* in English. The plan had been to dub it, but he and Boyer persuaded its American distributor to use subtitles. It would screen in 1,500 theaters across the country and earn $250,000—meager by Hollywood standards, but exceptional for a foreign film. Feldman had found Litvak a Hollywood employer in RKO, which wanted to remake *L'Equipage* (The Team), Litvak's film of a Joseph Kessel World War I air combat story. The director jumped at the chance, since opportunities in France were dwindling fast. Pommer had folded Fox-Europe and moved to England, forming Mayflower Films with Charles Laughton. Pathé/Natan, where *L'Equipage* was made, had closed, and Natan was in prison for fraud.

Fortuitously, the release of *Mayerling* coincided with the abdication of Britain's newly crowned Edward VIII. Like the film's Rudolf, Edward was perceived as a young ruler with revisionist views who surrendered his throne rather than give up the woman he loved because the establishment disapproved of her. RKO cashed in on the event by calling its *L'Equipage* remake *The Woman I Love*, a quote from the king's farewell speech to the nation. The title resonated with Litvak, as he was sleeping with the earlier film's star, Miriam Hopkins, whom he would later marry.

After wrapping *The Woman I Love*, he signed with Warner Brothers. This deal was also brokered by Feldman, who had convinced Jack Warner that Litvak was Europe's latest wunderkind. Warner proposed a film about Joan of Arc starring Claudette Colbert in a role that she hoped would establish her as a serious actress. Instead, to her bitter disappointment, he changed his mind and decided on Jacques Deval's *Tovarich*, a French stage success adapted for Broadway by Robert E. Sherwood.

Robert Lord, assigned to *Tovarich* as producer, was among the first to experience the results of Feldman's efforts on Litvak's behalf. "Warner summoned me into his office," he recalled:

> "I am going to do you a big favor," he said. "I'm going to let you work with the best director in the world. Have you ever heard of Anatole Litvak?"
>
> I said, "No."
>
> He said, "Well, I am sorry for you. He is under contract here and he is going to make a picture, *Tovarich*, from a French play by Jacques Deval. This is a great privilege, because you will learn from this man; we will all learn from him. Go to New York to see the play."
>
> I saw the play and said, "I can write this. It really doesn't take much writing."

Warner said, "No, no, no! We don't want you to write this. We don't think you have the finesse. Casey Robinson is going to write it." I knew Casey, and why he had more finesse than me I didn't understand.

At any rate I asked, "Do you want me to go over to RKO and meet Mr. Litvak?"

He said, "Oh, my God, don't disturb him. He is quite sensitive. Don't call him. He has accepted you." They really had the red carpet out for him.[2]

Tovarich is set among the Russian refugees who poured into Paris after the 1917 revolution. As France was the spiritual home of tsarist aristocrats and French was their second language, some newly penniless grand dukes and princesses found jobs in the hotels and restaurants where they had once been guests, a situation also exploited in Lubitsch's *Ninotchka*.

Prince Mikail and Grand Duchess Tatiana live in poverty but refuse to dip into the millions entrusted to them by the tsar for safekeeping. Instead, they take jobs as butler and maid to the bourgeois Dupont family, whom the Russians transform with their dignity, style, and impeccable manners. Soon Madame Dupont has swapped her Pekinese for a Russian wolfhound, the son is taking fencing lessons from Mikail and sighing over Tatiana, while both he and his sister sneak into the kitchen at night to drink vodka, play poker, and learn Russian. The good manners of the new domestics are tested to the limit when their former torturer Gorotchenko, now a commissar, turns up as a dinner guest. Against all expectations, he convinces the prince that the new Russia deserves the fortune he and his wife are protecting, and they surrender it to him before returning joyously to their new lives as servants.

Feldman negotiated a generous contract for Litvak, including approval of cast and key technicians. In turn, Litvak promised to deliver Boyer for the role of Mikail. Lord, feeling marginalized, protested that Boyer, whom he called "a sad, meek little man, adored by women," was wrong for the part and suggested the more virile Fredric March, but Warner prevailed.[3]

Even though Litvak was an old friend, as was Deval (he would join the movie colony at the outbreak of war), Boyer hesitated. Unsure of his ability to play comedy, he also worried about the incongruity of being surrounded by actors pretending to be Russian and French but speaking modern English, while he would be the only character with an accent. Even Basil Rathbone, though playing a Russian, speaks British English. Feldman persuaded him it would make no difference. His accent was part of the Boyer persona. Audiences would accept it, just as they accepted Garbo, accent and all, as Polish, Spanish, or French.

There was no shortage of candidates to play Tatiana, among them husky-voiced Kay Francis, whose $3,000-a-month contract with Warner was up for renewal. Determined to leave the studio, she was dissuaded by Jack Warner, who, she claimed, promised her the role of Tatiana if she stayed. Warner had no such intention. Behind her back, he was negotiating with Marion Davies, who had been his first choice for Tatiana when he bought the rights to the play for $185,000. That deal was interrupted when Litvak demanded that his new wife, Miriam Hopkins, get the part. Warner haggled with Hopkins for a few weeks before refusing to meet her price. Then, having demonstrated who was boss, he approached Paramount and asked to borrow Claudette Colbert. Following her success in Frank Capra's *It Happened One Night*, she demanded a whopping $150,000. Warner's erratic behavior irritated Litvak, angered Hopkins, drove Davies to quit the studio, and spurred Francis to sue him for fraud.

Meanwhile, the Warner publicists fretted about the title. As few people knew that *Tovarich* means "comrade," they proposed to exploit Colbert's success in *It Happened One Night* by changing the title to *Tonight's Our Night*. Litvak and Boyer protested the foolishness of throwing away the name under which the play had become famous. The compromise was a title sequence in which the unexplained subtitle *Tonight's Our Night* dangles below a more prominent *Tovarich*.

The joke of *Tovarich* lies in Mikail and Tatiana remaining unchanged while those around them go to pieces. Not until some bewildered dinner guests explain who is serving the soup do the Duponts discover the identity of their servants. Even then, neither breaks character, responding to their flustered employers with the same sangfroid they brought to their roles as courtiers of the tsar. The confrontation with Gorotchenko, played by Rathbone with icy punctilio, only confirms their conviction that to bear tribulations with fortitude, even pleasure, is the fate of all Russians. "Misery and hunger," says Tatiana, "the great luxuries of our race. We're born to suffer, and to love it."

Boyer wisely shades his character with a touch of the rogue. He never smiles but exploits the frowning romantic intensity he would use to advantage in *Gaslight*. Mikail has no compunction in fleecing the son at poker, and he naps at every opportunity, leaving Tatiana to do most of the housework while fending off the amorous advances of both father and son. He knows himself well enough to admit that his refusal to dip into the tsar's money is more practical than patriotic. Had they spent even a few francs for food, it would only be a matter of time before they moved into the Ritz.

Shooting *Tovarich* involved enough suffering to satisfy even the most masochistic Russian. The cinematographers' and editors' guilds resented a director who flouted their traditional prerogatives and used the cameraman and editor he preferred: Charles Lang and Henry Rust. The cast bridled as Litvak tried to introduce Ufa's methods at RKO, including detailing the day's work each morning, shot by shot. "Litvak had it all on paper; he planned every move," complained Bette Davis when they worked together on *All This and Heaven Too* a few years later. "There is no spontaneity or flexibility."[4] Even Boyer resisted, having become accustomed to discussing his motivations with the director. According to Lord:

> Tola [Litvak] would get a bitchy hate on Charles for a couple of days. He punished him by shouting, "*Non, non, non: coupez, coupez, coupez*" [No, no, no. Cut, cut, cut]. It was almost always in French. Then he and Charles would have it out. "*Dites moi que tu veux*" [Tell me what you want]. "*Je veux . . .*" [I want . . .]. And they'd go on and on. Charles would storm off to his dressing room. Tola would go in and fifteen minutes would go by while everybody sat around on the set and they'd come out and do the thing again and it was exactly the same thing as before.[5]

Still smarting over Warner's rejection of Hopkins, Litvak did not hide his dissatisfaction with Colbert. Both Boyer and Colbert believed their faces photographed better from one side than the other, but Colbert, citing a minute bump from her sinus operation, had a stipulation in her contract that she could never be shot in right profile. Setting up shots to accommodate both stars slowed down the meticulous Lang even more, and Warner ordered him off the film. Given the news, Lang simply walked off the lot. Colbert took this as a signal for her to go home as well, causing even more delays.

Tovarich marked Boyer's first appearance as the character type with which he would increasingly be identified: the displaced person. The term came into general use during World War II and attained official recognition with the Displaced Persons Act of 1948. Unlike "refugee," "displaced person" carried connotations of an exceptional social and cultural status that might never be restored. In playing Mikail, Boyer applied a comic twist to the character, whereas in *Arch of Triumph,* he would skew it toward tragedy. His accent—far from being an impediment, as he had feared—became an emblem of his displacement. He may have learned to think in English, but he would always do so as an outsider.

22

Lazy and Hot and Happy

With *Tovarich* in the hands of Litvak and his editor and nothing planned with Wanger, Boyer accepted an offer to make another film in France.

After Fox-Europe broke up, André Daven joined Marc Allégret to produce films featuring Allégret's current protégée, Michèle Morgan. Their next film, a version of Henry Bernstein's 1927 success *Le Venin* (Venom), needed a big name, and Boyer was among the biggest. *Conquest, History Is Made at Night,* and *Tovarich* had not yet opened in France, but *Mayerling* and *The Garden of Allah* were more than enough to convince the press, the industry, and the public that Boyer was an international star. Between 1936 and 1938, the most popular French stars with French audiences were Jean Gabin, Fernandel, Raimu, Harry Baur, Victor Francen, Tino Rossi, and Boyer. Whereas people had seen Maurice Chevalier's return to France in 1934 as an admission of failure, Boyer's return to appear in *Le Venin* was regarded as a victory lap.

As the Boyers sailed for Paris on the *Normandie, Tovarich* was released in the United States. Litvak had overspent the $1 million budget by $400,000, and its mediocre returns and modest reviews clouded his subsequent Hollywood career. For Boyer, however, the film was a personal success, establishing him as an actor who could play light comedy as skillfully as historical romance. "Charles Boyer is an admirable prince," wrote Frank Nugent in the *New York Times,* "having but recently been an admirable Napoleon."[1]

Paris in December 1937 reminded Boyer of *Tovarich,* except that the refugees wandering the streets and arguing in cafés were not Russians but fugitives from the Spanish Civil War and German Jews fleeing Hitler. France offered them a grudging haven but no hope of a permanent home. Gendarmes made no secret of their contempt, stopping and searching everyone who looked as if they didn't belong.

Boyer took the opportunity to catch up on recent cinema, including Jean Renoir's World War I film *La Grand Illusion,* starring Gabin and Boyer's longtime rival Pierre Fresnay, playing, inevitably, an aristocrat. Gabin also appeared in Julien Duvivier's *Pépé le Moko,* set in the native quarter of Algiers. Wanger had seen this film too and, unknown to Boyer, was mulling over an American remake with him as Pépé.

Daven introduced the Boyers to Marc Allégret, who immediately charmed them. Literate and urbane, he was a celebrity in France, having been the teenage lover of the much older writer André Gide before renouncing homosexuality and becoming one of the most skilled star makers of the European cinema. Daven, Allégret, and Boyer were soon the closest of friends. For the rest of their lives, the three would seek one another's company, both in France and later in Hollywood, where Daven fled during the war.

Boyer had such faith in Daven that he agreed to appear in *Le Venin* without reading the script—a gesture that, as work began, he came to regret. Onstage the play had created a sensation with its dark view of sex and marriage. Gabriel, a successful author, is married to Gisèle, who is fragile, docile, and pregnant. He also has a mistress, Françoise, about whom he is obsessively jealous—the "venom" of the title. Weary of her husband's misery, Gisèle tells him to go to Françoise. Once they are alone, the lovers' physical passion, infected by Gabriel's jealousy, turns violent. Françoise encourages Gabriel to beat and degrade her, after which, satiated, he returns home and starts work on a new book, while Gisèle finds consolation in having a successful husband and the expectation of becoming a mother.

Le Venin brought into the open the widespread but unacknowledged existence of kept mistresses and complaisant wives. Sophisticated stage audiences took such material in their stride, but Daven, doubting that the less worldly cinemagoers would be so accepting, had Marcel Achard and German émigré screenwriter Jan Lustig tone it down. Once they finished, little remained of the play but its title, and that too would soon fall victim.

The screenplay's main character, André Pascaud, is no longer an intellectual author but a no-nonsense engineer. His brother-in-law Gilbert loves the young and promiscuous Françoise but cannot convince her to settle down and marry him. André agrees to act as matchmaker. Inevitably, he and Françoise fall in love. Not revealing that he is married, André takes her to the country for a carnal weekend. Back in Paris, he pines for Françoise until his wife gives permission for the relationship to continue. The lovers meet, but when Françoise learns that André is married and his wife is expecting a child, she kills herself.

Furious at the emasculation of his work, Bernstein demanded that Daven change the title. *Le Venin* became *Orage* (Storm). Boyer plays André as a loving husband going through a midlife crisis who, with the connivance of his wife, finds relief and reassurance with a younger woman. There is little excitement and no sexual violence—just the interaction between two people of different ages and backgrounds. Having tracked Françoise to her disordered loft, André stumbles around in the dark, glimpsing her only in flashes from the neon lights outside her window, unsure whether to stare or look away as she crawls out of bed and pulls on her stockings. The candlelit apartment gives cinematographer Armand Thirard an excuse to craft some flattering low-key close-ups, the candles illuminating Morgan's luminous eyes while leaving the rest of her face in shadow. But Boyer dominates the film, as it is evident that Morgan cannot hold her own in face-to-face confrontations. He always seems to be lighting, drawing on, or ashing a cigarette, a trick to catch the audience's attention. Morgan confessed to being overawed by Boyer and unable to do her best work in the scenes they shared. "On the first day of filming," one profile recounted, Morgan "had to play a love scene with Charles Boyer while she had only exchanged a few polite expressions with him during the presentations. During shooting, Boyer kept the same hostile coldness towards her."[2]

Orage convinced neither audiences nor critics. One of the latter, Emile Vuillermoz, wrote that, "anxious to prune everything that could create *longeurs,* Marcel Achard and Jan Lustig have deprived us of indispensable information on the mentality and the origins of this engineer and this student. We are asked to accept, without explanation, that, in one minute, an energetic, loyal and conscientious man who adores his wife and is passionately interested in his profession can become lazy, selfish and indifferent to everything, simply because he encounters an attractive young woman." Graham Greene was more generous, contrasting the realism of the bedroom scenes with the artificiality of such films as *Queen Christina:* it was "the difference between literary and living passion—Garbo dangling the grapes and fumbling whimsically along the walls, and these two, lazy and hot and happy among the cigarette ash and the too many flies."[3]

23

"Come with Me to the Casbah"

While Boyer was in France, Wanger commissioned John Howard Lawson to translate the script of Julien Duvivier's *Pépé le Moko* into English. Lawson, who understood little French, worked from a literal translation. When his version failed to capture the spirit of the original, Wanger called in James M. Cain to polish the first twenty minutes. In the process, the title became the more accessible *Algiers*.

Jewel thief Pépé, nicknamed *Le Moko,* is on the run and has gone to ground with members of his gang in Algiers, capital of the French colony of Algeria. The old native section—the casbah—where he hides is a virtual city within a city. Tourists enter freely, but the locals repel police raids with contemptuous ease. Only Slimane, the lone Algerian detective in a force recruited largely from Paris, slips in and out, taking coffee with Pépé and watching for the error that will destroy him. It comes in the person of Gaby, one-time Parisian shopgirl and now the companion of a rich businessman. Pépé spots her when she and her friends, passengers on a cruise ship, arrive in the casbah for an evening of slumming. He is attracted by her jewels but even more by what she represents.

"You know what you are to me?" he asks her. "You're Paris. The subway . . . and potato chips . . . and coffee on the boulevard." To be reminded of Paris—his spiritual home—is, to Pépé, a torment, which makes Gaby even more seductive. She accepts his tributes indifferently, as her right, which disturbs him even more.

"You're all silk, and you jingle when you walk," he says. "What did you do? Before the jewels?"

"I wanted them," she says simply—an impulse both share.

When her ship is about to sail, Pépé leaves the safety of the casbah and runs to the port—where, in Duvivier's version, he slashes himself with a razor and bleeds to death. In the American film, he is shot by the police.

The script tells us almost nothing about Pépé. *Moko*, a slang term in the Occitan language, indicates that he is associated with the port of Toulon; Pépé, a shortening of Giuseppe, suggests Italian ancestry. But Paris is Pépé's great good place, and he invests it with an almost mystical charm. His life in exile means so little that he carelessly gambles it, his very existence a game of Russian roulette in which the odds diminish with every spin of the chamber.

Wanger initially struggled to see Boyer in the Jean Gabin role. Boyer typically played educated men ruled by reason and intellect and accustomed to taking charge, particularly with women. His Pépé might be a thief, but he would also be a gentleman. Gabin, in contrast, came from the world of music hall and operetta (like Chevalier), trailing a whiff of the barroom and the brothel. For a while, Wanger considered casting French actor Fernand Gravet, already known to American audiences from *The Great Waltz*. He even approached Gabin, who turned him down. "I'd already played the part," Gabin explained later, "and America was too far away." But Wanger always circled back to his first choice.

Boyer had to be convinced to take the part. To repeat, word for word, the performance of another actor would be degrading. Who knew why Gabin had played the character in that particular way? As with any role, Boyer had to find his own motivation, and his understanding of Pépé might yield a totally different interpretation. "Gabin is too special," he said. "He is unique. When he plays a role, it stays played. Others should not tamper. I will not tamper with a Gabin performance."[1]

Boyer eventually came around, but he demanded approval of both leading lady and director. As the latter, he nominated John Cromwell. A former actor, Cromwell had appeared on Broadway in a number of plays by George Bernard Shaw, the writer Boyer most admired, and had gone on to a respectable directorial career.

Both Cromwell and Wanger recognized that *Algiers* required a female lead of exceptional seductiveness. Louis B. Mayer had seen nineteen-year-old Hedwig "Hedy" Keisler in Gustav Machaty's *Ecstasy* during a European buying trip. On the basis of a scene in which she swims naked and then enjoys a cunnilingual orgasm *en plein air* as the camera lingers on her delighted face, he put both Machaty and the young Austrian actress under contract and brought them to Hollywood. However, aside from changing Hedy's surname to Lamarr—Keisler was too close to "keister" (slang for backside)—and ordering her to lose some weight, he gave her nothing to do.

Hedy quickly acquired a lover, English actor Reginald Gardiner. He took her to a party attended by Wanger and Boyer, who noticed her immediately. Eavesdropping, she overheard Wanger say to Boyer, "She has small tits but a magnificent face."[2] By the end of the party, she topped Wanger's short list for Gaby, above Dolores del Rio and Sylvia Sidney.

Cromwell could have worked with Sidney or del Rio, both proven professionals. But Lamarr presented difficulties. Her face was indeed magnificent. No actress in Hollywood possessed that high forehead or those arched eyebrows, that mane of dark hair, those luminous eyes and moist lips that seemed to murmur, "Not now, but soon. . . ." It was left to Cromwell to articulate the unpleasant truth behind this ravishing façade: "The problem was that she couldn't act, and we knew it before we started shooting or even rehearsing. After you've been in the business for a time, you can tell easily enough right when you meet them. I could sense her inadequacy, Wanger could sense it, and I could see Boyer getting worried even before we started talking behind Hedy's back. Hedy also had no personality. How could they think she could become a second Garbo? I'll take some credit for making her acting passable but can only share credit with Boyer fifty-fifty."[3] Their solution was for Boyer to take charge of Lamarr, reassuring her offscreen and controlling the tempo of their exchanges with a lift of his eyebrow or the modulation of his voice onscreen.

"Boyer was the unhappiest man in southern California," recalled Cromwell. "He felt doomed to imitate a Jean Gabin performance, and never appreciated how different his own Pépé was from Gabin's. Boyer showed something like genius to make a difference. It was a triumph of nuance. The shots are the same, the dialogue has the same meaning, but Boyer's Pépé and Gabin's Pépé are two different fellows, though in the same predicament."[4]

Algiers is less a remake of *Pépé le Moko* than a copy. There are long scenes in which Boyer imitates Gabin step for step, and the two films are often virtually identical in lighting, framing, cutting, and camera movement. Cromwell also uses Duvivier's exteriors, particularly within the casbah, and recycles most of the music by Vincent Scotto and Mohamed Ygerbuchen. Except for the two central performances, the most noticeable differences are in costuming and minor casting. Duvivier's extras and character actors are authentically unglamorous, wearing rags that look like rags. Even former music-hall star and Chevalier partner Fréhel is barely recognizable in a brief cameo. In Hollywood, however, it was a point of honor among casting, costume, and makeup departments to expend as much time and effort in creating a beggar as a baron. Even the cats in *Algiers* look well fed.

Algiers opened at New York's Radio City Music Hall to coincide with France's national holiday, July 14. The *New Yorker* saw it as a film about the "handsome and gallant" Boyer, dismissing Lamarr as no more than "orchidaceous." *Time* magazine thought differently: "Actor Charles Boyer's confident, romantic, tragic Pépé le Moko, and Joseph Spurin-Calleia's unhurried, calculating Slimane are cine-memorable. But best of all is the smoldering, velvet-voiced wanton-mouthed *femme fatale* of *Algiers,* black-haired, hazel-eyed Viennese actress Hedy Keisler (Hollywood name: Hedy Lamarr). Her coming may well presage a renewal of the sultry cinema of Garbo and Dietrich."[5]

David Selznick cited *Algiers* as an example of how remakes of foreign films—notoriously unreliable—could be profitable if the filmmakers copied the original's dialogue, design, music, and editing. This reduced shooting time and the need to tie up high-priced technicians, as any journeyman could imitate. "*Algiers,* contrary to general belief," Selznick wrote, "was not a success at the box office. It did below-average business almost every place, and yet Wanger will come in with a nice profit, whereas if he had not done a frankly duplicating job and had gone to the expense of a more creative job on the script and on the shooting, he would undoubtedly have come out behind the eight ball."[6]

In one sense, Boyer regretted *Algiers*. Generations of impressionists would make a fumbling stab at mimicking him by thrusting out their lower lip in imitation of his characteristic moue and murmuring, "Come with me to the casbah." His sole complaint was that he would be followed and plagued by a line he never said. Yet nothing muted the power of the film and of Boyer's characterization, which has found new admirers in every generation. Boyer also received his first Academy Award nomination, along with Alexander Toluboff for the sets, James Wong Howe for cinematography, and Gene Lockhart for his performance as the cringing informer Regis.

Behind the scenes, Wanger—having bought *Pépé le Moko* and everything connected with it—was rounding up and destroying all prints of the Duvivier film, which, for more than half a century, would effectively disappear. To him, this was merely good business; he was preventing exhibitors from re-releasing the original to compete with his production. Duvivier and Gabin may not have realized that Wanger would so thoroughly suppress their work. Shortly after the release of *Algiers,* the French trade magazine *Cinématographie Française,* under the headline "Be Careful with Remakes. Selling the Story Rights Can Destroy Your Overseas Career," warned, "It's a new procedure. Instead of selling *Pépé le Moko* in America, we are selling the story rights. *Algiers* with Charles Boyer will replace the French film in cinemas everywhere."[7]

24

Sex on the High Seas

In Europe, the pace of political events accelerated throughout 1938. Fascist Francisco Franco now governed Spain. In March, Hitler annexed Austria. As the German army marched into Vienna, 40,000 Austrian Jews were detained in "protective custody." Others fled; many went to South America, hoping eventually to reach the United States. Those with a police record or a history of political radicalism would spend years on the Mexican border, waiting for a visa.

A revival of European nationalism encouraged foreign governments to challenge America's annexation of their film industries. For decades, Hollywood had brought the best talents of Europe to California, then sold their work back to their home countries through its cinema chains. Now the tide was turning. Britain passed legislation forcing Hollywood to invest some of its profits in local productions, and France imposed a 50 percent limit on the number of foreign films shown there.

Nations also stepped up protests at Hollywood's readiness to parody and traduce their customs and history. As early as 1930, France's ambassador to the United States, poet and playwright Paul Claudel, complained to Will Hays, head of Hollywood's censorship authority, about French characters in Hollywood movies using "truly despicable language as it is spoken in the circles of *apaches* and prostitutes." He went on to condemn "so-called Parisian plays, the main character of which is their heartbreaking stupidity and shocking immorality."[1]

Studios continued to ignore such protests until foreign governments learned to go over their heads to the US State Department and threaten reprisals that could affect business or diplomatic relations. Spain hinted that trade negotiations might be adversely affected unless Paramount withdrew von Sternberg's *The Devil Is a Woman*, which it felt slighted its Guardia Civil. In a ceremony reminiscent of an auto-da-fé under the Inquisition, the studio was forced to ceremonially burn a so-called master print of the film in front of Spain's Washington embassy. Without conscious irony, Paramount founder Adolph Zukor whined apologetically, "We do not make pictures with any idea of depicting real life."[2]

In 1938 RKO announced *Love Match*, with an original screenplay by Delmer Daves based on a story he had heard on the *Ile de France* while returning from Europe. It involved a scandalous nineteenth-century affair between an American woman and a French diplomat, hushed up for fear of an international incident. A reader in the Breen office described the script as "violently in conflict with both the spirit and the letter of our Production Code [and a] low-toned, sordid story of gross sexual irregularities, without even a semblance of what we call 'compensating' moral values."

The French first learned of *Love Match* when RKO approached their embassy to clarify some historical facts. Two weeks before shooting was to begin, they threatened reprisals, including a public demonstration in Washington. Daves and magazine writer Mildred Cram hurriedly rewrote the script with help from Leo McCarey, who had been assigned to direct. From MGM, the studio borrowed Donald Ogden Stewart, its top writer of social comedy, to punch up the dialogue. The new version updated events to the present day, turning the ambassador into a playboy, the woman into a night-club singer, and their relationship into a bittersweet romance. Daves even revised his explanation of the story's origins, telling the press it had been inspired by his first glimpse of the Manhattan skyline as his ship sailed into New York.

The resulting confection went into production in the fall of 1938 as *Love Affair*, with Boyer and Irene Dunne as the leads. Shooting began without a complete screenplay. Anxious as always about his ability to play comedy, Boyer took long walks around the studio, struggling to find a motivation for his character. He rewrote his lines repeatedly and persuaded the rest of the cast to rehearse with him, a practice almost unknown in time-conscious Hollywood and seldom instigated by an actor.

A film buffeted by political pressure, commercial considerations, and censorship—and one that was partly improvised during production—seemed certain to fail. Yet it became the lightest and most charming of romances, much imitated and remade. It was a favorite not only among audiences but also among the performers themselves. Boyer repeatedly cited it as one of the films that gave him the greatest satisfaction. A history of RKO, its authors apparently unaware of the film's chaotic beginnings, calls *Love Affair* "one of the most carefully constructed and skillfully executed love stories in the history of the cinema. Sensitive, poignant, heartbreaking, and heartening at the same time."[3] Made for $800,000, it even turned a profit of $122,000.

Probably with thoughts of *History Is Made at Night*, McCarey begins the story on an ocean liner traveling from Paris to New York. Michel Marnay (Boyer), at one time a painter but now described vaguely as a "sportsman," meets Terry McKay (Dunne), a singer turned fashion buyer, and they fall in love. If Michel is a sportsman, his sport is sex, which is explicitly acknowledged at their first meeting. A telegram from one of Michel's lovers blows through a porthole and into Terry's cabin. Before returning it, she playfully demands that he describe the romantic events it recounts. Michel appears reticent, even ashamed, to do so, but as his explanation segues into a sexual advance, we realize that it is all part of his technique. Terry, however, treats his slick overture with the scorn it deserves. Sex without love is all nonsense anyway. As she says dismissively, it will never replace baseball.

Although Michel is engaged to an heiress and Terry has a wealthy protector in New York, the two are drawn together, bantering and flirting like skilled tennis players warming up between matches. McCarey sometimes frames them at full length, the better to illustrate their physical ease with each other. As they sway together, then part, one senses a magnetism that waxes and wanes with proximity. Play is suspended when the ship docks at Madeira, where Michel introduces Terry to his grandmother, Janou, played by the durable Maria Ouspenskaya. She urges Michel to abandon his playboy life and concentrate on his painting and on Terry. The lovers agree to extricate themselves from their other relationships. Barring any change of heart, they will meet in six months on top of the Empire State Building. Terry leaves her protector and starts singing in a nightclub, while Michel tries to make a go of his art, albeit by painting billboards part time. Six months later, both are on their way to their rendezvous when Terry is hit by a car. Confined to a wheelchair, she is too noble to inflict herself on Michel, but after a series of coincidences that we willingly accept, even while acknowledging their absurdity, they are reunited.

Boyer urged McCarey to expand the sequence where Terry meets Janou, which adds to the backstory about Michel's character and displays some of the devoutly Catholic McCarey's favorite imagery. It also gives Dunne a chance to show off her voice when Terry sings (in French) Martini's "Plaisir d'Amour." This, however, is not the song most associated with the film. That distinction goes to Buddy DeSylva's "Wishing," which Terry performs with a group of children. It was nominated for an Academy Award, as were Dunne, Ouspenskaya, Mildred Cram and Leo McCarey for best original story, and Van Nest Polglase and Al Herman for best interior decoration. None of them won, since that was the year of *Gone with the Wind.*

Following *Love Affair,* the Boyers and Dunnes became friends. In a 1939 interview, Boyer characterized Dunne, unconventionally, as resembling "a gracious house" in which "the best room would be the music room. Great music, and the best of good swing, and things by Gershwin would sound there always. The acoustics would be perfect. Guests in this house would be relaxed and happy but they would have to mind their manners." The comparison seems even odder because Boyer disliked swing and popular music in general, and the comment is best seen as illustrating his well-known awkwardness when being interviewed.

Ironically, given the frothy nature of *Love Affair* and its avoidance of political relevance, at least two members of the production team were active in left-wing causes. Editor Edward Dmytryk would be jailed as one of the Hollywood Ten in the postwar anticommunist witch hunts. Cowriter Donald Ogden Stewart, president of the Hollywood Anti-Nazi League, the American League of Writers, and the Anti-Franco League, fled to Europe in 1951, one step ahead of arrest.

Real life also intervened when Boyer got news of his former lover Lida Baarová. While *Love Affair* was in production, Joseph Goebbels announced that he was leaving his wife and children to live with her. Hitler, an admirer of Frau Goebbels, ordered him to end the affair, and the *Reichminister* reluctantly complied. At the same time, it was rumored that a Hollywood studio was about to offer Lida a seven-year contract. Boyer knew what damage might be done to his marriage and his career by the arrival of a former lover who had recently warmed the bed of Hitler's right-hand man. Fortunately for Boyer and his marriage, Lida chose to remain in Europe. No longer under Goebbels's protection and persona non grata in Germany, she moved to Italy. Inconsistent with the traditions of Hollywood romance, but to Boyer's relief, they never met again.

Meanwhile, Pat was experiencing belated regret at her lost film career and asked Feldman if there was any market for her services. The short answer was no, but friend Norma Shearer found her a small role in her next film, Clarence Brown's version of Robert E. Sherwood's *Idiot's Delight.* She played half of a newlywed couple stranded in the middle of a European war with, among others, Clark Gable as a song-and-dance man. As a farewell to show business, it was an anticlimax, but having got it out of her system, Pat announced that she was going to concentrate on starting a family. Boyer, privately gratified by her retirement, said nothing at the time but conceded in a 1959 interview, "Without doubt, it was better that she stopped making films."[4]

Boyer was now a regular at the high-stakes poker games hosted by former Fox president Joe Schenck at his palatial home, a Spanish Revival–cum–mock Renaissance mansion on South Carolwood Drive in Holmby Hills, one of the city's most select districts. A 1941 court case related to Schenck's finances would name Boyer and Twentieth Century–Fox president Darryl Zanuck as major winners at his table. The parties attracted a floating population of wealthy businessmen, politicians, and the occasional crime figure, as well as so-called gin rummy girls—wannabe actresses, models, and girlfriends who served the champagne, lit the cigars, and generally made themselves agreeable. Boyer was not slow to utilize the opportunities, both professional and social, offered by his new friends. Rumors of clandestine affairs grew in frequency, though the evidence was always sketchy, with famous names mentioned but never confirmed. Most people found it inconceivable that a man renowned for his onscreen success with women did not have his share of illicit sex. Pat had her suspicions, but, as the perfect Hollywood wife, she knew better than to ask for specifics.

25

The Gathering Storm

When Boyer finished *Love Affair* at RKO, he never imagined he would soon be replicating it a few miles away at Universal. He had no shortage of offers. André Daven had signed a deal with RKO to make two films in France, both to be shot at the Victorine studios in Nice, and both with Boyer: *Ariane* and *Le Corsaire* (The Pirate). Anatole Litvak also wanted him for *Confessions of a Nazi Spy*, intended to be Hollywood's first overtly anti-Nazi film. This project was especially attractive to Boyer, given his detestation of Hitler.

But Hollywood was obsessed with the success of *Gone with the Wind*. It had made period films fashionable again. Warner Brothers bought Rachel Field's best-selling *All This and Heaven Too*, set in nineteenth-century Paris, and offered Boyer the starring role. It was too big an opportunity to turn down. He accepted, leaving *Confessions of a Nazi Spy* to Edward G. Robinson.

Throughout the spring of 1939, Boyer followed the news from Europe, where British prime minister Neville Chamberlain and his French counterpart, Edouard Daladier, were turning a blind eye to fascist expansion. It seemed the worst time to take a European trip, but for Boyer, his two months off in the summer were an important break from the stress of filmmaking.

In Hollywood, however, actors were at the disposal of the studios. Irene Dunne owed a film to Universal, which saw an opportunity to cash in on the success of *Love Affair*. A screenplay provisionally entitled "A Modern Cinderella" was ready to shoot, and the studio wanted Boyer and Dunne to star. It even agreed to pay Boyer the $100,000 Feldman demanded. Boyer shrugged. *All This and Heaven Too* would take months to prepare, and Daven could begin shooting *Le Corsaire* in his absence, leaving his scenes until last.

With the benefit of hindsight, the Universal project, bad as it was, ended up being more successful than the others on which Boyer might have worked. *Ariane*, based on a film starring Elizabeth Bergner about a love affair between a young girl and a philandering older man, was not made until 1957, when

Billy Wilder filmed it as *Love in the Afternoon*. *Le Corsaire* would start but never be completed. As for *Confessions of a Nazi Spy*, Litvak went ahead with the film, despite a warning from Joseph P. Kennedy, former US ambassador to Great Britain (and father of the thirty-fifth president). Like many American businessmen, Kennedy was an eager appeaser. He urged Hollywood to placate the Nazis, even going so far as to suggest that it remove or disguise Jewish names. Failure to do so risked reprisals from a regime notorious for its lack of scruples. Many expatriates, including Marlene Dietrich, declined to appear in *Confessions of a Nazi Spy*, fearing for the safety of family members still in Europe. German exhibitors refused to screen the film, and some of those in Poland who did show the film were singled out after the Nazi invasion. There were stories, unconfirmed, of managers being hanged in their own cinemas.

Universal's *When Tomorrow Comes* (called at various times *Possessed*, *Seventy-Two Hours*, *Three Nights*, and *Give Us the Night*) originated as James M. Cain's "A Modern Cinderella." Even though Cain's greatest successes (*The Postman Always Rings Twice, Mildred Pierce, Double Indemnity*) were still in the future, Hollywood already valued his narrative ability and hard-boiled journalistic style. But it is hard to tell how much of the film is actually his work, as no fewer than twenty-one writers worked on the screenplay.

The film's Cinderella, Helen Lawrence (Dunne), waits tables in a restaurant with a dismal record of labor relations. She is busy encouraging the other waitresses to strike when she meets her Prince Charming in the person of Philip Chagal—a character Boyer dismissed as "really the same chap" as Michel in *Love Affair*. He invites Helen out on his yacht, moored off Long Island. A storm forces them to retreat to his luxurious home, where she discovers that he is a famous concert pianist with a mentally ill wife (Barbara O'Neil) who is periodically hospitalized and whom he cannot, by law, divorce. As the storm becomes a hurricane, Helen demands that he drive her home, but a falling tree crushes Philip's car, and he and Helen take refuge in a flooded church. After they are rescued in the morning, Philip's wife makes it icily clear that she will destroy his career rather than give him up. Husband and wife sail for Europe, with Philip making vague promises to Helen that he may return someday—when tomorrow comes.

Love Affair had been saved from the worst influences of studio and censor interference by the chemistry between the two central performers, but the writers, director, and key technicians of *When Tomorrow Comes* seemed determined to erase all memories of that rapport. The direction is perfunctory.

During their yachting excursion, Boyer makes no effort to control the boat, concentrating on Dunne while ignoring sails and rudder. Despite his dereliction, the vessel glides along on a back-projected Long Island Sound as smoothly as a punt on a pond. When, back at the mansion, he tries to create a romantic mood and demonstrate his keyboard skills, he does so not by playing a little Chopin but by pounding the piano in the midst of a thunderstorm. No wonder Dunne runs for cover.

The one sequence that creates any atmosphere, in the flooded church, was not part of Cain's original story. One of the film's regiment of writers, Dwight Taylor, poached it from Cain's 1937 novel *Serenade*. Taylor picked the wrong man to cross in this way. Cain had already tried to create an agency to police the industry's indiscriminate misuse of intellectual property, and he took Universal and director John M. Stahl to court. But the case backfired when the judge sided with the studio. His decision established in law that certain concepts, settings, and devices are common to all fiction and therefore in the public domain, able to be used freely without acknowledgment or payment. It made Hollywood studios effectively immune to charges of plagiarism.

Political tensions in Europe made Boyer more determined than ever to maintain ties with his fellow exiles. On the set of *When Tomorrow Comes,* he avoided socializing with the cast, preferring to play chess with his old friend Fritz Feld, who had a small role. A press report credited each with two wins in their little tournament, but Boyer privately conceded that he was out of his league. Feld, a strong amateur player, was good enough to hold his own with international grand masters.

Suzanne Charpentier (aka Annabella) had come to Hollywood at the same time as Boyer to appear in *Caravane,* and she remained friends with the Boyers. She had done a few mediocre films for Twentieth Century–Fox but clashed with Darryl Zanuck about their quality. Their relationship soured even further when she and twenty-five-year-old Tyrone Power fell in love. She was seven years older than Power, recently divorced from Jean Murat, and had a child—not the wife Zanuck wanted for his biggest star. He did his best to separate the couple by sending her to Europe on location. But Boyer and Pat helped the lovers get a special license to marry. Only after the ceremony took place under the palms in the Boyers' garden on April 23, 1939, did Zanuck admit defeat.

The marriage had an unexpected bonus for Boyer. Beginning in the late 1930s, radio occupied an increasing amount of his time. In addition to repeating his movie roles in such programs as *Lux Radio Theatre,* he appeared in *Hollywood Playhouse,* a half-hour anthology drama series originally created as a showcase for Power. Boyer took over the second series that ended its run in September 1939, but he was never happy with the format. "It is an open secret," reported a trade publication, "that he doesn't like the present policy of a different story and characters each week. Boyer would prefer a program in which he could develop a permanent characterization."

26

Blood, Toil, Sweat, and Tears

On July 1, 1939, the Boyers left on what would be their last holiday in France for some years, although they did not know it at the time. The *Normandie* carried a record 1,386 passengers, including Tyrone Power and Annabella, who were on their honeymoon, as well as Edward G. Robinson, Gary Cooper, Norma Shearer, Bob Hope, and many other stars. Most of them were headed for the inaugural Cannes Film Festival, which the Boyers also hoped to attend, as *Love Affair* was among the films being shown.

Scheduled to open on September 1, the Cannes Festival of Free Nations was France's hasty response to the Venice Film Festival, launched by Italian dictator Benito Mussolini the previous year. A showcase for his fascist regime, it was staged in a new purpose-built cinema complex at the Lido de Venezia, Venice's premier beachfront resort. The Cannes festival was ostensibly a rebuke to the politically biased Venice event, but the Côte d'Azur was also keen to reassert itself as Europe's premier tourist destination.

Europe basked in its most idyllic summer for decades. After being mobbed at Paris's St. Lazare railroad station, Boyer spent a few days giving interviews and catching up with friends. Among them was novelist and director Marcel Pagnol. They had known each other since 1928, when Pagnol had considered casting Boyer in his play *Marius*. Ultimately, Pierre Fresnay played the role of the young son of a Marseilles bar owner who runs away to sea. Pagnol now offered Boyer the lead in *La Prière aux Étoiles* (The Prayer to the Stars), which he was about to shoot at Victorine. Boyer promised to consider it once *Le Corsaire* was finished. There was also talk of reviving Bernstein's *Mélo* for a short Paris season.

Boyer and Pat traveled to Figeac, where his mother and stepfather were spending the August holidays. While they were there, news came that *When Tomorrow Comes* was a box-office success, despite being dismissed by the *New York Times* as a film that attempted to capture the "heartbreak of *Love Affair* but

112

only succeeded in being silly."[1] It outgrossed even Universal's major 1939 release, the Deanna Durbin musical *First Love*. Cheered by this news, Boyer went on to Nice, where Marc Allégret and André Daven had been shooting *Le Corsaire* since August 1. After wrapping at Victorine, the unit planned to shoot for a few days on the Atlantic coast near Brest in Brittany, but Boyer expected to finish in time to meet up with Pat (who had gone to England) for the Cannes festival.

Le Corsaire was a Marcel Achard play within a play of the kind pioneered by Luigi Pirandello in *Six Characters in Search of an Author*. It follows an American film crew as they become caught up in the real historical events behind a pirate movie they are shooting. With an eye to a US release, the modern action is set in Hollywood, with Boyer playing pirate Kid Jackson, alongside Michele Alfa and the handsome Louis Jourdan. The play had been a success onstage with Louis Jouvet, who expected to repeat his role in the film. He was furious when Allégret and Daven chose Boyer instead, and he ended their association.

Shooting had hardly recommenced when events intervened to stop it. All year, the governments of Britain and France had surrendered territory after territory to Hitler. Now, with the German army massed on the border of Poland, it was clear that Hitler had no intention of halting his acquisition of *lebensraum* for the German people.

As the news became more ominous, Boyer delayed his departure for Cannes and missed the opening gala. On the Croisette (Cannes' beachside promenade), guests of the festival, including the Duke and Duchess of Windsor and most of the Hollywood contingent, danced under the stars to the music of five orchestras and watched a show hosted by France's most popular comedian, Fernandel. Then, a sudden squall interrupted the fireworks that ended the fete. In an omen of imminent disaster, icy air rushed off the Mediterranean, accompanied by flashes of lightning, sending the celebrities fleeing to their hotels.

The next day dawned calm and sunny. Boyer was still at his hotel in Nice with Daven and Allégret when the radio announced that Hitler's panzers had crossed into Poland. All three realized that, with both Britain and France committed by treaty to Poland's defense, war with Germany was now unavoidable. A formal declaration came on September 3, followed by the general mobilization of France's armed forces. In Cannes, the first festival intended to celebrate the cinema of free nations never took place.

As technicians and actors dispersed to join their families or report for military service, Daven suspended work on *Le Corsaire,* with only about forty minutes shot. In Cannes, the stars hurriedly packed up and headed for home. Many expatriates with residences along the Côte d'Azur closed them up and piled onto any vessel heading for England or neutral Portugal.

Boyer was ordered to report to the town hall in Figeac, the rallying point for men of military age. "Nobody knows yet what the future may be," he wrote to Feldman on September 2. "France's courage and calm and England's are really admirable, in front of the infamous attitude of Hitler." He hoped he would be allowed to return to America. "It is obvious that I could be of more use over there, but I must naturally follow the orders I receive." He concluded, "Tell Darryl [Zanuck] and Joe [Schenck] I played poker last night and still hope to beat them 'when tomorrow comes.'"[2]

Given his celebrity, mediocre physique, and age—he had just turned forty on August 28—Boyer expected his appearance in Figeac to be a formality, but his failure to perform national service at age twenty came back to haunt him. Men who had completed basic training were sent home to await call-up, but Boyer, an untrained civilian, became "a victim of army bureaucracy and incompetence," in the words of Daven. Sent with other raw recruits to Agen, sixty-five miles away, Boyer was issued a shapeless uniform by harassed clerks who had never heard of him and was enlisted as a private second class in the Twenty-Seventh Colonial Artillery. He was shipped to Lyon for training in military communications and then sent back to Agen to serve as a telephone switchboard operator. The gambler in Boyer was reminded how swiftly one's luck could change.

Pat returned from England and took a hotel room in Agen, where they could be together when he was off duty. Meanwhile, they appealed to friends to pull whatever strings they could to get him released. Fortunately, the army decided that men over forty were more use on the home front than on the front lines, and in November 115,000 of them were demobilized, including Boyer. By then, the press had learned of his plight. Newspapers published photographs of Boyer in a baggy uniform that, as one caption put it, did not flatter "our seductive and celebrated movie star."

The invasion of Poland inaugurated what became known as the "phony war." With winter looming, Hitler's generals counseled him against attacking the Netherlands, Belgium, and France until the spring, particularly since the Maginot Line of fortifications, protecting France's eastern border, was regarded as impregnable.

Hollywood, like many American businesses, saw the war in Europe mostly as an opportunity. Walter Wanger owned the rights to *Personal His-*

tory, Vincent Sheean's account of his life as a foreign correspondent. Now he set Ben Hecht and Richard Maibaum the task of adapting it into the story of a journalist reporting on the present European crisis. He wanted Boyer and Claudette Colbert in the leads.

As many somewhat embarrassed Riviera residents returned to their villas, Victorine also came back to life, but it was too late for *Le Corsaire.* Nevertheless, its sets survived on the back lot for decades. *La Prière aux Étoiles,* which Pagnol began filming with Pierre Blanchar in the role intended for Boyer, would never be finished either.

Belatedly, the army tried to repair its public relations gaffe with Boyer by announcing that he would tour France, lecturing to women's groups. "One of the constant problems that beset the war-lords," explained a news report, "is the feminine antipathy to war, particularly in the ranks of mothers."[3] Supposedly his soothing voice and seductive manner would put their minds at rest— a ludicrous hope, under the circumstances. There is no evidence that Boyer ever seriously considered such a plan.

In Paris, he met Colonel Charles de Gaulle and finance minister Paul Reynaud, who would briefly serve as prime minister. Neither held out much hope that France alone could resist blitzkrieg. Profoundly depressed, the Boyers took a boat from Lisbon and arrived back in Los Angeles in time for a subdued Christmas. Before leaving Paris, Boyer had arranged that any money owed to him by French producers would be paid directly to the town of Figeac for humanitarian use. Figeac eventually benefited to the tune of 30,000 francs—$100,000 in today's money.

27

The World's Best-Dressed Governess

While Boyer was in France, Universal provisionally announced that he would appear with Deanna Durbin in *It's a Date.* When it seemed he might be there indefinitely, Walter Pidgeon took over that role; Joel McCrea replaced him in the Sheean film, now called *Foreign Correspondent;* and Herbert Marshall stepped in to record *Hollywood Playhouse.* This left Boyer free, when he did return, to appear in *All This and Heaven Too.* Years later, Litvak furnished an epitaph for the film: "I'll tell you what was wrong with the picture," he said. "*Gone with the Wind* was wrong with it. The picture was overproduced. You couldn't see the actors for the candelabra, and the whole thing became a victory for matter over mind."[1]

With the success of *Gone with the Wind,* David Selznick served Hollywood a meal of humble pie and crow, to which Warner Brothers responded with sour grapes. A year earlier, one of Warner's biggest stars, Bette Davis, had been the popular choice to play Scarlett O'Hara, and the film had almost been within the studio's grasp. Then Jack Warner overplayed his hand by demanding that Selznick cast Errol Flynn as Rhett Butler. Determined to use Clark Gable, Selznick took the film to MGM. In revenge, Warner bought the Civil War story *Jezebel,* a property he had previously rejected, and cast Davis in a role that was almost a copy of Scarlett. But even Davis's Academy Award for best actress was cold comfort for Jack Warner.

Still in pursuit of a project that would trump Selznick, he paid $100,000 for Rachel Field's best-selling *All This and Heaven Too*—which, he insisted, should always, in imitation of *GWTW,* be referred to as *ATAHT.* Davis appeared in the film grudgingly. During *Jezebel,* she had given birth to a daughter by director William Wyler, with whom she would soon work on two of her finest performances in *The Letter* and *The Little Foxes.* It was galling that, instead of Wyler's sensitive perfectionism, she would be subjected to Litvak's schematic methods. It was all the more infuriating because he too was a former lover. According to Basil Rathbone, who visited the set, their arguments could be heard by the entire cast and crew.

Boyer joined the production just after Christmas 1939, still disoriented by his army experiences and his glimpse of a very different way of life. Bereft of Hollywood glamor, he had become an ordinary man, and not a particularly impressive one. When he arrived on the set for the first time, Davis didn't recognize the balding, paunchy, middle-aged gentleman with the dazed expression and ordered him escorted off the lot. Her later comment that he was "the finest actor with whom I ever worked" took none of the sting out of the experience, as she also called him "the most vain man I worked with. Terribly serious about his looks. A wig, corset, lifts in his shoes, and so on."[2]

All This and Heaven Too owed much to *Jane Eyre* and every other governess–master romance, but Rachel Field claimed it drew on her own family history—specifically, the 1848 murder in Paris of the Duchess de Choiseul-Praslin by her husband, who committed suicide while awaiting trial. It was rumored that he had killed her out of love for his children's governess (Field's ancestor) Henriette Deluzy-Desportes and took poison rather than implicate her.

In the film, Henriette (Davis) is hired to care for the children of Praslin (Boyer) and his pathologically jealous wife (Barbara O'Neil). As Praslin and Henriette grow closer and she wins the affection of his children, the duchess becomes increasingly paranoid. Even though Henriette and Praslin never share a moment of romantic intimacy, let alone anything as flagrant as a kiss, the duchess, helped by her wealthy father, personal chaplain, and malicious servants, forces Henriette to resign and then prevents her from getting another job by maligning her to potential employers. After some bitter confrontations, Praslin batters his wife to death, then takes poison and dies without confessing his crime.

Casey Robinson struggled to squeeze all this into a screenplay. His first version clocked in at four hours, and no amount of cutting could get it to down to less than two and a half. Boyer did his best as Praslin, but Barbara O'Neil stole most of their scenes. (Litvak would have preferred his ex-wife, Miriam Hopkins, in the role. "The Duchess is a heartless venomous bitch," he said. "Miriam would be perfect.") Because the real-life duchess had borne ten children, O'Neil thought she should be played as older and dowdy. Instead, she was fitted with gowns appropriate to a production designed to make a splash. Davis was also absurdly overdressed. Rather than the "plain gray alpaca *basque*" that Field described as Henriette's "badge of discreet servitude," Davis spent forty minutes each morning being laced into a multitude of petticoats. Litvak agreed that she was the world's most expensively costumed governess.

In May, the Germans launched their offensive, flooding into the Netherlands, Belgium, and Luxembourg. Confounding all predictions, they bypassed the Maginot Line, cutting instead through the rugged, heavily forested, but lightly defended Ardennes, then pivoting north toward Paris and the English Channel. The fall of France, followed by Britain's invasion and defeat, appeared to be just a matter of time. Boyer always had his radio tuned to the news, and he ate in his dressing room rather than in the commissary with the rest of the cast. Fellow actor Walter Hampden said, "I hardly knew Charles Boyer when the production commenced, and I knew him not one whit better when it was over." He even took his radio to the set and listened between takes, until Litvak objected. "Yes, the war news is destroying my ability to concentrate," he admitted. The radio disappeared, and Boyer asked the cast not to discuss the war in his presence, but his anxiety only increased.

Frustrations and humiliations continued. Boyer's corset compressed his diaphragm, stifling his voice. In moments of high drama, he could do little but glare. "Charles was a happy fellow in the other pictures we made," Litvak said, "but in *All This and Heaven Too* he was surely the least contented man with whom I've ever worked." He lost ten pounds during the five months of filming. Twice, a doctor was called after Boyer suffered panic attacks, but the barbiturates he was prescribed made it difficult for him to perform in some key scenes, including the murder of the duchess. Boyer had never played a scene of physical violence, least of all toward a woman, and he was even less inclined to do so at a time when many of his friends in France might be dying. Litvak had to make do with close-ups of his tormented face.

After British prime minister Winston Churchill refused France's request for more troops and aircraft, Paul Reynaud admitted defeat, and Charles de Gaulle flew to London to set up a government in exile. Boyer was being dressed for more retakes when Churchill made his famous speech on May 13 promising only "blood, toil, tears, and sweat" and warning that "without victory, there is no survival." No longer willing to stand aside, Boyer stormed out of the studio still in costume. A few days later, he and Pat took the new Clipper flying-boat service from New York to Southampton, England. Pat joined her family in Bradford, while Boyer arranged his mother's passage to America on the *President Washington* sailing from Genoa, Italy.

The Boyers were still in London at the end of May when a fleet of small boats crossed the English Channel to rescue 330,000 British troops from the beaches at Dunkirk, leaving 40,000 French soldiers to become prisoners of war. Boyer met with de Gaulle in his London headquarters. Reynaud had promoted de Gaulle to brigadier general in one of his last acts as president, but even to the French, he remained an obscure military officer. His fame began with the speech broadcast on June 18 and its stirring conclusion: "Whatever happens, the flame of the French resistance must not be extinguished and *will* not be extinguished!" The BBC signal reached only northern France, so almost nobody heard it, and because of an oversight, the speech was not recorded. A similar speech four days later was more widely broadcast. An English translation, read by Boyer, was the version heard around the world.

Boyer, like Frenchmen everywhere, seethed as Hitler stage-managed the surrender of the defeated France. Troops broke down the wall of the museum containing the railway carriage where, in 1918, Germany had signed the armistice. They hauled it to Compiègne, in the woods outside Paris, which had since become a memorial. Scores of foreign journalists were summoned to witness the ceremony, which the Germans filmed to the music of a military band. Afterward, in their customary response to things that offended them, they dynamited the monument.

As the Germans advanced toward Paris, clogging the roads with refugees, Minister of Propaganda Jean Giraudoux commissioned Julien Duvivier to make the film *Untel Pere et Fils* (Mr. Someone and Son) to encourage resistance. Originally called *Le Reléve* (Continuation), it told the story of a typical Montmartre family, the Froments. Charles Spaak's script dramatized how the French had resisted German aggression in the past, first in the Franco-Prussian War of 1871 and then in 1914–1918. Duvivier had hoped to cast Jean Gabin, Françoise Rosay, and Pierre Blanchar, but Gabin was on his way to America, Blanchar was working with Pagnol, and Rosay and Feyder had fled to neutral Switzerland and then North Africa. Duvivier compromised with Raimu, Suzy Prim, Louis Jouvet, Louis Jourdan, and Michèle Morgan, all of whom played different generations of the Froments. The production values throughout are impressive, re-creating not only Montmartre over the course of a century but also the African jungle for a sequence in which engineer Jouvet goes mad with malaria while building a railroad. About an hour had been filmed when the Germans entered Paris in June 1940. Goebbels ordered all footage destroyed and the filmmakers imprisoned. Fortunately, a German officer and cineast helped Duvivier, his Jewish wife, and their son reach Lisbon and then the United States, where, with help from Boyer, Duvivier completed the film.

Germany declared France neutral and set up a puppet administration in the spa town of Vichy, with World War I hero Marshal Philippe Pétain as president. In Africa, General Henri Giraud continued to command the remnants of France's African army, in uneasy cooperation with Pétain. Both Giraud and de Gaulle claimed to represent unoccupied France, but the world would eventually accept de Gaulle as the de facto leader of Free France, the official nation in exile.

Friends who had fled to Britain appealed for Boyer's help in getting to the United States. He flew to Lisbon, accompanying émigrés and putting them on ships to New York. Among them were André Daven and his wife. Others, including director Jean Renoir and writer and aviator Antoine de Saint Exupéry, made their own way.

Returning to Hollywood, Boyer felt he had entered another world. Most Americans had only the vaguest sense of the world beyond their own hometowns. To Hollywood, war in Europe mattered less than the week's box-office receipts. He felt increasingly alienated. The dislocation reached comic proportions when Litvak asked Boyer and Davis to revoice some scenes from *ATAHT*. Davis was on holiday in Honolulu and Boyer was in New York, recording a radio dramatization of the film, so a three-way hookup was arranged with Litvak in Burbank. Alert to a publicity opportunity, Warner Brothers invited journalists to listen in. All was going well until Davis and Boyer found they had been sent different versions of the script and their dialogue didn't match. The resulting chaos did nothing to improve the film's prospects.

28

The War at Home

With war, Europeans in Hollywood were confronted with a dilemma. Most of the men should have gone home and presented themselves for military duty, but the German advance had happened so quickly that their countries were overrun before they had the chance. A few Britons, including David Niven, went anyway. Many, however, breathed a sigh of relief when the ambassador, Lord Lothian, assured them that "the maintenance of a powerful British nucleus of older actors in Hollywood is of great importance to our own interests, partly because they are continually championing the British cause in a very volatile community which would otherwise be left to the mercies of German propagandists."[1]

For years, the Nazis and their sympathizers had been busy across the United States. Information centers (known as Brown Houses) opened in some of the larger cities, including Los Angeles, offering German food, German beer, and Nazi ideas. The lesson of such places was not lost on Boyer, who knew that if France wanted a hearing in isolationist America, it would have to speak for itself.

A few months after his return from England, he launched the French Research Foundation (FRF). From his own pocket, but with additional covert funding from diplomatic sources, he purchased an unprepossessing building at 411 North La Cienega Boulevard. His friend André David became the foundation's director, with a staff of three, and they started to create a reference library. Ostensibly, the foundation would collect information on France's historical, artistic, and cultural achievements and disseminate it through the media, but its more serious function was to circulate pro-French propaganda and aid those in exile or seeking sanctuary.

In issuing visas, the United States still adhered to quotas set early in the century, when most immigrants came from Ireland, Poland, and Russia rather than Germany, Austria, and France. Exceptions were made if the applicant had a sponsor or a job offer—a loophole that Hollywood's German and Austrian community was adept at exploiting. Ernst Lubitsch and William Dieterle started the European Film Fund to acquire work permits for immigrants, even if that meant a former professor of literature would be shelving library books or a famous composer would be transcribing Serbian and Croatian folk songs, as was the case with Béla Bartók. A network of volunteers guided newcomers to those who could help them. New arrivals in Los Angeles with no English or no money were directed to Salka Viertel's Santa Monica home, while Fritz Feld and Herman Bing, who had come to Hollywood years before and made their names as character actors, now extended helping hands to their one-time bosses.

Boyer hoped the FRF would do the same for French artists. Some didn't wait for assistance. Jean-Pierre Aumont was acting in a play in Cannes when a fan came backstage to get his program autographed. Noting that the fan was consul for the Central American nation of Honduras, Aumont managed to obtain a Honduran visa authorizing his entry into the United States. Marcel Dalio, with his teenage wife, fled to Lisbon. After purchasing visas issued by Chile, they arrived in Mexico to find that the documents were forgeries. Fortunately, Victor Francen got Dalio an acting job in Canada. The couple then made their way to California, where Dalio, with help from Boyer, found regular work. His wife, Madeleine Lebeau, also appeared in a number of films, including *Casablanca.*

The foundation opened officially on October 15, 1940—two days before Pétain announced that Jewish artists would no longer be permitted to work in France. Privately incensed, Boyer said nothing. To be effective and maintain the trust of the still-neutral US government, the FRF could not take sides. Like Rick's Café in *Casablanca,* its doors had to be open to every-one, regardless of their political views or the lack thereof. Publicly embracing any faction could have immediate and drastic financial repercussions. In September 1938 actress Myrna Loy had cabled her support to Jan Masaryk, president of Nazi-occupied Czechoslovakia. "He told the press of my mes-sage," she said. "The news got back to Germany, and my pictures were banned."[2]

In Boyer's office, portraits of de Gaulle and Pétain hung next to those of Giraud and military hero Marshal Lyautey. The rest of the building conveyed an illusion of peaceful cultural unanimity, with bronze busts by sixteenth-century sculptor Antoine Coysevox and other examples of France's artistic heritage. Moise Kisling, who had fled France at the same time as Boyer and settled in Los Angeles, created a painting for the lobby. Boyer's detachment impressed Kisling. He confided to David, "He's not an actor, this man, but a philosopher."[3]

Boyer finally broke his silence in July 1941. After the isolationist America First movement, spearheaded by aviator Charles Lindbergh, drew 20,000 people to the Hollywood Bowl, Boyer joined other celebrities before a crowd of 19,000 at the same venue to speak in support of former presidential candidate Wendell Willkie, who had made a case for intervention. Japan's attack on Pearl Harbor on December 7, 1941, settled the argument decisively. On December 22 Boyer joined the fifteen-member Actors' Division of the Hollywood Victory Committee, which met at the Beverly Wilshire Hotel to plan the industry's contribution to the war. Among his first acts was to collaborate with Merle Oberon on *Calling All Aliens!* a short film explaining how to register as an alien.

Setting up and operating the foundation cost an estimated $2 million, much of it from Boyer's own pocket. In addition to donating his French earnings to the people of Figeac, he gave large sums to the French Red Cross, which shipped food parcels to French prisoners of war. French nationals working in the movies were urged to donate 5 percent of their salaries to French war relief. But getting Hollywood's French community to agree on anything was virtually impossible, as Boyer discovered when he convened a meeting of its members. Among those present was producer Henri Diamant-Berger. He recalled: "There is no very deep political unity in the group of French exiles. We are twenty-eight of our profession and this represents at least five or six different tendencies. Jacques Deval willingly admits de Gaulle but does not like the English much. René Clair and Duvivier are reluctant, not wanting to hurt their families in France. Renoir, with his usual violence, puts everyone in the same bag: Pétain, de Gaulle, the Communists who ruined him. He swears by the Americans only."[4]

Many exiles preferred to lie low and enjoy the hospitality of Francophile Americans. Jean Renoir scorned a group that hung out at The Players, the club high above Sunset Boulevard owned by director-screenwriter Preston Sturges. "Wonderfully victorious attacks were launched on Vichy from this Sunset Strip café," he wrote sarcastically. "It's not hard to be a hero when the enemy is 10,000 kilometres away." Even Boyer's mother preferred not to get involved. Despite taking lessons, she never learned English. "If you go to a certain Hollywood pastry shop any afternoon," wrote Annabella, "you will encounter, amid the brioches, three ladies, no longer young, exchanging the latest gossip. They are mesdames Chauchoin, Rossignol and Charpentier. Madame Chauchoin is the mother of Claudette Colbert, Madame Boyer-Rossignol that of Charles, and Madame Charpentier is mine."[5]

Because of his many years in America, Boyer was the acknowledged leader of the French community. Aumont praised him for creating "a welcoming center for the French of California. In his home he had judiciously and lovingly compiled an abundant library of French books. Playing the roles of judge, ambassador, priest and philosophy teacher all at once, he received with patience all of his countrymen who came to him in order to plead their case and demand justice."[6] Dalio called him "the Governor General of our little French colony."[7] It was a barbed compliment, since governors-general were seldom native to the colonies they controlled. Having arrived before the war, Boyer, in Dalio's opinion, had little understanding of those with families and loved ones still in occupied France.

Dalio, Aumont, Renoir, Clair, and Kisling were regular visitors to the Boyer home, where André Daven and his wife lived for a while as houseguests. Pat helped the newcomers rent homes, find doctors, and open bank accounts. In return, the expatriates were expected to behave themselves.

Aumont, a noted ladies' man, was flirting at a party with actress Gene Tierney, then married to couturier Oleg Cassini, when Boyer took him aside. "Watch your step," he warned. "She's a married woman. It just isn't done here."

"What a strange country," Aumont mused. Undeterred, he would go on to have affairs with Joan Crawford, Hedy Lamarr, Vivien Leigh, and Barbara Stanwyck. When he married Maria Montez in 1943, Boyer, pleased to see him settling down, accompanied the couple to a jeweler to choose a ring and acted as best man at the wedding. When their first child was born, he became godfather.[8]

Jean Gabin, who made it to Hollywood with the help of then-lover Marlene Dietrich, steered clear of the group. He made no attempt to hide his dislike of Boyer, which went back to the controversy over the suppression of *Pépé le Moko*. The trade press tried to create a rivalry between the "great lovers," but Gabin had no desire to stay in Hollywood any longer than necessary and made only two films there. As soon as he could, he returned to Europe, joined Giraud's Free French forces in North Africa, and drove a tank during the liberation.

Louis Jouvet remained in South America, where he formed a troupe with other French performers. Weary of touring, he appealed to Boyer for help in acquiring visas for himself and the group. Boyer, Renoir, Aumont, and others signed a petition, and Aumont was designated to go to Washington and appear at the hearing to determine whether the visas would be issued. Aumont recalled:

> I found myself at the Department of Justice, in front of a
> commission of about ten members: agents from the FBI, OSS,
> Army Intelligence, Navy Intelligence, the State department and
> others. They overwhelmed me with questions. Who did Jouvet vote
> for in 1936? What would Jouvet do if the Germans were
> threatening to kill his children unless he agreed to blow up some
> factories in America? What do you think of De Gaulle, Petain,
> Giraud, Maurice Chevalier? Will France become Communist?
> Does the Resistance really exist? And so on. Despite my efforts, the
> commission refused Jouvet his visa. The reason? His troupe was
> too large. How could they ever be sure that some spy hadn't slipped
> into it?[9]

Not all French artistic refugees chose to reside in California. Painters and writers preferred the more cosmopolitan New York. Some lived in comfort on their American royalties, as did *Liliom* author Ferenc Molnar at the Plaza Hotel. Paintings by Toulouse-Lautrec and Édouard Manet decorated Henry Bernstein's suite at the Waldorf Astoria, and its door was answered by a servant in traditional striped waistcoat and white gloves. Bernstein disparaged those authors whose work was translated into English, such as Jules Romains, André Maurois, and Antoine de Saint Exupéry, who privately opposed Vichy but refused to say so publicly. Undeterred, he published a scathing attack on Pétain, *Portrait of a Defeatist*, which caused him to be stripped of his French citizenship and membership in the Academie Française.

Many among the New York contingent made a point of speaking only French. Some in Hollywood, including long-time residents Émile Chautard and director Jacques Tourneur, followed suit. Tourneur had lived in America for so long that he spoke French with an American accent, yet he insisted that, as long as the Nazis occupied France, it would be the only language heard in his home.

Producer Henri Diamant-Berger was among those who thought the community should support de Gaulle more openly. Paul Périgord, professor of French cultural studies at UCLA, started a group called France Forever and enlisted Diamant-Berger to publicize the general and his work to business and veterans' groups. Paradoxically, this faction protested when Warner Brothers hired William Faulkner to develop a film about the general called, variously, *Journey to Dawn, Journey to Hope, Free France,* and *The de Gaulle Story.* Faulkner used the FRF to research the general's life and career, and although he wrote more than 1,200 pages, apologists for de Gaulle ensured that the film would never be made.

This factionalism came to a head when liberals formed a chapter of the Free World Association (FWA), launched by Louis Dolivet. He had landed in New York in June 1940, limping on crutches and claiming to be an air gunner wounded in battle. Dolivet started a magazine, *Free World,* and launched the FWA, which was committed to the ideals of the defunct League of Nations. Orson Welles, whom Dolivet befriended and urged to run for Congress, helped form a Hollywood chapter. Boyer, Lubitsch, Arthur Hornblow Jr., Dory Schary, Dudley Nichols, and Walter Wanger were among those who joined. In response, the industry's right wing, including Walt Disney, director Sam Wood, Robert Taylor, and Boyer's friend Adolphe Menjou, founded the Motion Picture Alliance for the Preservation of American Ideals, which stigmatized the Free Worlders as communists. The lines had been drawn that would lead to the worst excesses of the blacklist. (Embarrassingly for Boyer and the other FWA members, Dolivet was unmasked as a Soviet agent with a history of infiltrating liberal movements.)

Boyer's neutrality made it easier for him to broadcast on the government-funded Voice of America. He produced radio versions of the screenplays of films in which he had appeared and arranged for them to be transmitted in Francophone countries. He added a French commentary to the 1944 documentary *The Fighting Lady,* produced by Twentieth Century–Fox for the US Navy, and revoiced Frank Capra's *Why We Fight* documentary series, during which he and Capra became friends.

Boyer even let himself be mocked on such radio programs as *The Burns and Allen Show* and *Amos and Andy,* if it would help sell war bonds. In one episode, Gracie Allen assumes blithely that Boyer will appear in her amateur theater production without payment "because he's Free French." And Andy takes a job as Boyer's valet to acquire more "couth." Boyer agreed to endorse Magnavox record players if he could be photographed listening to one at the

FRF. The resulting advertisements inspired the *New Yorker* to publish a poem by Leah Curran Wright that inquired:

> What is the matter with our friend Charles Boyer?
> Why doesn't he have a radio-phonograph in his own foyer?
> I hate to think of Charles' having to run clear down to the
>   Foundation
> Every time he feels the need of a little musical titillation.

29

A Voice Singing in the Snow

Reviewers were kinder to *All This and Heaven Too* than it deserved. *Variety* called it "film theatre at its best."[1] Audiences, however, found it a bore. The *New York Times* opined: "Miss Davis and Mr. Boyer put all the 'soul' they possess into the playing of the principal roles. Under the slow-paced direction of Anatole Litvak, they carry through mainly on one somber key—Miss Davis with her large eyes filled with sadness and her mouth drooping heavily with woe, Mr. Boyer with his face a rigid mask, out of which his dark eyes signal pain. Barbara O'Neil as the termagant duchess considerably overplays the part."[2] But it was O'Neil who earned the film's only Academy Award nomination for acting—the ultimate humiliation for Bette Davis.

Litvak was generous in his assessment of Boyer's performance, which, he said, "transcended the curse of over-production. He was easily the best actor I ever directed, although in the three pictures we made I didn't direct him once—he was his own creative artist. Possibly *All This and Heaven Too* was the best work he ever did. It was a much more complex performance, certainly, than for *Mayerling* or for *Tovarich*. It also shows that the great performances are not given by contented actors."[3]

No longer under contract to Walter Wanger, Boyer was free to work elsewhere. Ideally, he wanted more control over his roles. An actor who is waiting for the right script too often accepts the first one offered. As his own producer, he could acquire properties and develop them. His agent, Charles Feldman, was dabbling in production too, and he encouraged Boyer to do the same.

Jean Renoir and screenwriter Dudley Nichols sent Boyer a script called *The Children*, which would pair him again with Michèle Morgan, this time as a schoolteacher in a small town occupied by Nazis. The local gauleiter urges him to collaborate and use his position to influence others to follow suit. He is tempted to do so as a means of winning the love of a spunkier female colleague, but instead he denounces the Nazis, even though it means death.

RKO, to which Morgan was under contract, agreed to produce *The Children* but would not pay Boyer's $100,000 fee; nor would it lend Morgan to another studio to make the film. At this point, Walter Slezak, cast as the Nazi commander, and Charles Laughton, newly arrived from Britain, met on the Twentieth Century en route to Hollywood. Slezak showed Laughton the script, which the latter thought would be an ideal vehicle to relaunch himself in the American market; there was even a good part for his protégée, Maureen O'Hara. RKO was interested, particularly since neither actor was as expensive as Boyer, so Morgan and Boyer bowed out rather than deprive the others of a "go" project. Renoir made the film, changing the title to *This Land Is Mine,* while a disappointed Boyer let Feldman negotiate deals for two films at Universal and another at Paramount.

Every lover needs a love object, but among Hollywood's many actresses, only a few could convey those elusive emotional states of yearning, obsession, and sacrifice demanded by such roles. The best of them excelled not in acting but in reacting. Any director could, like Josef von Sternberg, order an actress to "count to ten, then look at that light as if you couldn't live without it." But it took a Marlene Dietrich to achieve the effect and repeat it to order.

Such actresses were often highly strung, with the Thoroughbred's tendency to nervousness. Margaret Sullavan's wistful look, air of isolation, and husky voice—which Louise Brooks described as "strange, fey, mysterious, like a voice singing in the snow"—hid chronic anxiety. Troubled marriages and a progressive hearing loss frequently interrupted her career, which would end prematurely at age forty-nine in suicide. In 1941, however, Sullavan's marriage to agent Leland Hayward seemed to have stabilized her, although she remained prone to depression. "Perhaps I'll get used to this bizarre place called Hollywood," she said morosely, "but I doubt it." She had taken a break after the birth of her second child and was preparing to sign a deal with MGM when Universal enforced an old contract that committed her to make two films. By then, she was pregnant again, which complicated the production of the first film, a remake of *Back Street.*

Fannie Hurst's novel, which Universal had already filmed successfully in 1932, was, like *A Star Is Born,* a perennial. Divorce and infidelity no longer carried the same stigma as when the novel appeared in 1931—let alone when it is set, in the early 1900s—but audiences in 1941 could still relate to a woman who sacrificed her life for a man who was too selfish to reciprocate.

Fortunately for first-time producer Bruce Manning, Sullavan was happy to work with Boyer, in part because his resonant voice suited her faulty hearing.

Eyeing her expanding waistline, Manning hurried the film into production under British director Robert Stevenson. Boyer signed on October 10 for a film due to open in February.

Fannie Hurst protested, in vain, at the changes made to her novel to accommodate the political and social realities of 1941, as well as the casting of Boyer and Sullavan. Their characters, Walter Saxel and Ray Smith, no longer belong to Cincinnati's German community; nor is Ray the tough, independent girl of the novel, ready to share a beer in a bar as she fends off passes from her drinking pals. The settings and characters in Stevenson's version are decidedly Anglo-Saxon, and Ray has become quiet and demure, resigned to languishing for decades in her backstreet apartment, mooning over Walter's portrait while he enjoys his prestigious job and loving family. Boyer does his best with an unsympathetic role, portraying Walter as not so much heartless as a victim of circumstance. Because the censors insisted that the relationship between Walter and Ray be shown as clandestine and degrading to both, there could be none of those intimate scenes in which he excelled. The effect was to make this Sullavan's film, an opinion endorsed by the reviews, a few of which deprecated Boyer's overly romantic attitude compared to Sullavan's reticence.

These comments gave Boyer pause. Perhaps he should play more roles in which he dials down the soft-eyed admiration and murmuring endearments. Wanger's old ambition to make him the modern Valentino did not preclude a little menace. With all these options to consider, Boyer asked Feldman to press Universal to use him on both sides of the camera. Within a few months, the agent had drawn up a deal under which Boyer would become, in name at least, his own producer.

Boyer and Hedy Lamarr in *Algiers* (1938, Walter Wanger/United Artists). "You know what you are to me? You're Paris."

Boyer and Angela Lansbury in *Gaslight* (1944, MGM).

Ingrid Bergman revenges herself on Boyer in *Gaslight* (1944, MGM).

Boyer (*foreground*), age five or six, in front of his father's factory in Figeac. His parents watch from the balcony.

Boyer and Florelle in *Tumultes* (1932, Ufa).

Boyer as a Romani fiddler in *Caravan* (1934, Fox Film Corp.).

Boyer and Jean Parker
in *Caravan* (1934,
Fox Film Corp.).

Boyer (*right*) with
producer Walter
Wanger (*center*) and
Columbia boss Harry
Cohn (*right*), 1936
(UPI).

Boyer clowns with Sophia Loren during the filming of *What a Woman!* (1956, Lux).

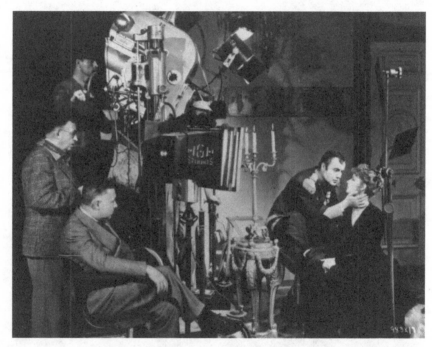

Clarence Brown directs Boyer and Greta Garbo in *Conquest* (1937, MGM).

Boyer and Greta Garbo in *Conquest* (1937, MGM).

Boyer (*center*) with his close friend Maurice Chevalier (*left*) and an unidentified man, circa 1970.

Boyer as the High Lama in *Lost Horizon* (1973, Columbia).

Rock Hudson (*right*) about to do Boyer *A Very Special Favor* (1965, Universal).

Boyer in native costume and Loretta Young as a Manchu princess in *Shanghai* (1935, Walter Wanger/Paramount).

Boyer (*left*) plays chess with old friend Fritz Feld on set of *When Tomorrow Comes* (1939, Universal).

Boyer narrating *The Louvre* (1964, NBC).

Boyer (*in the hat*) with Marc Allégret (*left*), Michèle Morgan, André Daven (*right*), and an unidentified man during the production of *Orage* (1938).

Boyer aged five or six.

Boyer's earliest mentor Raphael Duflos in *La Travail* (1919).

Boyer in a rare costume part as the Duc de Vallombreuse in *Le Capitaine Fracasse* (1929, Lutèce Films).

Boyer as Napoleon and Reginald Owen as Talleyrand in *Conquest* (1937, MGM).

Boyer in French army
uniform, 1939.

Boyer and son Michael on
Ischia, circa 1957.

Boyer as Yorisaka in *La Bataille* (1934, Gaumont).

Boyer, Alan Marshal, Marlene Dietrich, and Joseph Schild-kraut enjoy the hospitality of Dietrich's silk-lined tent on location in Arizona for *The Garden of Allah* (1936, Selznick/United Artists).

Boyer and Joan Fontaine in *The Constant Nymph* (1943, Warner Brothers).

Boyer (*right*) with Robert Florey (*center*), Jean Renoir (*seated*), and Louis Verneuil,
Hollywood, circa 1944 (Robert Florey).

Boyer ponders the many depictions of Napoleon Bonaparte during the production of *Conquest* (1937, MGM).

Hedy Lamarr in *Algiers* (1938, Walter Wanger/United Artists).

Boyer in *Algiers* (1938, Walter Wanger/United Artists).

Boyer (*right*), Conrad Veidt (*center*), and Hans Albers, who played the aviator Ellisen in the French, English, and German versions, respectively, of *F.P. 1 Antwortet Nicht* (1933, Ufa).

Henry Bernstein (*center*) with the Boyers in London, circa 1940.

Boyer (*right*) with Ruth Chatterton and Tyler Brooke in *The Magnificent Lie* (1931, Paramount).

Gaby Morlay as Clara in *Le Bonheur* (1934, Pathé-Natan).

Boyer as the anarchist Philippe in *Le Bonheur* (1934, Pathé-Natan).

Women with the "Boyer look": Renee Falconetti, Alice Field, and Nathalie Paley.

"It will never replace baseball." Boyer and Jean Arthur "meeting cute" in *Love Affair* (1939, RKO).

Marcel L'Herbier.

Boyer and Pat about to move into their new house in Beverly Hills, 1934.

Liliom is carried into the afterlife by "God's police" (*Liliom*, 1934, Fox Europe).

The Boyers lay flowers on the grave of their son, Michael. Behind Boyer are Michael's roommate Jon Kirsch and Monsignor Daniel Sullivan (Associated Press).

Boyer registers as an alien, 1940 (International News).

Boyer as a *jeune premier*, circa 1930.

Tilly Losch vamps Boyer in *The Garden of Allah* (1936, Selznick/United Artists; photos by William E. Thomas).

The Boyers arrive at a Los Angeles church to say the rosary for the soul of their son, Michael.

Charles Laughton (as Otto Haake) tries to recruit Boyer (as Ravic) as an informer in *Arch of Triumph* (1948, Enterprise/United Artists).

Boyer with his mother, Louise Boyer-Rossignol, in Hollywood, shortly after her arrival in 1940 (Universal).

Boyer doesn't disguise his irritation at having to show visiting dignitaries around Universal in 1943. They are Celia Villa, daughter of notorious Mexican bandit Pancho Villa, and Jackson Leighter, coordinator of Latin American relations (Universal).

The Boyers at their new
Beverly Grove Drive home,
1937.

Boyer as Paul Dumond, "the
best headwaiter in Europe,"
impersonating a burglar to
rescue Jean Arthur from her
homicidal husband in
History Is Made at Night
(1937, Walter Wanger/
United Artists).

Boyer in 1939, rehearsing for his appearance on the radio drama series *Hollywood Playhouse* (NBC).

30

The Golden Door

Sullavan's pregnancy dominated *Back Street*'s postproduction. She skipped the gala premiere in Miami because flying might have induced labor. Boyer was also absent, pleading influenza. In fact, he had a recurrence of the panic attacks and palpitations experienced during *All This and Heaven Too*. Doctors found no major illness but urged him to reduce his smoking habit, now up to four packs a day.

Back Street had barely opened when Sullavan's baby boy arrived, accompanied by extensive publicity. For the Boyers, it once again raised the idea of having a child. Pat planned no more film appearances after *Idiot's Delight,* so the moment was propitious. With fingers crossed, they began another attempt. Partly to ensure that the child would be born American, they renewed their applications for citizenship.

Paramount was the most "European" of the studios, with the largest number of émigrés on staff, so it had no lack of stories about refugees. Billy Wilder alone could have provided a score. The Austrian-born former journalist had spent six months in the border town of Mexicali before convincing an immigration official that keeping him there was depriving the world of great films. "Write some good ones," the officer reportedly said as he stamped Wilder's passport.

One of Wilder's best refugee screenplays, cowritten with regular partner Charles Brackett, began with a treatment by Ketti Frings, a journalist who wrote for fan magazines. Called "Memo to a Movie Producer," the story was autobiographical: Katherine "Ketti" Hartley met former German boxing champion Kurt Frings in 1937, when he was a ski instructor at Saint Moritz. They married, but the US Immigration Service blocked Kurt's admission to the country until 1940 because he had falsified some details on his visa application. Kurt sat out the delay in a community of refugees on the Mexican border. Ketti spent weekdays in Los Angeles but made the two-hour drive back to the border on weekends. She persuaded producer Arthur Hornblow Jr. to give her fifteen minutes to pitch her idea for a film. At the appointed time she walked into his office, laid the treatment on his desk, said "Thank you," and left, hoping he would use the remaining fourteen and a half minutes to read it. He did and was immediately intrigued. Two days later, Paramount bought the story for $50,000 and assigned it to Wilder and Brackett. Meanwhile, Frings began writing a novel using the same material.

In Frings's novel, the husband is an amiable jock, and the couple's marriage, despite its long-distance aspect, is happy but strained by the need to convince immigration authorities that the husband has cut all ties to his shady past. The screenplay would go through a succession of titles, including *Ensenada* and *The Golden Door*. Frings called her novel *Hold Back the Dawn*, and since it sold well, Paramount adopted the same title.

To direct, Hornblow assigned Mitchell Leisen. Wilder protested, since he had clashed with Leisen on an earlier collaboration, the comedy *Midnight*. An elegant and unapologetic homosexual who began his career designing costumes for Cecil B. DeMille, Leisen was an affront to the hard-bitten fraternity of writers typified by Wilder, who dismissed him as "a window dresser."

Feldman sent Boyer an early version of the script. He liked its dry, cynical tone—a Wilder trademark—but thought the character was too sporty for him and insufficiently romantic. Hornblow asked the writers to rethink the project with Boyer in mind. This irritated them, but they had to admit that an older, more thoughtful, and perhaps more devious main character increased the dramatic possibilities. Drawing on his knowledge of con men and the European demimonde, Wilder created a character who is a fraud and a liar—his favorite type. In the new version, Ketti disappeared and Kurt morphed into a version of Wilder himself, who, during his checkered prewar career, subsisted for a brief time as a paid dance partner. (The Frings protested this rewriting of their characters and threatened to sue, but to no avail.)

Georges Iscovescu is an aging adventurer who has spent years living off women in the capitals of Europe. He bluffs his way onto the set of director Dwight Saxon (played by Leisen) to pitch a story that, it turns out, is his own. He explains that, while stranded in Tijuana and facing an eight-year wait for a visa, he looked for an American to marry. His choice was Emmy, a frazzled schoolteacher too frightened of sex to have ever explored it. Once they were married, he intended to dump her, but events forced a change of heart that drove him to try to sell their story as a screenplay.

Wilder and Brackett fleshed out the cast with a rich collection of individuals. Avuncular immigration agent Hammock (Walter Abel) covertly observes the exiles by randomly visiting them on the pretext of having one of them give him a haircut. Anita (Paulette Goddard), Georges's former mistress, explains how she acquired a visa by marrying a vertically challenged jockey. "Once over the border," she says, "I went to a judge. I said, 'A woman wants a man, not a radiator cap.' Divorce granted. Fifty dollars."

Victor Francen, whom Boyer had helped restart his career in Hollywood, plays another refugee: the pious and patient van den Luecken. He has one of Wilder's most pointed scenes, a reminder of how far short of its ideals America has fallen. When the refugees complain about delays in getting visas, van der Luecken suggests that they "remember the words on the Statue of Liberty."

"Life, liberty, and the pursuit of happiness?" Hammock suggests.

"No," chides van der Luecken. He then quotes the poem of Emma Lazarus: "'Give me your tired, your poor / Your huddled masses yearning to breathe free / The wretched refuse of your teeming shores. / Send these, the homeless, tempest-tossed to me. / I lift my lamp beside the golden door!' Or is it 'the shining door,' Mr. Inspector?" Hammock, discomfited, admits he isn't sure.

Using a technique he would refine in such films as *Double Indemnity* and *Sunset Boulevard,* Wilder gives Iscovescu a cynical voice-over in which he reflects on the decline in his fortunes. Once a guest at the Ritz, he now lives in the ironically named Hotel Esperanza—Spanish for "hope"—where he gets a room only because the previous tenant hanged himself. Rather than champagne, he drinks tequila bought with a borrowed peso. And instead of his complaisantly carnal lover, he has a dowdy schoolteacher whose one appeal is her passport. (Not that Olivia de Havilland, who plays Emmy, is actually dowdy, but we willingly suspend our disbelief.)

There is nothing glamorous about Boyer's first appearance in the film. His black and white oxfords set exactly the right sleazy tone. They echo the hair—too full and a little oily—and the day-old stubble. Later his character will smarten up, get a haircut and a shave, and put on a suit, but that first image stays in our minds, signifying that desperation is Iscovescu's primary impulse.

Wilder and Brackett document the entrapment of Emmy in a manner that makes us both despise and admire Georges. Likewise, when Anita maliciously alerts Emmy to his treachery, we detest rather than applaud her. Boyer invests his character with all the charm and intensity of his former work, but amplified here by conflicting emotions. Georges is perturbed by his growing affection for Emmy, and even Anita feels compassion and regret. Boyer manages to pull off a difficult change of heart in the last third of the film, when Emmy lies comatose in a hospital after a car accident and we learn that Georges is trying to sell his story to Saxon to pay for the medical care that will save her.

Having taken charge of his performance and established his motivation, Boyer was in no mood to fall in with Wilder's sometimes inappropriate ideas—most notably, when a despairing Georges talks to a cockroach in his hotel room. "Where do you think you are going," he demands of the bug as it climbs the wall. "You're not a citizen, are you? What is your quota number?"

According to Brackett, Wilder encountered Boyer eating lunch at Lucey's, near the studio, and learned that the actor insisted on this scene being cut. It was not the first time Boyer had defied the writers. He had earlier refused to shoot a restaurant scene because the fish being served was pompano, which he disliked. Seeking a compromise, Brackett suggested that they rewrite the cockroach scene to make it more intense, but Boyer was adamant. He didn't like cockroaches and asked, "Why would I speak to one?" According to legend, Wilder then told Brackett, "If that son of a bitch won't talk to a cockroach, he won't talk to anybody!" and cut most of Boyer's dialogue from the last third of the film.[1] (Inconveniently, neither the film nor Brackett's published journals support this. If anyone is marginalized in these scenes, it's Emmy, who lies comatose while Georges tries to raise money for her treatment.)

Wilder was further incensed when his work and Brackett's was credited as "based on a story by Ketti Frings," since little of it remained. When Hornblow refused to amend the credits, Wilder asked that his be changed from "Screenplay by . . ." to "Written by . . .," as the scenario wasn't entirely his and Brackett's work. This incident strengthened Wilder's resolve to direct. He refused to accept his next assignment, *The Major and the Minor*, unless he also directed it, which was the start of a distinguished directorial career. An early shot in *The Major and the Minor* shows a newspaper headline advertising an article entitled "Why I Hate Women by Charles Boyer."

Rumors circulated during the production of an affair between Goddard and Boyer, but similar stories cropped up about Goddard on every film. Pat shrugged them off. Anyone who knew her husband would recognize that the dark-eyed brunette wasn't the "Boyer type." In fact, de Havilland and Boyer would have made more convincing lovers. Watching the dailies, de Havilland confided to Brackett that it was difficult to remain in character when acting with Boyer because she found him so attractive.

The censors' misgivings about sexual improprieties were easier to deal with than an unexpected intervention by Harry J. Anslinger, commissioner of narcotics in the Treasury Department. A chronic grandstander, Anslinger claimed to have proof that Kurt Frings was "a notorious international character" who had rightly been denied entry to the United States. He also suggested that the film risked impairing US-Mexico relations, which the government was striving to improve with its Good Neighbor policy. When the Breen office seemed inclined to investigate these charges, Kurt Frings, who was about to start a business as a Hollywood talent agent, threatened a lawsuit for libel. Producer Hornblow stepped in, and the matter was quietly buried. However, Anslinger's comments alerted Mexico, which complained to the US State Department about the film's depiction of its citizens as venal and of Tijuana as squalid. So the sets were spruced up and some diplomats were given token jobs as "advisers."

The film previewed at a suburban cinema in Long Beach, California. "Never approached a preview with more agony," Brackett wrote in his diary, but he was agreeably surprised when it was a success. "The audience was absorbed from the start to the finish—an almost tangible absorption, which was catnip to the worried hearts. The [audience comment] cards were excellent and I drove home in high good humor."[2]

Hold Back the Dawn was nominated for an Academy Award as best picture. Also nominated were Olivia de Havilland's performance, the Wilder-Brackett script, Leo Tover's cinematography, Victor Young's music, and the art direction of Robert Usher and Sam Comer under Paramount's head designer Hans Dreier. Boyer was ignored, and the film won nothing. They all might have saved face had they lost to that year's stellar nominee, *Citizen Kane,* but the big winners were John Ford's folksy *How Green Was My Valley* and Gary Cooper in the patriotic *Sergeant York.*

Boyer continued to aid friends who were seeking safety in the United States. But his help came too late for former lover Renée Falconetti, who frittered away the fame she had achieved in *The Passion of Joan of Arc* and, despite many offers, never made another film. During the occupation, she fled to South America; from there, she hoped to relaunch her career in the United States. However, she died destitute in Buenos Aires in 1946 from an overdose of amphetamines, said to be ingested as part of a crash diet.

31

The Most Popular Frenchman
in America

The French word for actor is *comedien,* which can mislead Anglophones into assuming that all French performers consider themselves comics. In fact, the specialist in comedy, known as a *farceur,* is entirely distinct, and the two seldom overlap. "In France there is a chasm between music-hall artists and real theatre actors," explained Maurice Chevalier. "The latter are educated people, whereas in my time most music-hall artists were not."[1]

Boyer approached comedy with caution. Even his roles in *Tovarich* and *Together Again* are played for irony, not laughs. But occasionally he was tempted. Following *Back Street,* he "mentioned to Maggie [Sullavan] that I was about to drown in all the tears my pictures were causing, and I would like to do a comedy, just for a nice change. They had been trying to talk her into making a farce that she thought had possibilities, but she chose *Back Street* instead. However, she would agree to make the other picture if I would be in it."[2]

Ladislao Bus-Fekete's *Heartbreak* was hardly a farce, so the film Universal wanted Sullavan to make was probably not the one she and Boyer ultimately appeared in. Charles Feldman is prominently credited as the owner of the rights, suggesting that Boyer brought the project to Universal as part of his production deal. The comedy of marital discord and confusion was a specialty of central European writers, a legacy from Viennese operetta; the plots often turned on love affairs complicated by inheritance, profession, or class. Boy-meets-girl was less common than prince-meets-waitress or, as in the case of *Heartbreak,* playwright-meets-doctor. In a feeble pun on the Sullavan character's profession as a physician, the film was called *Appointment for Love.*

Despite its title, the film has surprising charm due to the chemistry between Boyer and Sullavan, which was as potent as anything he developed with Claudette Colbert or Irene Dunne. Director William A. Seiter, who had come up through knockabout comedies featuring the Marx Brothers, Wheeler and Woolsey, and Laurel and Hardy, tried to influence Boyer to play the script more broadly. That he and Sullavan ignored his advice gives the film its appeal.

At the premiere of his new play, a successful Broadway author (Boyer) is distracted during his curtain speech by a woman in the front row (Sullavan) who appears to have fainted. The call, "Is there a doctor in the house?" reveals that she *is* a doctor and hasn't fainted but fallen asleep because of the long hours she works. They fall in love and marry, after which Sullavan, determinedly rational, keeps her own apartment so as not to disturb her husband with her late-night arrivals and departures. He is used to partying until dawn and breakfasting at noon, so the two seldom meet.

Their professional and emotional lives finally intersect in a scene that is among Boyer's most touching. Called to the hospital in the middle of a date, Sullavan tells her husband to go home, since she may be in surgery all night. However, when she leaves the hospital in the small hours, he is still on the steps. Leaning wearily against him, she asks, "How did you know I wanted you to be waiting there?" Her defenses down, she tries to explain her elation at the act of healing—the sense of willing someone to live. Her senior colleague had been with her at the patient's bedside, "but I couldn't tell him," she says. "I couldn't tell anybody. Anybody but you."

Julien Duvivier was already known in Hollywood, having directed *The Great Waltz* for MGM in 1938. Even though some of that film had been reshot after his departure, his credentials were sufficient, with Boyer's help, to revive his American career, beginning with *Tales of Manhattan*. The project originated with Russian-born Boris Morros, a musical director at Paramount for many years (and, unsuspected at the time, a Soviet spy). Morros had produced a couple of films when Sam Spiegel approached him with a project. (Spiegel had responded to the hostility toward Jewish and German names by styling himself "S. P. Eagle," while composer Max Steiner became "Main Steyner.") Spiegel proposed a film similar to Duvivier's 1937 *Carnet de Bal,* in which episodes with different casts are linked by a common object. In *Carnet de Bal,* the object is an ancient dance card, and in *Tales of Manhattan,* it is a tailcoat, supposedly cursed, that passes from hand to hand. (An early working title was *Tails of Manhattan.*)

Paramount turned the project down, but Twentieth Century–Fox accepted, subject to Spiegel's ability to find a satisfactory cast and crew in a community depleted by war work and the draft. Publicity claimed that the resulting roster of stars and writers constituted the greatest assembly of talent in a single production up to that time. Boyer was joined by Charles Laughton, Edward G. Robinson, Henry Fonda, Paul Robeson, Rita Hayworth, W. C. Fields, and Ginger Rogers, with screenplay contributions from Ben Hecht, Donald Ogden Stewart, Billy Wilder, Buster Keaton, and others.

Boyer was an obvious choice for the opening story, playing matinee idol Paul Orman, for whom the coat is tailored. Duvivier enlivens this segment with audacious visuals, beginning with a quartet of tailors, including the portly Robert Greig, arriving at Orman's luxurious apartment and, with the help of his equally ample valet (Eugene Pallette), reverently unveiling the coat for his approval.

Following that night's performance, Orman hurries to meet his mistress (Rita Hayworth), the wife of big-game hunter Thomas Mitchell. Tony Gaudio's camera follows him in sweeping crane and tracking shots as he leaves the theater and heads for Mitchell's country mansion. It is there that the husband confronts the lovers in his circular trophy room, its walls lined with the antlers of animals he has killed. (This may be Duvivier's joke, a pair of horns being the traditional symbol of a deceived husband.)

Cigarette always in hand, voice modulating from theatrical declamation to intimate murmur, Boyer is at his suave best and more than earns top billing. Even when Mitchell shoots Orman through his new coat, inaugurating its history of ill fortune, he maintains his sangfroid. Pretending the bullet missed him, he strolls to his car, only to collapse and order his chauffeur to rush him to the hospital.

The episode's one discordant element is a miscast Rita Hayworth, borrowed from Columbia to replace Irene Dunne. To Boyer's irritation, she was afflicted with the giggles, supposedly over his accent, which she described, inaccurately, as "thick enough to cut with a knife." Orson Welles, her future husband, implies that it was not Boyer's accent but his image as a great lover that amused her. "They went a day over," he recalled, "because every time Boyer gave her the *ooh, ooh* look, she broke up. *Broke up!* The thing that all the women were panting for struck her as funny. And poor Boyer, a very sweet fellow, didn't know what he was doing wrong. He would just talk with his French accent, and away she'd go!"[3]

Boyer, who often played poker with Darryl Zanuck and Fox president Joe Schenck, persuaded them to hire André Daven as the film's producer.

Daven remained at Fox after the war, part of Zanuck's inner circle. Boyer was also responsible for the inclusion of African American singer, actor, and left-wing activist Paul Robeson in the film. Late in 1941 Robeson wrote to his wife from Hollywood: "At a British benefit (swanky) I met all the stars and had a special chat with—breathe hard—*Mr. Charles Boyer*. He came to my recital and told Morros that he has all my records. So the ground is laid."[4]

Robeson appears in the final episode in which the coat, filled with money, falls from a plane into an impoverished community of sharecroppers. They use the windfall to buy their land, and the coat's curse is neutralized when it is draped over an inanimate scarecrow. Bad luck lingered, however. The episode's cliché racism offended Robeson, who never appeared in another film, and the speech in which he urges his neighbors to form a collective would be used against him when he was blacklisted.

In the wake of Pearl Harbor, *Thunder in the East* (the remake of *La Bataille*) was recut into an anti-Japanese propaganda film called *Hara Kiri*, with an introduction that compares Yorisaka's treachery to that of modern Japan. Angered that he was not consulted on this decision, Boyer signed a three-year contract with Universal in January 1942 that committed him to producing nine films and appearing in at least four of them. He would not be asked to act in any film against his will and was promised approval of script, director, and costar. He would not need to put up any money nor deal with the nuts and bolts of production. These details would be left to Universal. But in matters concerning his appearance onscreen, Boyer's decision was final. On paper, it seemed to offer the autonomy he had long desired, but in essence, it did not differ from Irving Thalberg's proposal to place him under long-term contract as a "charter performer" during the making of *Conquest*. Such nebulous deals gave the studio first call on the artist's services and a preferred position in salary negotiations but offered the performer only the illusion of power, which cost the studio nothing.

Boyer had ideas about the kind of films he wanted to produce. One was Henry Bernstein's *Le Venin*, which Marc Allégret had bowdlerized into *Orage*. With a better actress than Michèle Morgan, Boyer believed it could be a powerful drama. He discussed it with Bernstein in New York, who gave his approval, but when he suggested it to Universal, the studio responded with the standard stall: "Let's make that our *next* project." With *Tales of Manhattan* grossing $2.8 million, the studio wanted another one just like it. If Boyer and

Duvivier coproduced, the studio wheedled, each would pocket a hefty $125,000. Once again, the actor's proposal was disposed of by the studio.

Although 1942 was a busy year for Boyer, it began unpromisingly. Until he became an American citizen, he sometimes returned to the United States through Canada. In January, as part of the panic following the Japanese attack on Pearl Harbor, he and other foreign nationals were denied entry by nervous American border guards. Antoine de Saint Exupéry was among those turned back at the US-Canada border and complained in a letter to his agent, "That idiot Charles Boyer was pinched in the same way but telephoned Madame Roosevelt and was passed through in a perfectly illegal manner."[5]

The First Lady's intervention had an element of self-interest. Boyer was part of the Hollywood Victory Caravan, a two-week cross-country tour to sell war bonds. In April he joined Cary Grant, Bing Crosby, Bob Hope, Merle Oberon, Humphrey Bogart, James Cagney, Laurel and Hardy, and other stars in a special train lent by the Santa Fe Railroad. Its fourteen cars carried two prefabricated dance floors, collapsible rehearsal stages, two pianos, and room for a ten-man band. Organized by Charles Feldman and featuring many of his clients, the tour began in Los Angeles on April 26 and traveled to Washington, DC, where Mrs. Roosevelt hosted a tea party at the White House for the cast on April 30. They went on to play in twelve cities, netting more than $700,000.

The Boyers officially became American citizens in February. Only a week later, one of Boyer's favorite writers, Stefan Zweig, and his wife committed suicide in Brazil, where they had joined a German community so they could live among people who spoke their language. Their deaths suggested Boyer's contribution to the Victory Caravan show: In his first public act as an American citizen, he adapted *The Last Class,* a short story by Alphonse Daudet dramatizing the value of language in defining a culture. Using a blackboard, a few desks, and a single student to suggest a classroom, he played a French schoolteacher in Alsace following Prussia's seizure of the region in the Franco-Prussian War of 1871. On orders from Berlin, French is banned beginning at noon that day. As the clock strikes, he defiantly writes "Vive la France!" on the blackboard.

André David, who accompanied the tour, wrote: "It's too seldom said that, since Sarah Bernhardt, no artist has done more in the United States for the prestige of our culture. Sarah only had to propagate our glorious art. Boyer had to restore confidence at a somber time when the face of France was covered in ashes. The most popular Frenchman in America, he has succeeded in becoming a veritable tower of strength. From town to town, crowds cry in his passing 'Vive la France!'"[6]

On July 24 Boyer participated in another ceremony that, even more than his naturalization, confirmed his status as a true citizen of the United States. His hand- and footprints were impressed in cement next to those of other stars in the forecourt of Grauman's Chinese Theater on Hollywood Boulevard.

32

Love and Death

Being a star/producer for Universal meant more work, but little of it was creative. Boyer entertained foreign dignitaries who visited the studio and did guest spots on radio shows, as well as acting in dramatized versions of recent films for Cecil B. DeMille's *Lux Radio Theatre*. His likeness, sometimes with Pat beside him, appeared in glossy magazines with a "mild, cool" Chesterfield cigarette or a bottle of Pabst beer in hand. But when he tried to discuss specific projects with Universal, cornering the relevant executives proved to be just as difficult as it had been at MGM.

The sequel to *Tales of Manhattan,* initially called *For All We Know* but retitled *Flesh and Fantasy,* originally contained four episodes, separated by interludes featuring actor David Hoffman and writer-comedian Robert Benchley as clubmen discussing predestination. Books from the club's library provide the cue for each story, including a version of Oscar Wilde's *Lord Arthur Savile's Crime* featuring Edward G. Robinson. When Universal deemed the film too long, the fourth episode, starring Alan Curtis as a criminal on the run who takes shelter with an old friend and his blind daughter, was deleted. The salvaged footage became the basis of a new feature, *Destiny.*

Progress on the film was sluggish as actors dropped out to do war work or serve in the military. Boyer and Duvivier signed their contracts in June 1942, but filming did not begin until the fall. Boyer hoped Charles Laughton, Adolphe Menjou, Deanna Durbin, and even Greta Garbo might participate. Instead, he had to be content with whoever could spare time between their other commitments. Robert Cummings and Betty Field, who appear in the first story, came on board in March 1943. Edward G. Robinson and Barbara Stanwyck also signed on (at $50,000 each), but Stanwyck had to squeeze in her appearance between two of her most memorable roles in *The Lady Eve* and *Double Indemnity.*

Also in March 1943, the Academy of Motion Picture Arts and Sciences presented Boyer with a special award. Though not quite an Oscar—there was no statuette, only a certificate—it acknowledged "his progressive cultural achievement in establishing the French Research Foundation in Los Angeles as a source of reference for the Hollywood motion picture industry." It wasn't quite the unique recognition it appeared to be; rather, it was part of the Academy's attempt to encourage patriotic effort. Careful not to play favorites, it gave the same award to British playwright and actor Noël Coward for celebrating the Royal Navy by starring in and codirecting *In Which We Serve* and to MGM "for its achievement in representing the American Way of Life in the production of the Andy Hardy series of films." These feature Mickey Rooney as a small-town teenager and Lewis Stone as his father, a judge with whom Andy has an inspirational tête-à-tête in each film.

As *Flesh and Fantasy* dragged on, Duvivier used Universal's facilities to complete *Untel Pere et Fils,* the propaganda feature cut short by the war. He shot additional episodes with Michèle Morgan, as well as the linking scenes with Boyer that he had been unable to film at Victorine. As *Heart of a Nation,* the film received some screenings in 1943 and would appear again after the liberation as *Immortal France.* For the later versions, Duvivier replaced Boyer's links with a filmed introduction telling the story of the film's rescue and eventual release.

Meanwhile, Warner Brothers recruited Boyer for Edmund Goulding's troubled adaptation of *The Constant Nymph,* a 1924 novel and play by British author Margaret Kennedy. Negotiations on the film were long and tortuous, particularly with the Breen office, as the film deals with a sexual relationship between a fourteen-year-old girl and a man twice her age. In most of the Anglo-Saxon world, such a liaison constituted statutory rape.

Tessa Sanger is the youngest daughter of an elderly composer. They live in the Swiss Alps, mainly for Tessa's benefit, as she suffers from tuberculosis. The precocious girl has a crush on her father's protégé, English composer Lewis Dodd. Lewis marries Florence Creighton, one of the Sanger cousins, but both the marriage and his music languish. When Tessa runs away from school and hides out with Lewis, they become lovers. She inspires him to create his masterpiece, after which they flee to the more liberal Brussels, where she dies, leaving Lewis emotionally and artistically enriched.

The first two candidates to play Lewis, English actors Robert Donat and Leslie Howard, refused to travel to California. (Had Howard done so, he might have survived the war, but his plane was shot down over the English

Channel in June 1943.) Goulding signed Errol Flynn as Lewis and eighteen-year-old Joan Leslie as Tessa, but negotiations on the film took more than a year, by which time both of them were unavailable. At this point, Jack Warner invited Boyer to portray Lewis. Although older than Goulding would have liked, Boyer could play the piano and fit the popular image of a composer. But the actor had his doubts, which were shared by leading British film critic C. A. Lejeune. Why, she asked, did the film transform Dodd from "a young and rather Bohemian British composer, living in a modest home at Strand on the Green [into] a suave, mature Continental [who] spoke English with a French accent [and] lived in Kensington in a house as big as the Albert Hall and almost as ugly."[1]

Boyer also found the screenplay unsatisfactory. Emasculated by the censors, Lewis has little to do but feed lines to Tessa and Florence. As for the sensational love affair, the Breen office would not even allow Tessa and Lewis to kiss. She has to be satisfied with a "dream vision" of them coming together while she listens to a radio broadcast of the composition she inspired.

Boyer also protested the casting of newcomer Alexis Smith as Florence. They were the same height, but because of her upright stance, she photographed taller. Smith had developed a technique she used with shorter actors. "I would stand up straight in long shot," she explained, "but as I walked towards the camera I'd throw out my right hip and slump. That took inches off my height."[2] But to Boyer, it was just one more argument against the film. Grudgingly, he told Feldman to accept but to demand $150,000. Both were surprised (and Boyer was a little disappointed) when Jack Warner agreed.

Finding a replacement for Joan Leslie further delayed the start of shooting. Goulding claims he discovered the film's eventual star in Romanoff's restaurant, where he saw actor Brian Aherne eating lunch with a companion, both of them wearing leather flying suits. (Aherne piloted his own plane.) Goulding told Aherne about his problems. "Jack Warner wants a star," he said, "but she has to be consumptive, flat-chested, anemic, and fourteen!"

"How about me?" said the woman in the flying suit. Goulding had not recognized Aherne's wife, Joan Fontaine. She was cast the next day, and shooting began almost immediately. (This story has more than a whiff of the publicity department. Aherne had played Lewis Dodd in an earlier film version of *The Constant Nymph* and likely thought of Fontaine for the role independently.) The twenty-five-year-old Fontaine throws herself so energetically into impersonating a teenager that Boyer can barely stay out of her way as she leaps, sprints, falls down, jumps up, and generally embodies vitality and good health—all belying the fact that Tessa is fatally ill.

Goulding was Boyer's least favorite kind of director, notorious for controlling every performance. A trailer for the film shows Goulding demonstrating to Boyer exactly how to play a scene, even draping his head in a scarf and taking Fontaine's part. Even so, the *New York Times* wrote, "Charles Boyer's interpretation of the unhappy musician is played with an understatement that effectively reflects the bitterness and the torment of his predicament."[3] But this was Fontaine's film. Academy members nominated her for a best actress Oscar, the second year in a row. To the end of her life, she rated *The Constant Nymph* the best assignment of her career and Boyer her preferred actor.

Goulding, who was as much a theater person as a movie person, suggested forming a company to produce plays featuring movie stars. These performances would be filmed before a live audience and sold to one of the major studios. It was an idea ahead of its time, anticipating the twenty-first-century practice of transmitting stage performances to cinemas. Boyer and a few other stars expressed interest, but few were willing to take the time to rehearse and refine a role for the stage when it was so much easier and more lucrative to do it onscreen.

Meanwhile, Boyer returned to *Flesh and Fantasy*. His episode was the last in the film, and though it matched him with Barbara Stanwyck, one of the biggest names in the cast, it was also the weakest. His character, Paul Gaspar, is a high-wire walker who performs in the circus as the "Drunken Gentleman," pretending to walk the wire while inebriated. His performance climaxes with him jumping from one wire to another. After a persistent dream in which he botches the jump and a woman in the audience screams as he falls to his death, Gaspar decides to drop the act, only to meet in the flesh the woman of his dream (Stanwyck) on a boat taking him to America. After the baroque excesses of the first episode, with its New Orleans setting and grotesquely costumed revelers, and the expressionist chiaroscuro of the second episode, in which Edward G. Robinson is pursued by his fears through a blacked-out London, this rather tepid story falls flat.

The frustrations of *Flesh and Fantasy* further embittered Boyer toward Universal, which had exploited his prestige but offered nothing of substance in return. The breaking point came when studio head Martin Mayer ignored Boyer's suggestions for future productions and asked him to appear in *The Climax* as a homicidal physician obsessed with a singer. Adapted by Curt

Siodmak and Lynn Starling from a 1930 play, it imitated *The Phantom of the Opera*, a recent Universal hit, and even featured the same actress, soprano Susanna Foster. The director was George Waggner, a B-movie specialist in westerns and horror films. Boyer refused. In the midst of the subsequent acrimony, he and Universal tore up their contract.

Boyer could now devote more attention to Pat and their desire for a child. When he confided to Frank Capra that their efforts had so far failed, Capra, who fathered four children and came from a family of seven, suggested that they were being too systematic. "The cure is to go home for lunch," he said, "when your wife is not expecting you. Then grab her, tear off her clothes, her panties, and ravish her right where you catch her; on the floor; in the kitchen; on the stairs. The excitement and the ecstasy will shock the body juices out of their contraceptive syndrome, and they'll respond again."[4] Whether Boyer tried the Capra method isn't known. However, in July 1943, Pat announced she was pregnant.

33

Not What It Looks Like

Part of the reason Boyer declined *The Climax* was his reluctance to play a villain, something he hadn't done since *Le Capitaine Fracasse*. That his next film offered the opportunity to play someone both seductive and sadistic had a perverse appeal.

Gaslight revels in the claustrophilia of Victorian England, a society of drawn curtains, averted eyes, and closed doors. Singer Paula Alquist is swept off her feet by dashing musician Gregory Anton, who insists that they abandon her sunny Italian home and move into the gloomy London mansion where her aunt, a famous diva, had been murdered. Soon after, Paula begins to experience inexplicable phenomena: the gaslight dims without reason; she hears footsteps on the floor above, where her aunt's possessions are stored; letters and pieces of jewelry disappear and reappear without explanation. Both Gregory and the servants, including an insubordinate young maid, deny hearing or seeing any of these things, and Paula believes she is going insane. She is rescued by one of her aunt's fans, who discovers that Gregory, the aunt's former accompanist, killed her and spends his nights searching the house for her jewels. Bound and waiting for the police, Gregory makes one last attempt to manipulate Paula, which she uses to torment him as he tormented her.

The story had already been filmed in Britain as *Angel Street,* with Anton Walbrook and Diana Wynyard, but Hollywood became interested only after the play enjoyed a run of 1,295 performances on Broadway, with Vincent Price in the lead. Columbia bought the rights in 1940, planning to reunite Boyer and Irene Dunne from *Love Affair,* but Louis B. Mayer offered $150,000 for the film rights, intending to have his latest protégée, Hedy Lamarr, play Paula. While Walter Reisch wrote a script, Mayer ordered the British film suppressed. It was thought that all copies had been destroyed, but some cans carrying the title *Angel Street* were overlooked, and the film was later reissued as *The Murder in Thornton Square.*

On reflection, Mayer decided that Lamarr couldn't handle the role, so he restored Irene Dunne to the part, with Melvyn Douglas as Gregory and Vincente Minnelli directing. MGM announced this version in October 1942, but by December, Douglas had dropped out to join the army. Wiser heads suggested that he be replaced by the undraftable Boyer. Broadway playwright John van Druten, who had been brought in to polish Reisch's script, lobbied for George Cukor to direct. Cukor agreed, but he pushed producer Arthur Hornblow Jr. to ask David Selznick for the loan of Ingrid Bergman, whom he knew had been eager to play Paula ever since seeing the production on Broadway.

Selznick had also seen the play on Broadway and knew that it would make an effective film. One scene impressed him above all others: Paula's savior almost gives himself away by leaving his hat in the house. "Never have I witnessed anything in the theatre remotely approaching the effectiveness of this particular scene," he wrote. "The audience was so terrified that part of it literally stood to its feet and screamed at the stage 'The hat! The hat!'"[1] Once Selznick agreed to loan Bergman, he extracted an unprecedented $323,000 from MGM, only $69,500 of which went to the actress. He also demanded that another of his contract players be given a part: the young Joseph Cotten. So the middle-aged policeman who rescues Paula became twenty years younger and a potential love interest.

Boyer's accent and manner played into the xenophobia that, to the Victorians, made Europeans seem both menacing and alluring. That Gregory is a musician made him even more appealing because music, like sex, was an area in which Europeans conventionally excelled. The archetype of continental seducers, Gerald du Maurier's Svengali, exercised his powers of domination through music, a comparison Selznick used in commenting on an early cut of *Gaslight*. "The picture is in desperate need of at least two more scenes in which we see the husband as a lover," he wrote, "in which we see both his tenderness and also the Svengali-like sex hold that he has over her. Boyer is at his best in such scenes. [They are] great showmanship and what audiences will expect of Boyer and Bergman."[2] Cukor followed this advice and went even further, expanding Gregory's scenes with Nancy, the hoydenish housemaid played by eighteen-year-old Angela Lansbury in her first film.

The need to make Boyer seem taller than Bergman adds power to his performance. Cukor consistently shoots him from a lower angle, while his close-ups of Bergman look down on her, emphasizing her weakness. Sneering, snapping, snarling, cajoling, Boyer uses every expression in his repertoire, every curl of the lip or twitch of an eyebrow, to reduce his victim to cowering helplessness. Physical violence is unnecessary. His voice is enough, and every intonation has the cruelty of a whip.

Selznick also urged Cukor to cut a final exchange in which Gregory tells Paula that he always loved her but let greed overcome those feelings. "As a member of the audience," he wrote, "I found myself seriously resenting the attempts to soften Boyer at the finish. The character is that of a no-good son-of-a-bitch, a monster and a murderer, and as a member of the audience I don't want him soft-pedaled at the end. He is getting his just deserts."[3] Boyer concurred. Mixed motives of this kind had made it difficult for him to play Duc de Praslin in *All This and Heaven Too* with any kind of truth. To be credible, Gregory Anton needed to be a fiend.

Behind the showbiz *gemütlichkeit*, Boyer and Bergman were far from friendly. "In the Selznick projection room, she ran all of Charles Boyer's pictures before commencing *Gaslight*," recalled her personal publicist Joseph Steele. "She scouts her leading men the way a football coach scouts the opposing team, by seeing them in action."[4] These in-depth assessments sometimes culminated in sexual relationships. Bergman became the lover of directors Victor Fleming and Roberto Rossellini and reportedly offered herself to a nonplussed Alfred Hitchcock. Rossellini apparently told Marlene Dietrich that initially he was not interested in Bergman sexually, but she seduced him. Cukor's homosexuality meant that he was not an option as a lover, but it is conceivable that she tried to seduce Boyer and was rebuffed. If so, that would explain her subsequent hostility toward him.

Bergman preferred to do love scenes only after she had rehearsed them, and by chance, her first onscreen kiss with Boyer permitted no such rehearsal. Deprived of her customary sexual edge, she turned to mocking him and his physical deficiencies. In memoirs and interviews, she repeatedly mentioned that he stood on a box for some scenes and wore built-up shoes. (In fact, she and Boyer were the same height: five feet nine inches.)

Because of Pat's previous miscarriages, Boyer was on tenterhooks throughout the shooting of *Gaslight*. On December 7 she went into labor two weeks early. Two days later, a phone call summoned Boyer from the set, and he returned in tears to announce that he had a nine-pound son. Cast and crew applauded. Production was halted for the day, and Hornblow broke out the champagne. But Bergman was dismissive. "He had a son!" she scoffed. "Everyone had to have champagne! More champagne, and Charles's tears falling into every glass. You'd think that no one in the world had ever had a son before."[5]

34

Love in a Cold Climate

Flesh and Fantasy opened in October 1943 and became Universal's second-highest-grossing film of the season, making $1.5 million. The news barely registered with Boyer, who was preoccupied with Pat's recovery. "My wife almost died when Mike was born," he said. "I prayed from the bottom of my soul and made a vow to believe [in God] if she was saved."[1] He didn't become a regular churchgoer, but when in Paris, he made a point of attending mass every Sunday at the Church of the Madeleine.

Following the tensions of *Gaslight* and the birth of their son, christened Michael Charles, the Boyers had little desire to travel, so Boyer took a break during 1944 to enjoy fatherhood. The time was all the more precious because postpartum complications meant that Pat could never conceive again. During the break, he recorded commentaries for *Congo,* a short film by Belgian traveler André Cauvin, and for *La Bataille du Rail,* René Clément's film about the resistance activities of French railway workers, but he refused all acting offers.

Like everyone else, but more so because of their émigré status, the Boyers closely followed news of the war in 1944, unaware of behind-the-scenes activities in France. Hitler had envisaged France as the holiday playground of the Reich, but as the war turned against him, he became vengeful. He ordered Paris's military governor, General Dietrich von Choltitz, to mine the most important buildings and, in the event of invasion, to destroy them, as the Germans had done at the Compiègne surrender site and, in 1943, the casbah-like Vieux Port district of Marseilles. Demolition of Paris should have begun in June 1944 as the Allies advanced toward the capital, but von Choltitz had been persuaded not to make a hopeless situation worse. When Hitler phoned to demand, "Is Paris burning?" the general and his staff were already fleeing the city. When Paris was liberated in August, newsreel scenes showed ecstatic Parisians thronging the familiar boulevards and de Gaulle striding down the

Champs-Elysées. This revived Boyer's hope that he might soon return to France. His mother was equally anxious to go home. But the vast international machine that was the war could not be halted overnight.

While shooting *Gaslight* at MGM, Boyer sometimes ran into Irene Dunne, who was working on *The White Cliffs of Dover*. Mayer hoped to sign her to a long-term contract, but she had no desire to become another of the "more stars than there are in the heavens" he bragged about. Meanwhile, Harry Cohn at Columbia noted that Boyer and Dunne, already a proven duo, had just appeared individually in major box-office hits. He asked Virginia Van Upp, his right-hand woman, to find a project in which they could team up again. (Van Upp, one of only three female producers in Hollywood at the time, would eventually produce such classics as *Gilda* and *The Lady from Shanghai*.) She unearthed *A Woman's Privilege*, by veteran F. Hugh Herbert, and rewrote it for Boyer and Dunne, borrowing liberally from Dunne's 1936 success *Theodora Goes Wild*, in which the pillar of a starchy community anonymously writes a steamy best seller and is romanced by an artist.

Packaged under the smug title *Together Again*, the new film has Dunne playing a widowed Vermont mayor who finds love with sexually liberated artist Boyer when he arrives to work on a statue of her late husband. Such an attractive property, offering both stars an easy ride and the promise of a generous payday, was too tempting for Boyer to turn down. To remind audiences of their previous teaming, the film reprises the 1927 tango "Adios, Muchachos," to which they danced in *History Is Made at Night*. Later popular in English as "I Get Ideas," it is repeated frequently, and Dunne even sings a verse and a chorus in Spanish, accompanied by her character's daughter on the piano.

In the absence of a complex story, Van Upp and director Charles Vidor pack the film with comic incidents. After mistaking her for a model and asking her to undress, Boyer takes Dunne to a nightclub, where she is confused with a stripper and jailed for the night. When he turns up in Vermont, Dunne's teenage daughter (Mona Freeman) mistakenly believes that he is in love with her. Charles Coburn as Dunne's father-in-law contributes his customary turn as a curmudgeon. A motif of storms and rain is slightly more original. Lightning blasts the head off the original statue, mandating its replacement, and Boyer and Dunne have their first romantic interlude trapped in a sculpture yard during a storm.

In the spring, shortly before filming began, Boyer was in Washington, DC, to make a speech for the French Research Foundation and also to promote

Gaslight. He was invited to the White House and personally thanked by the president for his war work. The shooting of *Together Again* coincided with the election that gave Roosevelt an unprecedented fourth term. Both Boyers were registered Democrats and campaigned on his behalf, but Coburn was a fervent Republican, as were Dunne and Vidor, which led to political disputes on the set. After Roosevelt's landslide victory, Boyer sent Coburn a tongue-in-cheek telegram of condolence, a gesture he did not appreciate.

Gaslight made more than $1 million profit on its first release. "Gaslighting" also entered the lexicon to describe psychological manipulation or intimidation. The 1945 Academy Awards further enhanced its reputation. It was nominated for best picture; Boyer, Bergman, and Lansbury were nominated for their performances; and the cinematography, screenplay, and black-and-white art direction were also honored. Only Bergman won. Boyer lost to Bing Crosby in that year's sentimental favorite *Going My Way.* It was cold comfort that *The Fighting Lady,* for which he had recorded the French commentary, was honored as best documentary.

The collapse of his production deal with Universal made Boyer more receptive to Edmund Goulding's idea of filming stage plays. Charles Feldman, along with Howard Hawks, suggested an alternative: a company that would discover promising new performers, train them, and then lease them to the studios. Although Boyer and Hawks made some progress toward setting up such a company, provisionally called B-H, the idea never panned out. However, it encouraged Feldman to become more proactive. Alerted by Hawks's wife, Slim, who had spotted her on the cover of *Life* magazine, Feldman signed nineteen-year-old model Betty Joan Perske to a personal contract. Rechristened Lauren Bacall, she made an auspicious debut under Hawks's direction in Warner Brothers' adaptation of Ernest Hemingway's *To Have and Have Not,* costarring Humphrey Bogart.

Still unsure of this novice actress, Warner labeled her "The Look" and rushed her into *The Big Sleep,* again with Bogart and directed by Hawks. While this film was still in postproduction, Jack Warner decided that since Boyer was, like Bogart, forty-six years old, he and Bacall might make an effective team. That decision ignored the intense emotional bond between Bogart and Bacall, who married in January 1945.

Warner Brothers had bought Graham Greene's novel *The Confidential Agent* in 1939, intending for Paul Muni to star in it, but five years later, this Spanish Civil War thriller seemed stale. Anxious to get it off the books, Warner made a generous offer to Feldman for the services of both Boyer and

Bacall. The deal promised Boyer a payout of $207,500. At the same time, Feldman sold half of Bacall's contract to Warner for a rumored $1 million.

Greene had written the novel in only six weeks to support himself while he completed the more demanding *The Power and the Glory*. Sustained by amphetamines, he worked in a cheap London hotel, and details of his life appear in the story, including his seduction of the proprietor's daughter. The novel's protagonist, Spanish loyalist Luis Denard, is a former academic (played by Boyer and changed to a composer in the film). He arrives in Britain in 1937 with money to buy coal that would otherwise go to the fascists. He is thwarted by greedy mine owners, their racist cronies, and an enemy better organized than his own rabble of helpers. Denard succeeds, mainly by chance, but also with the help of Rose Cullen (Bacall), an English girl who accompanies him back to Spain at the end of his mission.

Director Herman Shumlin was a left-wing sympathizer who helped produce the anti-Franco Spanish Civil War documentary *Spanish Earth* with Hemingway. He knew Boyer from his war efforts, as did producer and screenwriter Robert Buckner, who had worked on William Faulkner's aborted de Gaulle biopic. Greene praised *Confidential Agent* as "the only good film ever made from one of my books by an American director."[2] Critic James Agee agreed, noting that Boyer "gives the agent a proper balance of incongruous frailty, incompetence, tragic responsibility and moral courage."[3]

In Greene's drug-skewed perception, London has more than a hint of the Berlin created by Fritz Lang in *M*. Killers lurk in dark alleys, and every knock on the door heralds some new and exaggerated character. Boyer's old friend Victor Francen is politely sinister as the chief fascist, and Wanda Hendrix, despite an unconvincing Cockney accent, is charmingly vulnerable in her screen debut as a brutalized maid. However, the film soon leaves reality behind with a visit to a language school where Peter Lorre, more pop-eyed and haunted than ever, tries to teach a baffled Boyer the rudiments of a synthetic international language called Entrenationo.

Greek actress Katina Paxinou delivers a bravura performance as the hotel proprietor who is also a turncoat spy. Boyer knew Paxinou from her war work on behalf of occupied Greece and had suggested that Warner borrow her from Paramount. She brings a quality of manic malice to the part, her face seeming to shrink to just a pair of mad eyes. Her schemes finally thwarted, she "succumbs to poison with beautiful grotesquerie," as described by Bosley Crowther of the *New York Times*.[4] With her last breath she laments, "All my life I've worked against clever minds, but in the end it's the fools that let you down." As she dies, Boyer, furious that she has murdered the maid, savagely and repeatedly slaps her face.

The studio press book for *Confidential Agent* raved: "When Boyer Looks at 'The Look' Bacall—Wow!" Backed with an image of Boyer in profile descending on a swooning Bacall, it promised exhibitors the same sexual electricity as *To Have and Have Not*. Instead, the inexperienced Bacall struggled. Unlike Hawks, Shumlin was no help, even refusing to let her see the dailies, which might have allowed her to modify her performance. She characterized his contribution as "much ego and no communication." Under different circumstances, Boyer might have been the rock she needed to steady herself, but he too was dissatisfied and preoccupied with Shumlin. The director, making only his second film, shot mostly in semidarkness and cast such actors as George Coulouris, Dan Seymour, and Peter Lorre in attention-grabbing but irrelevant roles that detracted from the central performances.

Boyer was exempted from the overwhelmingly negative reviews. Those who had hailed Bacall as a phenomenon after *To Have and Have Not* thought her poor showing in *Confidential Agent* reflected badly on them, and their reviews were malicious. Jack Warner tried to tough out the notices. "She's about a hundred times better in *Confidential* than in *Sleep*," he insisted. *The Big Sleep* had not yet been released, and Feldman stepped in to avert the destruction of a potential major moneymaker, warning, "If the girl receives the same general sort of reviews and criticisms on *The Big Sleep*, you might lose one of your most important assets." He urged Warner to add "at least three or four additional scenes with Bogart of the insolent and provocative nature she had in *To Have and Have Not*." Warner complied. They rescued Bacall's career, but *Confidential Agent* highlighted her deficiencies as a performer. She admitted later, "I would never reach the *To Have and Have Not* heights again."[5]

Boyer continued his propaganda activities right up to the last days of the war. He recorded an album of readings from French writers, ranging from Voltaire and Rousseau to a somewhat outclassed Charles de Gaulle. Orson Welles weighed in with texts by Thomas Jefferson, Abraham Lincoln, and Franklin Roosevelt. In 1946 Boyer narrated *Children of Tragedy,* a documentary about the plight of young refugees in the ruins of Europe.

His adoptive country, in the most backhanded of compliments, responded by turning Boyer into a cartoon figure. In January 1945, during preproduction of *Confidential Agent,* Warner Brothers released a Looney Tunes cartoon called *Odor-able Kitty.* Directed by Chuck Jones and voiced by Mel Blanc, it features a skunk named Henri who speaks with a parody of Boyer's French accent and behaves in a broad approximation of his screen persona. A cat acquires a white stripe down its back and is immoderately pursued by the amorous Henri. The cat in *Odor-able Kitty* is male, but in subsequent films in the series, the cat is a female christened Penelope Pussycat, while Henri is renamed Pépé le Pew. Pépé never utters the cliché "Come with me to the casbah," but his murmuring, heavily accented endearments, as well as the character's name and the cartoons' settings (always suggestive of Paris), clearly link them to Boyer. He must have been aware of the cartoons, but it is unknown whether he ever saw them. If he did, he said nothing for publication.

35

Stranger in a Strange Land

Confidential Agent opened in December 1945. Japan had surrendered in August, so the world celebrated its first Christmas at peace since 1938. Boyer was tempted to sit back and enjoy the moment, but the possibility of returning to France in the summer of 1946 spurred him to use the winter and spring to take stock.

As the parents of an infant son, he and Pat needed more space. They bought a house at 802 North Linden Drive, Beverly Hills, where they would live for the next twenty years. Neighbors included actress Maureen O'Sullivan, her director-husband John Farrow, and their seven children. The Farrows became the Boyers' closest friends in Hollywood, and daughter Mia, the same age as Michael, was a particular favorite.

Approaching fifty, Boyer had reached a difficult point in his career. For Clark Gable and Gary Cooper, gray hair and wrinkles enhanced their authenticity as men of action. But for romantic leading men, particularly foreigners, age made them less credible lovers. The tendency was to cast them as villains, priests, waiters, and the occasional head of state. Boyer would play all of these in time, but for the moment, he was ready to fight to keep his name above the title.

For a start, he needed to improve his appearance. Part of the impetus came from his baby son. "A boy," he reflected, "does not wish to believe that some nice old man is his father." Built-up shoes and a corset were facts of his working life, but developments in cosmetic surgery, accelerated by the war, offered a partial solution to his baldness. Transplanting individual hair follicles was not yet possible, but in a kind of reverse facelift, a portion of his bald scalp was removed and the remaining hairy section pulled forward. This restored at least the vestiges of his original hair. He continued to wear toupees in public and while filming, but at home he could display the approximation of a hairline.

Pat hoped that spending time at home would make Boyer more social, but for the most part, he continued to sit in his library reading. Pat took to attending parties without him, usually accompanied by a friend such as Jean Feldman. In 1945 Cole Porter listed his party guests as George Cukor, Edmund Goulding, Anita Loos, and Ernst Lubitsch, along with Pat and Jean. Pat enjoyed the village atmosphere of Beverly Hills and the domestic to-and-fro. Nobody came to the door to borrow a cup of sugar, but the Porters did inherit the Boyers' cook, who had previously worked for Annabella.

Through the spring of 1946, hopes dwindled for a speedy return to France. Most ocean liners were still in dock awaiting refitting, having been stripped down for use as troop transports. Some freighters ferrying materiel and personnel to and from Europe took a few passengers, but this was an uninviting prospect, as travelers had to absolve the owners in writing of all responsibility for accidental explosions or chance collisions with mines. Hoping the situation would improve by summer, Boyer looked around for a new film. Fortuitously, Ernst Lubitsch had a promising project.

The 1944 novel *Cluny Brown,* by English author Margery Sharp, satirized Britain's prewar landed gentry and their lifestyle of country-house weekends and cocktail parties—an existence made possible by an underclass of domestics and artisans who proudly "knew their place" in Britain's intricate social hierarchy.

Clover "Cluny" Brown is an orphan. Raised by her uncle, she lacks social skills but is ambitious to follow in his footsteps and become a plumber. By chance, she meets Adam Belinski, a Czech intellectual and fugitive from Hitler who is living alone in London during the last weeks of peace. They forge an eccentric relationship that concludes with them traveling to an unprejudiced America, where Cluny is considered exotic and charming.

Darryl Zanuck had bought the novel in a deal with David Selznick aimed at widening the appeal of Jennifer Jones, whom Selznick was about to marry. She had never played comedy, and the part of Cluny seemed suitable for a first attempt. John Cromwell was set to direct, with Lubitsch as producer, but when James Hilton failed to deliver an acceptable script, Selznick moved on to his epic western *Duel in the Sun.* By the time that film wrapped, Hilton and Cromwell had abandoned the project, leaving Lubitsch and Samuel Hoffenstein to rewrite the script, toning down its farcical elements, and Lubitsch to direct.

Boyer was already familiar with the novel. He and Pat had read it together as a magazine serial. In Adam Belinski, Boyer recognized another displaced person. He and Lubitsch knew many such people, having spent the war helping them find safety in the United States. Boyer's Belinski is stranded in London with only one suit and no money. Seeking an old friend in the hopes of borrowing enough to pay his rent, he finds the apartment occupied by a subtenant whose sink is blocked on the very afternoon he is hosting a cocktail party. An anguished call for a plumber produces Cluny Brown. Thereafter, her fortunes tangle with Adam's as she is sent to work as a maid in the country house where he is, by chance, a houseguest.

Although Lubitsch mocks a society where owning a dinner jacket is of greater significance than the activities of "that Hitler chappie," he also applauds the generosity and good nature of the gentry and their respect for the truly important things in life—notably, gardening and dogs. In the novel, plumbing is incidental, but Lubitsch makes Cluny's ambitions the film's central joke and a means of mocking Britain's snobbery. Her determination embarrasses her uncle and others of her class, including the village pharmacist, who sees her as a potential wife. The afternoon tea he arranges to introduce her to his family ends in disaster when a blockage in his pipes tempts Cluny to demonstrate her skills.

Jones shows little talent for comedy, but Boyer takes up the slack, helped by a strong supporting cast, most of them borrowed from MGM. Peter Lawford plays a young engagé aristocrat; Richard Haydn, speaking with his usual strangled affectation, is Cluny's pharmacist suitor; and C. Aubrey Smith also makes an appearance. But none of them rival Sara Allgood and Ernest Cossart as housekeeper and butler to Belinski's hosts and Cluny's employers. They deliver straight-faced, quietly horrified postmortems of the two outsiders' social blunders. "Her handling of the china has been sinister," says Cossart, choosing from among Cluny's numerous defects as a housemaid.

An English production would have made *Cluny Brown* a love letter to the old-fashioned values destroyed by the war, but Lubitsch and Boyer show more sympathy for Belinski. The film aroused unexpected hostility in Britain, which was still furious over Hollywood productions such as *Objective Burma*, which invented a role for Errol Flynn in the almost entirely British and Australian far-east campaign. One newspaper compared the incongruity of *Cluny Brown*'s view of class distinctions to "kippers fried in cream, an anchovy laid across a strawberry ice [or] any other simile that conveys complete and awful wrongness." Another complained of "caricatured aristocrats and adenoidal chemists and self-conscious 'characters' and upper classes all seen as amiable half-wits, while the lower orders are smugly servile morons."[1]

C. Aubrey Smith published a formal apology for taking part in the film. British cinemas pulled *Cluny Brown* after a week. Nor was it popular in America. Audiences had wept with Greer Garson in *Mrs. Miniver,* but the war was over, and so was Americans' sympathy for Brave Little Britain. Among studio bean counters, the failure of a second consecutive film for Boyer rang warning bells. His salary for *Confidential Agent* had been more than twice that of comparable performers. Now some muttered about him being overpriced.

A limited transatlantic service recommenced early in 1946, and the relaunch of the Cannes Film Festival, including a screening of *Gaslight,* provided the pretext for the Boyers' return to Europe. They found France bankrupted by four years of occupation, infested with recrimination and suspicion, and split by political rivalries that were encouraged by the communists, in the hopes of seizing power. In Paris, they left Michael with his grandmother and a nanny, Miss McGore. Though not hostile to Pat, Louise Rossignol-Boyer never hid the fact that she would have preferred a French daughter-in-law. To Pat's irritation, she also insisted on calling Michael "Michel," in the French style.

On the way to Cannes, the Boyers stopped in Figeac. Penicillin had been restricted to military use until 1945, but limited quantities were now becoming available. In memory of his father, Boyer arranged for the Figeac hospital to receive an advance supply to deal with the many cases of tuberculosis. Like many well-intended acts, Boyer's generosity was resented by those ready to feel slighted by even the most selfless of gestures. "The fact that he became American was not appreciated," said Philippe Calmon, a local historian, "and when he came after the war to distribute penicillin to the hospital, it was seen as an ostentatious gesture."[2]

For the festival, Maurice Chevalier had rented a villa outside Cannes, where he and Boyer hung out, playing *petanque* and giving occasional interviews. There was a poisonous residue of recrimination against those perceived as collaborating with the Germans during the war, and Committees of Liberation investigated anyone who had been allowed to work during the occupation. Boyer, whose credentials were impeccable, defended Chevalier against such accusations, even though his friend's behavior may have been questionable. But such local concerns were eclipsed by the films on display at the festival and the chance to meet old friends. For the first time in six years, Boyer saw Pierre Blanchar and his wife, Marthoune. Blanchar was winning praise for his role, costarring with Michèle Morgan, in Jean Delannoy's *La Symphonie Pastorale,* a version of an André Gide story of love and obsession in an alpine village.

Despite the collapse of his deal with Universal, Boyer still hoped to become his own producer. He had commissioned English-language treatments of *L'Éprevier* and *Capitaine Fracasse,* with an eye to remaking them in Hollywood. He had also persuaded Walter Wanger to buy the remake rights to Jacques Feyder's 1934 *Le Grand Jeu,* a melodrama set partly within the ranks of the Foreign Legion. But the fate of *Pépé le Moko* and other films bought by Hollywood made French filmmakers cautious. When Boyer raised with Gide and Delannoy the possibility of remaking *La Symphonie Pastorale* in America, he was met with a resounding *non!*

He encountered equal resistance from Louis Grué, author of the 1944 *Legende de Gaillardet,* which reconstructed life in medieval France as seen through the eyes of a goldsmith—a world of minstrels, knights, warring barons, and the occasional divine intervention. Boyer visualized a film like Marcel Carné's *Les Visiteurs du Soir,* which brought a modern sensibility to a fable of the Middle Ages. He suggested that Grué write a treatment, cutting some of the less visual incidents and inventing some dialogue. But when the author refused, Boyer dropped the project.

Back in California, he took to spending his days at the French Research Foundation. Like most men who become fathers in middle age, he lacked the temperament to be a toddler's playmate, so he left that to Pat and Miss McGore. The nanny had become a fixture in their household and would remain as Michael's governess and surrogate parent until he was fourteen. In his office at the foundation, Boyer could read in peace, handle his investments, and work on his book collection. He ate lunch, generally alone, at nearby Ernest's on North La Cienega, where a secluded table was permanently reserved for him.

Postwar Hollywood was going through one of its periodic upheavals. Many filmmakers returning from military service were resentful of studio control. Frank Capra, John Ford, and William Wyler all formed companies to produce their own films, but the most innovative was Enterprise, established by Charles Einfeld, David Loew, and actor John Garfield. Enterprise offered a new and enlightened environment. Creative staff enjoyed relative autonomy and shared in their films' profits. Fringe benefits included free life insurance. "There was coffee and doughnuts twenty-four hours a day," said editor and later director Robert Parrish. "They even washed your car!"[3]

Enterprise upgraded the former California Studios on Melrose Avenue, opposite the sprawling Paramount lot, to accommodate the set that William Cameron Menzies, an Oscar winner for *Gone with the Wind,* would design to re-create prewar Paris for *Arch of Triumph*. Erich Maria Remarque's best-selling novel of the same name was his most ambitious work since *All Quiet on the Western Front*. Producer David Lewis proposed a four-hour film to rival *Gone with the Wind*. Lewis Milestone, who had directed *All Quiet on the Western Front*, would be in charge, and Remarque was writing the screenplay with young novelist Irwin Shaw. To make the film, Enterprise formed a separate production company: it owned 15.5 percent, Remarque 20 percent, and investor Ingrid Bergman 37.5 percent. If the film succeeded at the box office, all of them would be rich, without the need to spend any of their profits on the expensive upkeep of studio facilities and personnel.

Before Boyer left for France, Feldman advised him that he had been offered the lead in this production. It promised to be his largest salary yet, since he would share in the profits. It seemed the best possible omen for a busy peacetime career. The project immediately interested Boyer. He had firsthand knowledge of 1938 Paris, where he had filmed *Orage*. He also knew Remarque from prewar Berlin. The writer was married to Paulette Goddard, Boyer's costar in *Hold Back the Dawn,* but for the story's central relationship, Remarque drew on his long liaison with Marlene Dietrich.

There were problems, however. Boyer's character, an embittered doctor named Ravic, was too close to Denard in *Confidential Agent*. Both lost a wife and child to the war, both encounter a woman who does them more harm than good, and both have a facial scar (although Milestone, like Shumlin, declined to condone anything more than a token scratch). Boyer also refused to play Ravic as a German. "I am a Frenchman," he told David Lewis. "For me to play a German, that would be ridiculous. And as for me playing a 'good' German, that would be impossible. I would not know how to begin to act such a part." His objections were as much technical as patriotic. He took lessons from a linguist, Dr. Simon Mitchneck, whose job "was to rid him not only of his own very famous accent but of certain American undertones."[4] Remarque and Milestone cooperated by giving the screen Ravic no precise nationality.

Boyer also persuaded them to remove scenes that reflected badly on the French and their prewar treatment of refugees, even though he knew, from his own personal observations, that they were accurate. To criticize France might trigger a backlash against both the film and himself. He knew that some of his countrymen already regarded him as a turncoat for becoming an American citizen, marrying an Englishwoman, and making his career in the United States.

As an emblem of misery, it would be difficult to find one more despairing than the opening of *Arch of Triumph*. The rain that drizzles from the nighttime Paris sky may fail to extinguish the flame on the Tomb of the Unknown Soldier, but a scattering of crushed wreaths and the looming bulk of the Arc de Triomphe mock its heroics. On the soundtrack, a portentous reprise of the first few bars of "La Marseillaise" underscores the message that although France has not yet suffered a military defeat in 1938, its moral collapse is already well advanced. Expressionless in sodden hat and overcoat, Ravic embodies Europe's spiritual bankruptcy. By chance, his path crosses that of Joan Madou, another drifter. Her lover has just died, and she is preparing to jump into the Seine. Against his better judgment, Ravic changes her mind, only to find himself increasingly involved in her aimless life. In their affectless passivity, the couple suggests the philosophy to which Jean-Paul Sartre, in the Paris of 1947, was about to give the name "existentialism." *Arch of Triumph* is not so much film noir as *film nul*.

A gynecologist living illegally in France, Ravic performs abortions and other surgeries that French doctors find too complex or unprofitable. The meager fees he charges keep him at the ironically named Hotel International, a hive of the stateless. His neighbors include Morosov, his only friend, a former Russian colonel who is now a nightclub doorman; a clique of Spanish fascists eager to return home to fight with Franco; and a miscellany of Czechs, Germans, and Austrians, alike only in their misery. Memory drags at them like a ball and chain. One man cannot forget the experience of having his fingernails torn out. Another is feared as a harbinger of death because, each time he moves to a new city, disaster strikes the one he just left. In pursuit of a sinister verisimilitude, Milestone filled these supporting roles with veteran German and Russian actors such as Willy Kaufman and Emil Rameau, themselves refugees from Hitler's Europe. Tongue in cheek, he gave the role of a café proprietor to Hollywood restaurateur "Prince" Michael Romanoff.

Production moved into high gear when Ingrid Bergman joined the cast. Newly independent of Selznick and riding high on the success of *Casablanca*, she had become one of Feldman's clients. Despite being an investor in the company making the film, she negotiated a $175,000 fee for her participation, plus 25 percent of the profits—the same deal as Boyer.

As the twelve-week shoot lengthened to twenty, David Lewis gave up hope that the film would be finished by the end of 1947 and qualify for the 1948 Academy Awards. Meanwhile, Milestone felt pressure to soften the relationship between Ravic and Joan into a love story with echoes of *Casablanca*.

Writers Remarque and Shaw protested. Turning them into lovers made non-sense of Ravic's character. Obsessed with the memory of seeing his wife tortured to death, he is incapable of love. In the novel, Joan's sentimentality simply exasperates Ravic. "He did not listen to what Joan Madou said," Remarque writes. "He knew all about that and no longer wanted to know about it. To be alone—the eternal refrain of life. . . . It wasn't better or worse than anything else. One talked too much about it."[5]

Ravic becomes entangled with Joan not out of love but out of expediency. When he learns that she has left the corpse of her lover in a hotel room, he realizes that by sheltering her, he risks becoming involved in a police inquiry. Impatiently, he hustles her back to the hotel, establishes that her lover died of natural causes, faces down the greedy proprietor, retrieves Joan's luggage, encourages her to empty the dead man's wallet, sends for a doctor to sign the death certificate, and slips away just as the police arrive. In these scenes, Boyer is in his element—peremptory, commanding, effective—but they are the exception. The expanding romance pushes other themes aside—notably, Ravic's revenge on Ivan Haake, the Nazi officer who killed his wife. Haake's protracted murder would have climaxed the four-hour version of the film, with Ravic luring the German out of Paris by promising sex with Joan, then brutally dispatching him and leaving the body naked and mutilated.

Shortly before the end of location filming in France, Michael Chekhov, who was set to play Haake, suffered a heart attack. Charles Laughton agreed to replace him, but some of the scenes involved Bergman, who by then was appearing on Broadway in *Joan of Lorraine*. Those scenes had to be shot in Hollywood on expensively re-created sets, including a ten-foot-high, four-ton plaster model of the Arc de Triomphe. After its use in a fund-raising parade for war orphans and attempts to install it in a New York park as a symbol of Franco-American relations, Enterprise broke it up at a loss of $35,000. It barely appears in the film because the Breen office demanded the removal of almost the entire subplot in which Ravic murders Haake. As compensation, the censors allowed Ravic to go unpunished for the murder, which they chose to view not as private revenge but as an act of war, since it took place just as Hitler invaded Poland.

Only fragments of this theme remain in the released film, including an almost comic café scene in which Haake enlists Ravic to arrange a sexual encounter with Joan. Failing to recognize Ravic as one of his victims, Haake also suggests that he become an informer on the émigré community. Ravic's slightly offended refusal convinces Haake that he is dealing with a man of honor. He even believes that, like himself, Ravic may be a former member of a Prussian military fraternity, his scarred face the result of a duel. Laughton had his customary problems in "finding the character" of Haake, and he spent many nights with actor Norman Lloyd, discussing Hitler's autobiography *Mein Kampf* over a bottle of whiskey. Laughton had recently begun working on a production of Bertolt Brecht's play *The Life of Galileo* and tried, unsuccessfully, to get Enterprise to hire Brecht as a writer.

It was soon obvious to Boyer that *Arch of Triumph* would be a colossal flop. Enterprise shared his opinion and, hoping to recoup even a fraction of its investment, slashed the running time in half. Remarque and Shaw resigned in protest, so newcomer Harry Brown (who would later cowrite the Oscar-winning *A Place in the Sun*) performed the butchery in collaboration with Milestone. Edwin Schallert of the *Los Angeles Times* asked Boyer if the film was better for the cuts. "They improved it considerably," he said wryly. "It was terrible for four hours. Now it is terrible only for two."[6]

Thinking a Broadway success might neutralize some of the inevitably negative press, Boyer looked around for a play. Sam Behrman was writing one with him in mind, but it was not yet ready. Some years later, it emerged as *Lord Pengo*, in which Boyer played art dealer Lord Duveen. The Theatre Guild offered *The Big Two*, a comedy with political overtones by Ladislao Bus-Fekete, but it would not provide the quick injection of positive publicity Boyer needed. Instead, he asked Feldman to find a film that could be in cinemas before Christmas. Universal proposed a modest drama based on "The Gioconda Smile," a short story by British novelist Aldous Huxley.

"The Gioconda Smile" was part of the 1921 collection *Mortal Coils,* which also became the working title of the film. The main character is a philandering country gentleman named Hutton (changed to Maurier to accommodate Boyer's accent). When his wealthy wife dies suddenly, Maurier marries his brother's teenage mistress, infuriating both the brother and Janet Spence, a neighbor who is hopelessly in love with him. Maurier, who fancies himself a connoisseur and often finds echoes of art in the physical features of his friends, sees something in Janet's smile reminiscent of the *Mona Lisa: La Gioconde.* In fact, it hides an icy fury. She spreads a rumor that he poisoned his wife, a crime for which he is wrongly convicted and hanged. Huxley had already successfully adapted the story for the stage, and Universal offered him $1,560 a week to rewrite the play as a film.

In 1940 Alexander Korda, having lost his company London Films, relocated to California to complete postproduction on *The Thief of Baghdad.* His younger brother Zoltan came with him, but when Alex returned to Britain, Zoltan remained, hoping the climate would aid his tuberculosis. Zoltan was tapped to direct *Mortal Coils,* which was renamed *A Woman's Vengeance.* He rounded up some of Hollywood's wartime European community who had decided to remain in America. Hungarian Miklós Rózsa wrote the melodramatic score. British actress Rachel Kempson plays Boyer's wife, and Sir Cedric Hardwicke is Libbard, a physician who quietly observes the evolving tragedy. Janet Spence is played by Jessica Tandy, who had just enjoyed a triumph on Broadway as Blanche Dubois in *A Streetcar Named Desire.*

Huxley's rewrite transformed Maurier from an intellectual snob and serial seducer into someone sufficiently sympathetic to engage an audience. He also added a scene that gave full rein to production designer Eugene Lourié. When Janet visits Maurier just before his scheduled execution, Lourié frames her in a tiny barred window that looks down into the cell of the condemned man. As she admits her crime and relishes her revenge, Maurier squirms in impotent horror while, behind him, two guards sit impassively, deaf to her admissions, having trained themselves to act "as if we just aren't here." Huxley had nothing but praise for Boyer's performance, which he described as "creating an atmosphere of simple tenderness without the least sentimentality."[7]

36

"Why, This Is Hell, nor Am I out of It"

S hortly after *A Woman's Vengeance,* Boyer had a car accident. Never much of a drinker and even less of a driver, he was returning home after dining with pianist Arthur Rubinstein when he rammed a car standing without lights. Pat, asleep beside him, was unhurt, but Boyer cracked two ribs and was briefly hospitalized. Shortly thereafter, he began to suffer from the neuralgia and leg pain that would trouble him for the rest of his life.

To Boyer's surprise, the French Research Foundation was experiencing a late spurt of activity as producers whose films were set in France, such as *The Razor's Edge, The Diary of a Chambermaid, The Song of Bernadette,* and *Monsieur Beaucaire,* asked for help. Director Robert Florey was among its most eloquent supporters. He wrote:

> The studios and their producers, writers, directors and technicians
> can obtain, in a few minutes and at no cost all desired information
> for the purpose of establishing the correct atmosphere for a historical
> or modern film in which the action takes place in France. If the
> accessories director for a film needs a Parisian *coupe-fil* or would like
> to know the form of French birth certificate, or a Metro ticket, he can
> contact the Foundation that will then give him the information. One
> may consult, in this building, all the books possible on French
> costumes, uniforms, or furniture throughout the ages. A director
> who contacts the Foundation is sure of not making any mistakes.[1]

But without its propaganda value and the funding that this attracted, the FRF was an impossible drain on Boyer's resources. *Arch of Triumph* was the first film to give screen credit to the FRF for its assistance. It would also be the last.

The reviews of *Arch of Triumph,* which opened in February 1948, were not as bad as Boyer had feared. Bosley Crowther mocked it as "a gold-plated, Chanel-perfumed version of down-at-heel boy-meets-girl, a full Hollywood intensification of the poignancies of a doomed romance. From within Lewis Milestone's roving camera, we watch love as it is made by two of the movies' most able craftsmen, repetitiously and at exceeding length."[2]

Others joked about its jumble of nationalities and accents, with Swedish Bergman playing an Italian, British Laughton a German, American Louis Calhern a Russian, and French Boyer an Austrian. Nobody liked the pervasive gloom. Writing in the *New Yorker,* John McCarten noted, "almost every time the characters get low in their minds, it starts to rain. Since they're a grim bunch, the film is one of the moistest that have come along in years." He acknowledged the effectiveness of Boyer's performance but agreed that it highlighted the inadequacy of Bergman's. "In their scenes together, [Boyer] tends to make Miss Bergman look very brash and immature, for his effective underplaying reduces her bouncy histrionics to the level of girlish antics."[3] The film earned only $1.5 million of its $5 million cost. United Artists refused to distribute any of the company's other productions—a fatal blow. It declared bankruptcy even before *Arch of Triumph* was released.

Feeling the need to get away, Boyer booked passage for the family to Europe. In Paris, his war work and twenty-five years of professional activity were recognized by his appointment as a chevalier of the Légion d'Honneur, which entitled him to wear its red ribbon in his lapel. After the ceremony, he stayed with his mother while Pat took Michael to England to visit her family.

To the alarm of his parents, Michael had developed a stammer. This speech impediment, which has no physical basis, generally manifests at around four or five years of age. It is marginally more common in bilingual children, who are conflicted by the need to speak two languages. Michael spoke only English with his mother and his governess, both English and French with his father, and only French with his grandmother Louise. Boyer's remoteness and Pat's maternal overprotectiveness may have played a part in inducing what Mia Farrow described as Michael's "heart-stopping anxiety-generating stutter."[4]

When Pat returned to Paris, she and Boyer visited Figeac. The local newspaper photographed him in front of the apartment where he was raised, and the town made a halfhearted attempt at a civic welcome, for which Louise rounded up a few old friends. One of his earliest friends, Philippe Gambon, now practiced law in town, but the two men had so little in common that they were reduced to the apparently inexhaustible subject of Greta Garbo. Boyer took Pat to the theater where he had appeared in *L'Aiglon* as a teenager and proudly showed her his inscription on the dressing-room wall. She added her own to commemorate the event.

Cultural life in Paris was reviving. It was the era of modern jazz in smoky cellars, the sweeping skirts and broad-brimmed hats of the New Look, and, among intellectuals, existentialism. In Saint-Germain des Prés, Jean-Paul Sartre, Simone de Beauvoir, and Albert Camus were instilling new life into literature, theater, and philosophy. Boyer dined with Joseph Kessel, Camus, and Sartre and saw Sartre's play *Les Mains Sales* (Dirty Hands), inspired in part by the 1940 assassination in Mexico of Leon Trotsky at the order of Joseph Stalin. It tells the story of Hugo and Jessica, a young communist and his wife, who infiltrate the home of Hoederer, a politician thought to have betrayed the party, with the intention of assassinating him. But both succumb to Hoederer's charm, and Hugo decides not to go through with the killing, until he sees Jessica kissing Hoederer—innocently, as it happens. His bourgeois instincts as husband and lover override his rational mind, and he commits the murder.

Boyer thought the play could succeed on Broadway, subject to a translation that stressed the love story. Producer Jean Dalrymple bought the rights and hired screenwriter Daniel Taradash to minimize what the *New York Times* called its "long arguments about abstract political ideas." Clashes with Sartre were inevitable. Like many French artists, he was reassessing his opposition to communism and found his former hostility embarrassing. To emphasize that the play was not only about politics, Dalrymple renamed it *Crime Passionel* and then *Red Gloves*. Neither title reflected what Sartre meant by the original—that those involved in politics have to get their hands dirty, including the use of violence, if necessary. When Dalrymple refused to restore the original title, Sartre sued in the American courts and won, but he later accepted *Red Gloves* as the title of the English translation.

For the family's return to America, Boyer quixotically canceled their airline reservations and booked passage on the *Queen Mary*. Holding up young Michael as they watched Le Havre receding, he hoped his son would remember the sight, which he might never see again. The failure of *Arch of Triumph*, in which Boyer had invested his hopes for continuing his acting career, was a warning that he could no longer expect the same fame and acceptance he had enjoyed before the war.

Back in Los Angeles, he and Pat attended the premiere of Bertolt Brecht's *The Life of Galileo,* directed by Brecht and Joseph Losey and starring Charles Laughton. Staged in the tiny 260-seat Coronet Theatre, the production had been pared down, in line with Brecht's theories about "alienation." The costumes were plain, the settings sparse. The first-night spectators, who included Charlie Chaplin, Billy Wilder, and Igor Stravinsky, were never allowed to forget that they were watching a play.

Bluster from those who called Hollywood the center of communist activity in America (including former friend Adolphe Menjou) encouraged Boyer to be more outspoken about his political beliefs. He had declined to join the Committee for the First Amendment, formed to oppose the House Un-American Activities Committee's probe into Hollywood, but his friends Van Heflin and Anatole Litvak were members, and they persuaded him to participate in *Hollywood Fights Back,* a two-part radio documentary broadcast on the ABC network in October and November 1947. Boyer's voice opened the program, explaining that "fourteen of the fifty stars you are about to hear are at this moment in a special plane flying to Washington to carry on in person the fight for our rights as American citizens. If it weren't for studio commitments, all of us here today, and dozens more, would be in the air as well as on it." Judy Garland, Robert Ryan, Richard Conte, Danny Kaye, and many others spoke vigorously in support of political and intellectual freedom. But like the Washington delegation's visit to observe the hearings, it achieved nothing. Photographs of the fourteen marching toward Congress, led by Humphrey Bogart and Lauren Bacall, were widely published, but once the press quizzed them about their personal political beliefs, their resolve crumbled. Two weeks later, Bogart and Bacall called their action "ill advised."

Maurice Chevalier made a calculated return to the United States in 1947, but on the stage rather than the screen. His one-man show sold out, which had an immediate effect on his overall popularity. In May the trade paper *Billboard* confirmed that RCA Victor had signed him to a record contract. Advertising agency J. Walter Thompson proposed to pay him $7,700 a week to host the *Kraft Music Hour,* but Chevalier held out for $500 more. His agent was, of course, the tireless Charlie Feldman.

The Boyers were there for Chevalier's opening night. The success of his old friend convinced Boyer to expand his horizons, and he agreed to play Hoederer in *Red Gloves.* It opened on Broadway in December 1948, with John Dall as Hugo and Joan Tetzel as Jessica. Boyer's Broadway debut guaranteed plenty of preliminary interest, and despite almost entirely negative reviews, the play ran for 113 performances before closing in March 1949. On the night Ingrid Bergman was in the house, she overheard two women commenting on Boyer's baldness and shortness. She turned to them and said, "Just wait until he starts to act." She then observed, "He acted as he always did, with such magic, and held the audience in the palm of his hand."[5]

In New York, the Boyers generally stayed at the Hotel Pierre and dined with friends, including former first lady Eleanor Roosevelt, at nearby restaurants such as the Penthouse. Rising above Central Park at the corner of Sixty-First Street and Fifth Avenue, the Pierre was the preferred residence for many celebrities, who appreciated the tight security that kept unwelcome visitors at a distance. As it seemed likely that he would now be doing more stage work, Boyer leased a suite there, which became his East Coast pied-à-terre. He had paintings and some favorite pieces of furniture shipped from Los Angeles. Boyer also bought an apartment in Paris for his mother and started shopping for the emblem of the truly successful French bourgeois: a country château.

Since the major radio networks generated their programs from New York, the move also facilitated Boyer's on-air work, which increased as he made fewer films. In 1950 NBC featured him in *Presenting Charles Boyer,* a summer replacement for the popular *Fibber McGee and Molly.* Unlike *Hollywood Playhouse,* the sixteen half-hour shows cast Boyer as continuing character Michel Bonet, a roguish boulevardier and raconteur reminiscent of Michel Marnay from *Love Affair.* A trade-press reviewer remarked, "The French actor's gift for authoritative characterization and his warm mike presence converts a shopworn *Raffles* type into a thoroly [sic] entertaining series, sparked by flashes of surprisingly sophisticated dialog." John Crosby in the *Boston Herald* called Boyer's radio persona "refreshingly different. [He] kisses the ladies' hands, bows from the waist, buys them violets and talks in a species of rich, complimentary prose that few other actors could get out of their mouths without suffering acute embarrassment." But the series never found a sponsor and was discontinued after one season.

When *Red Gloves* closed, Charles Laughton approached Boyer with a proposal. Following *The Life of Galileo,* Laughton had been looking for other properties that lent themselves to the same sparse Brechtian treatment but with the potential to attract a larger audience. He found one in George Bernard Shaw's *Man and Superman.* First performed in 1903, the play dramatizes the conflict between social convention and unbridled self-indulgence. Representing the latter is John Tanner, author of *The Revolutionist's Handbook and Pocket Companion.* A typical Shavian visionary, he believes himself descended from Don Juan Tenorio, the great lover condemned to damnation at the climax of Mozart's *Don Giovanni*. In a dream, Tanner imagines himself as his own ancestor in Hell. He is joined by the Devil; then by Doña Ana, whom Juan loved; and finally by her father, the Commander, whom Juan killed in a duel. The Commander was sent to Heaven, but he is visiting his daughter in Hell, where the company is more interesting. The four chat. As summarized by critic John Simon, "Juan, the Devil, the Commander, and Doña Ana debate for some eighty or ninety minutes the advantages of Hell (art, beauty, love, pleasure) and Heaven (rational discourse and promulgation of the Life Force). The Devil, of course, defends those hedonistic amenities, whereas Juan, a true Shavian, wants none of them, and heads for a thinker's Heaven."[6] Most productions of *Man and Superman* dropped this act, which is not directly related to the rest of the play. It was sometimes performed as a separate play, *Don Juan in Hell*.

Boyer had always liked Shaw's wordy, thoughtful plays with their long, complex speeches energized by the playwright's Irish love of language, but he had never had the chance to act in one. With Boyer on board, Laughton began to recruit the rest of the cast. His first choice for Doña Ana was the glamorous Madeleine Carroll, but she lacked stage experience. Laughton then suggested his wife, Elsa Lanchester, but producer Paul Gregory thought her voice was all wrong and that she lacked the necessary romantic quality. For a while they considered Fredric March and his wife, Florence Eldridge, as Juan and Ana, but by 1951, Gregory had what he called the First Drama Quartet: Boyer as Don Juan, Laughton as the Devil, Sir Cedric Hardwicke as the Commander, and Agnes Moorhead as Doña Ana.

Production could not have been simpler. The piece needed only two backstage workers. Shaw had specified no sets, so the play could be presented on an empty stage. To set the scene, Laughton simply read Shaw's stage directions. The four wore evening clothes and sat on tall stools; to speak, they stood at lecterns, where they appeared to read the text. In fact, all had memorized it. Turning the pages was simply for show.

The play opened with a preview in the small town of Claremont, California, on February 27, 1951. For the next three months, it toured across the United States and into Canada. Because of its simplicity, the play was well suited to a variety of venues, some of them extremely unlikely, such as the State College Theatre in Fargo, North Dakota.

Boyer had forgotten the discomforts of life on the road. "Charles developed into a mild hypochondriac," said Hardwicke, "and, like Agnes, spent most of the day resting." As with all touring shows, laundry was an ongoing problem. Boyer and Hardwicke competed to see how many wearings they could get out of one dress shirt. Mostly, the group traveled in a small hired bus. This was an unnerving experience for Boyer, who was more nervous on the road since his car accident. He sat behind the driver and protested if he went faster than forty miles an hour. Laughton finally told the driver that, whenever Boyer asked what speed they were traveling, to tell him thirty-five miles an hour, even if it they were going sixty.

In June the production moved to Britain. For a while, it appeared that Hardwicke might not be able to appear, since a bill for unpaid taxes was hanging over his head. Boris Karloff was announced as his replacement, but at the last moment, Gregory lent Hardwicke the money. The show opened in Birmingham and then proceeded to Manchester, Liverpool, Glasgow, and Edinburgh, with good but not full houses. It bypassed London, since John Clements was already performing *Man and Superman* as part of the Festival of Britain, and by tradition, no two companies ever presented the same play concurrently. Boyer would have to wait for his West End debut.

Doubting that Broadway audiences and critics would appreciate such an undramatic presentation, Gregory did not plan a Broadway run. However, a single performance at Carnegie Hall in October received such ecstatic notices that the group played on Broadway for thirty-eight performances in November and December 1951. During a six-week break to allow the others to fulfill film commitments, Laughton toured independently in a one-man show, giving readings from the Bible, Aesop, and Dickens. "Contrary to what I'd been told in the entertainment industry," he said, "people everywhere have a common shy hunger for literature."[7] For feeding that hunger, he pocketed $90,000.

Don Juan in Hell toured for three more seasons, earning profits of more than $1 million. The performance was also released as a recording, and in 1952 Boyer won a Tony Award for his part in the stage production. Laughton said, "It is a pity that George Bernard Shaw did not see and hear Charles Boyer as Don Juan. Shaw of all people knew how rare is the true intellectual actor. Boyer is that, besides which he is a considerable artist in other respects. I would call him a genius—yes, a genius who belongs on the stage."[8] Elsa Lanchester complimented her husband's performance in a way that applied to all four: "You have learned the very best thing an actor can learn; how to talk to an audience as if they were people in a room." One of the few dissenting voices was that of eminent British actor John Gielgud, who found the production "a perfectly terrible exhibition of fake spontaneity, and a terrific bore."[9]

37

No Fixed Place of Abode

In 1952 Boyer dissolved the French Research Foundation and sold the building to producer Sol Lesser. Its archives were presented to UCLA. They comprised "newspaper clippings, pamphlets, and photographs documenting occupied France, activities of the Free French movement, and the post-war diplomatic relations of France." Also included were "ephemera issued by the Free French organizations in London, New York, and Algiers."[1]

Boyer was rich enough to retire and briefly considered doing so. Pat would have been in favor of that decision. With no career of her own, and no longer kept busy helping new arrivals to the States, she got depressed during the periods of isolation when her husband was living within a character. Influenced by the devout Farrow clan, who attended mass every Sunday, she converted to Catholicism. Mia Farrow remembered Pat in those days as "highly strung, with a fluty English voice that went on and on. [She] focused on her son, fluttering over him, worrying about every move and word, every bite he ate. She made everybody nervous, especially Michael."[2] Perhaps as a result, Michael's stammer became more pronounced.

Farrow had become an honorary member of the Boyer family, and ten-year-old Mia considered Boyer her "favorite grown-up." He responded to the interest of this precocious child with polite attention, describing his travels and his memories of Paris. Occasionally she perceived a flash of his country childhood. Walking together one day near the Malibu beach house, Boyer noticed a fledgling that had fallen to the ground. Carefully wiping his hands with green leaves—"to take away the human scent," he explained—he restored the bird to the nest, and he and Mia waited to see the mother welcome it back into her brood.[3]

The European cinema was showing renewed life. Rossellini's *Open City,* DeSica's *Bicycle Thieves,* and Cocteau's *Orphée* were screened widely in the United States, courtesy of a new phenomenon: art-house cinemas. Friends in

Paris were doing well. Max Ophuls directed *La Ronde,* René Clair *La Beaute du Diable,* and Julien Duvivier *Sous le Ciel de Paris.* A new generation of continental leading men, including Jean Marais, Serge Reggiani, Daniel Gelin, and Gérard Philippe, was as hungry for fame as Boyer had been at their age. A few won Hollywood contracts. One was Louis Jourdan, whom Boyer had last met on *Le Corsaire.* With his career in transition, the older actor was not particularly welcoming of this younger rival. "Charles didn't give me any advice," said Jourdan. "That wasn't his style. I was never bored when we were together, but he said practically nothing."[4]

In Hollywood, agents were the new power brokers. Charles Feldman had produced film versions of Tennessee Williams's *A Streetcar Named Desire* and *The Glass Menagerie,* and within a decade, Lew Wasserman's MCA would own Universal. Increasingly, actors became their own producers, generally in partnership with someone well versed in business. For the second and last time, Boyer flirted with the idea of following suit.

Playwright Emmet Lavery was a friend whose left-wing political convictions Boyer shared, and Boyer had supported Lavery during his unsuccessful bid for Congress in 1946. Lavery knew Rudi Joseph, who had produced two films with German director Douglas Sirk, and he arranged for Boyer to meet the two men. Boyer "was disgusted with his recent picture *Arch of Triumph,*" Sirk recalled, "and he badly needed to move on to something entirely new to get his career going again. Now, it had been suggested earlier that I should do a film out of the play *The First Legion* by Emmet Lavery. Boyer liked the idea very much. I think originally Boyer was going to produce it, but then he told me he'd prefer me to produce it, which I did in the end, with Rudi Joseph."[5]

The First Legion, a Broadway success in 1934, takes place in a small Jesuit seminary in California; members of the order regard themselves as "the first legion" in the battle with evil. When the elderly Father Sierra, believed to be paralyzed, spontaneously recovers his ability to move and speak, members of the seminary proclaim a miracle. Other people desperately seeking cures gather at the gates, and young men line up to join the order. But Father Ahern (his name was changed to Arnoux in the film, to accommodate Boyer's accent), a former attorney, remains skeptical—and rightly so. Sierra's physician, Morrell, a onetime seminarian turned atheist, admits that he induced the "cure" medically. Up to this point, the story has the makings of an interesting ethical dilemma: Should Arnoux, for the greater good, let the false miracle be accepted, or does he have a higher loyalty to the truth? Lavery dodges the question. As Arnoux urges his colleagues to doubt Sierra's cure, a young paraplegic girl and friend of Morrell slips into the seminary's chapel and prays not for herself but for the soul of the unbeliever. This selfless act restores her ability to walk.

Sirk welcomed the change of direction, moving the film away from questions of belief and injecting an element of satire. "I wanted the picture to be very ironical," he said, "push it definitely towards comedy. There is a miracle that is not a miracle, but because of it, a lot of things happen to this little monastery, and then God says 'Now I'll send them a *real* miracle.'" He convincingly re-creates the tension inside an order that prides itself on intellectual rigor. In some cases, that tension affected the production. "The Jesuit fathers had to give the OK on everything," Sirk complained. "They were on the set the whole time, scrutinizing every line and implication. I think it could have been a sharper picture, more clearly in focus, if those goddam Jesuits hadn't been there."[6]

Sirk called Boyer "a great gentleman as well as an excellent actor."[7] For Boyer, the experience of working in an ensemble piece with such veteran character actors as Walter Hampden, George Zucco, Taylor Holmes, William Demarest, and Leo G. Carroll encouraged him to rethink his former insistence on star billing. None of them had been stars, yet they could all look back on rich creative lives. To Hampden, Boyer confided his relief at no longer having to play "charming continental gentlemen [in] silly romantic parts."[8] Many European stars of Boyer's age enjoyed long and successful careers in featured roles. It was Boyer's loss, and the audience's, that American films continued to revolve around virile heroes and seductive heroines, depriving him of vehicles in which he might have shown off his mature expertise.

Critics admired Boyer's understated performance in *The First Legion*. The *New York Times* called it "strong and keen" but agreed that the film's resolution was unconvincing. "Mr. Lavery and Mr. Sirk introduce us to such an interesting and genuine group of men, and to such a quietly provocative discussion in the better part of their film that it is mentally disturbing to find them ending up in a rush of sentiment."[9] A crass publicity campaign did not help. One poster, a triumph of misinformation, featured the ecstatic face of Barbara Rush, who plays the handicapped girl. A smaller image shows her being carried in the arms of a man dressed in an ordinary suit. There is not a single reference to paraplegia, priests, or the church.

Sirk wrapped *The First Legion* in May 1952 but had to wait a year for its release through United Artists. Once it appeared, Sam Goldwyn was among the producers reminded of Boyer's versatility. Norman Mailer was then enjoying success with his novel *The Naked and the Dead* and was anxious to cash in. Goldwyn proposed a backhanded take on Nathanael West's novel *Miss Lonelyhearts*. Rather than a newspaper columnist morbidly preoccupied with the desperate people who consult him, the film would focus on a radio personality who dispenses advice on the air, then tracks down the people he helps. Goldwyn saw Boyer as the guru, with Montgomery Clift in support, and although Mailer and Jean Malaquais wrote a screenplay, it was never produced.

The delay in releasing *The First Legion* emphasized the negative aspects of independence and influenced Boyer's response to the next script he received—this one sent by Twentieth Century–Fox. An approach from one of the major studios was heartening, even though the property had been kicking around for a while, and he was far from the first choice. Also, the director was Otto Preminger, a notorious bully. *The 13th Letter* was a version of Henri-Georges Clouzot's *Le Corbeau* (The Raven). In that film, produced in Nazi-occupied France, a rural community is plagued by poison-pen letters, mainly directed at the town's doctor. Clouzot based the film on an actual case in the town of Tulle, about sixty miles from Figeac. Boyer may have known of it. He certainly had knowledge of the kind of community in which such things occurred.

Preminger had persuaded Darryl Zanuck that shooting in French-speaking Canada would restore the immediacy of the French wartime setting. On location in Quebec's Saint-Denis and Saint-Marc-sur-le-Richelieu, he created a sinister environment of desolate and often empty houses where people subsist in a state of isolation and despair. In hopes of appealing to the reviving European market, *The 13th Letter* cast British newcomers Michael Rennie and Constance Smith and Boyer's old friend Françoise Rosay. But the impassive Rennie possessed none of Pierre Fresnay's humanity in the French version. His only response to the general paranoia is to pensively wind one of the clocks in his collection. Maureen O'Hara and Joseph Cotten were the original stars, but both were busy with other projects by the time Howard Koch finished the screenplay, delayed by Preminger's rewrites. Linda Darnell replaced O'Hara as a woman with a deformed foot and a yen for Rennie—glamorous casting that compromised Preminger's vision of a town mired in unrelieved ugliness and spite.

Boyer approached his role as the doctor with professionalism but little conviction. Discarding his toupee, he grew a halfhearted beard and affected a limp. His appearance over the opening credits, a dominating silhouette leaning on a cane as he arrives back in town by barge, implies a person of importance, but he is gradually marginalized. It was Boyer's first experience with a process familiar to all character actors: If a star objected to a particular line or action, it was changed. If a minor performer expressed such doubts, the actor was changed. Preminger directed with his customary arrogance, and Boyer struggled to remain civil. He was rewarded with respectful reviews. "Charles Boyer slips into the character of the elderly French-Canadian doctor with wonderful ease," wrote *Variety*.[10] The *New York Times* called him "intriguingly cryptic."

Paramount remained a power in the industry, but charges of monopoly and restraint of trade were eroding its independence. Its productions were no longer emblems of continental sophistication but more often comedy remakes of 1930s successes or lackluster retreads of antique themes. *Thunder in the East* (the same title as the English version of *La Bataille* two decades before) was based on an Alan Moorhead novel set during the 1947 partition of British India. However, if one substituted Pathan tribesmen or Chinese communist guerrillas for jihadi, the film could have been set almost anywhere in Asia and at any time since Queen Victoria.

Alan Ladd stars as a gunrunner who flies into the besieged Indian region of Gandahar with a cargo of weapons. The maharajah wants to fight, but Boyer's pacifist Prime Minister Singh, costumed and made up to look like India's Nehru, believes he can negotiate a peace. However, when he extends the hand of friendship, the Muslims literally amputate it. In brownface, Boyer makes a less convincing Indian than James Mason, originally cast as Singh. And Ladd, despite his braggadocio, is, to borrow Raymond Chandler's phrase, a small boy's idea of a tough guy.

Thunder in the East stayed on the shelf for two years, the second time this had happened to Boyer. It was dispiriting to be reminded that his work was of little relevance. So when he was offered another independent project, this time from producer Stanley Kramer, it did little to lift his spirits. Kramer would go on to make his reputation with such politically edgy projects as *The Defiant Ones* and *On the Beach*, but *The Happy Time* is the opposite of engagé. Boyer, in the role played by Claude Dauphin onstage, is the head of a French-Canadian family in 1920s Ottawa. When not leading a vaudeville theater orchestra, he must contend with a randy rascal of a father (Marcel Dalio, in an embarrassing wig), a priapic brother (Louis Jourdan) who lives up to all the clichés of the traveling salesman, and another brother (Kurt Kasznar) who is perpetually drunk. In the face of these bad examples, his adolescent son (Bobby Driscoll) struggles with puberty, particularly after the family takes in an attractive young soubrette as their maid.

In 1952 the Screen Writers Guild authorized studios to "omit from the screen" the names of any individuals who failed to "purge" themselves before Congress by naming colleagues they knew or suspected to be communists. Leftist Zero Mostel had originally been cast as the drunken brother, but Columbia boss Harry Cohn refused to employ anyone under investigation, so Kasznar was hired to reprise his Broadway performance. Cohn also required director Richard Fleischer to state in writing that he was not a communist.

Boyer's role, though not quite a stage Frenchman, is nevertheless a one-note depiction of the type: cheerful, philosophical, paternal, bland. Work as a character actor might have been easier to find, but the parts were smaller and allowed no room to exercise his virtuosity. Boyer felt a growing conviction that the American cinema had little more to offer him. During an interview in September 1950, he had acknowledged, without histrionics, that he wished to perform henceforth only as a character actor, to the best of his ability. Fortunately, it was at this moment that he found a new and lucrative outlet for his talent.

38

One Star Short

When *Don Juan in Hell* played in San Francisco, David Niven was appearing at the theater next door in F. Hugh Herbert's controversial sex comedy *The Moon Is Blue*. The two groups of actors and their spouses often dined together after their shows, and one night, the conversation turned to television.

Actors could already gauge from the empty cinema seats how much damage was being inflicted by the new medium, but they were uncertain how to respond. Most regarded working in TV as professional suicide, and cut-rate suicide at that: they were fortunate to earn $300 for a thirty-minute appearance. Television production, however, could be lucrative, as Lucille Ball and her husband, Desi Arnaz, discovered in 1950 when they launched Desilu Productions and created *I Love Lucy* and other TV series. They were followed into production by another husband-and-wife comedy team: George Burns and Gracie Allen.

Boyer had recently been approached by onetime singing star Dick Powell with the suggestion that they produce a fortnightly half-hour drama series for television called *Four-Star Playhouse*. Powell would manage the project and alternate with three other actors in the leading roles, sharing the income. He had already lined up a sponsor—the Singer sewing machine company— and actor Joel McCrea, richer than either Powell or Boyer thanks to his property investments, was on board. Boyer accepted and invited Niven to participate.

Niven became the most enthusiastic of the four. He told a journalist, "It is wonderful to be a producer at last, and in television. The schoolgirl jealousy of the film industry will have to end, and we can, with a little intelligent planning, actually help each other. Certainly it means a lot more work for actors and writers and directors, and as television is clearly not going to go away, now it's here we should all make the most of it."[1] He even speculated that cinema was a thing of the past—a phenomenon that, like vaudeville, would last for seventy or eighty years and then die off. Cinema had replaced vaudeville; now television would replace cinema.

Niven's commitment to the project's success mostly reflected his need for the money. He was thus quite distressed when McCrea dropped out at the last minute. Among those stars approached to replace him, Rosalind Russell dismissed the idea with contempt. Lauren Bacall also passed but lived to regret it. "David had gone into that Four-Star deal out of sheer desperation at the way his film career was moving—or rather wasn't," she recalled. "They asked me to join them, and like a jerk I refused, which shows you how lousy my professional instincts were."[2] The partners compromised by recruiting actress and director Ida Lupino, who, although a useful addition in terms of talent, had no capital to invest. William Frye, who produced the series pilot with Boyer and Andrea King, conceded that the title was a misnomer, as there were really only three stars.

As Four-Star International, the partners leased the former studios of low-budget Republic, originally built for Mack Sennett's Keystone. Each of the three male members acted as producer of the episodes in which he appeared. Niven found this aspect of the job worryingly onerous. "The auditions would make me a nervous wreck," he said. "I'd sit there looking at these poor devils trying to get work and then remember what it was like for me in the 1930s. I finally worked out a system. When an actor and actress came in for a part, I would have my secretary hear them while I stayed in the inner office and watched them through the keyhole. Then I could telephone through and say yes or no without having to get into embarrassing confrontations."[3]

Playhouse ran from 1952 to 1956, first as a single thirty-minute show each fortnight, then, from the fall of 1953, once a week. For the first year, Boyer sometimes had to write personal checks to cover the payroll, but in 1954 *Billboard* magazine voted *Playhouse* the second-best TV drama series, and more generous sponsors came on board.

The series worked on a production line. Between them, Robert Florey (thirty-one episodes) and Roy Kellino (forty-one episodes) handled the bulk of the direction, augmented by younger directors such as Robert Aldrich and Blake Edwards, who would later make names for themselves. The latter wrote and directed seven episodes between 1952 and 1954.

Costs limited the kind of stories the series could use. Most involved fewer than six characters. Location shooting was too expensive, so episodes generally took place on two or three interior sets. For "Moorings," in the second season, Boyer plays a shipping magnate humanized by his encounter with a blind woman (Dorothy Malone) and her son, who is fascinated with ships. A room with a model ship and a wall map had to stand in for his office; the beach set, though well furnished with rocks and sand, lacked an ocean.

Scripts were generated in-house. Staff writer John Bagni wrote fifteen episodes, often working with his wife, Gwen. Following Bagni's death in 1954, Richard Carr took over for thirteen episodes, supplemented by such established names as Seeleg Lester and Octavus Roy Cohen. Lupino contributed two original stories for the 1956 season.

Actors were hired for three or four episodes at a time. Most were familiar faces, including such veterans as Florence Bates, Allen Jenkins, and Una Merkel. There were no continuing characters, although in eight of Powell's episodes he played gambler Willie Dante, a character that was later the basis of the NBC series *Dante*. Boyer appeared in thirty episodes. The lesson he had learned from Bernstein—that he was unconvincing playing anyone weak or tentative—also applied to this new medium. He told story editor Coles Trapnell that he didn't care if he projected a negative image, as long as it was one of authority. In a few stories he played a tyrant or a bigot, but most often he played a successful businessman or artist jolted out of complacency by a random encounter or discovery.

Though satisfied with the success of his investment, Boyer did not share Niven's enthusiasm for television as a medium. As the most serious actor of the three, he disliked the anthology format, just as he had in radio. The twenty-two minutes remaining after eight minutes of preliminaries and commercials allowed little time to create a character.

A typical episode was "Backstage," the fourth in the first season. Directed by Florey from an original script by the Bagnis, it ingeniously riffed on the recently successful *All About Eve*. Theater star Boyer prevents a young woman from jumping off a bridge, only to discover that she is an actress who has staged the encounter as a kind of audition. In "My Wife Geraldine," he is a bachelor who invents a wife in order to get a job, but he does so with such effectiveness that he is suspected of murdering her. When his landlady offers to play the part in real life, he declines, having fallen in love with his fantasy.

Boyer found episodes directed by Aldrich more challenging. "The Bad Streak," broadcast in January 1954, cast him as a professional gambler whose casino is failing. At the climax, he is pitted in a crucial game against his wastrel son, who tries to break the bank. After defeating him, Boyer puts a coin into a slot machine and hits the jackpot; his streak of bad luck is over. The moral of the story is one Boyer knew from personal experience: if you're going to gamble, you've got to be ready to lose.

Playhouse was the first of many series Four-Star produced. Within a few years, it was one of American television's most active production companies, with a dozen hit shows to its credit. Niven boasted that, in five years, it had turned out 1,800 episodes of various programs, making its principals comfortably rich. They had confounded the pessimists who thought that three actors could never collaborate. Their secret, Niven explained, was not to spend too much time together. Meetings were conducted by telephone, and decisions were made over dinner by two partners, on the assumption that the third would agree. Powell, the best businessman of the group, revealed his personal recipe for the trio's success: he had one partner—Niven—who could never be serious, and another—Boyer—who could never be anything else.

The series also introduced Niven and Boyer to a younger audience that was largely unfamiliar with their films. Among the teenagers who first saw Boyer on TV was future star Warren Beatty, who admired and sought to emulate his apparently effortless success with women. The *Playhouse* programs led Beatty to discover *Love Affair,* and he would make his own version of it in 1994.

Before the Boyers left New York in July 1953 for their annual trip to France, Boyer closed a deal to appear on Broadway in *Kind Sir,* a play by screenwriter Norman Krasna. Krasna, who had just enjoyed a hit with the film *White Christmas,* was itching to get back to Broadway. Producer Jean Dalrymple saw it as an ideal project for Mary Martin, who was about to end a record run in *South Pacific* with Ezio Pinza. Audiences who had enjoyed the romance between an American girl and an older Italian would surely queue up to see her matched with an equally seductive Frenchman. Martin had always played in musicals but was eager to establish herself as a comedienne. She also liked the story, particularly because it called for a wardrobe of eye-catching Mainbocher costumes. Boyer saw it primarily as an investment, and he, along with Martin, put up most of the $75,000 budget.

In Paris, Boyer met with Max Ophuls, who had just bought the film rights to a literary success of two years earlier, the novella *Madame de . . .* by Louise de Vilmorin. Ophuls offered Boyer a part in the film. The actor recognized the value of reviving his European career, but also the risks. In George Cukor's *A Star Is Born,* when failing star Norman Mayne suggests that he might work in Europe, "where they are doing some awfully interesting things," it is seen as professional suicide.

Back in New York, Boyer started rehearsals for *Kind Sir*. On paper, it had all the ingredients of a hit. A successful actress is introduced to an attractive diplomat, who tells her that he is married, though estranged from his wife. They begin an affair, meeting only when their busy schedules intersect. Then she discovers that he isn't married at all, just unwilling to accept the responsibility of matrimony. She plans to punish him for his deceit, but it ends when he unexpectedly proposes.

To direct, Mary Martin suggested Joshua Logan. Since his days as a voice coach with Walter Wanger, Logan had become one of Broadway's most sought-after directors, winning a Pulitzer Prize for his work with Martin in *South Pacific*. All were unaware of his chronic manic depression. During rehearsals for *Kind Sir,* he became increasingly irrational, suggesting that Martin enter the stage turning a cartwheel, and throwing pebbles at the actors when he was displeased. "It was a nightmare," said Martin. "We kept trying to get him to seek medical attention, but he wouldn't go. He said, 'If I go in, I'll never get out of the hospital.'"[4]

Logan's condition deteriorated when the play went on the road prior to opening on Broadway. During the first preview in New Orleans, Boyer crossed the stage by walking in front of a sofa. From the back of the theater, Logan screamed, "I told you *behind* the sofa!" and ran down the aisle toward the stage, yelling. He was taken from the theater in a straitjacket, having suffered a complete mental breakdown, and spent several weeks in a sanatorium. To keep working under such conditions demanded all of Boyer's professionalism.

The play opened in New York on November 4 to notices that paid more attention to Martin's wardrobe than to the performances. *Time* magazine called it "a sumptuous bore and a gilded vacuum." On the bright side, the $700,000 in advance ticket sales guaranteed a profit. *Kind Sir* ran for 166 performances and closed, to Boyer's relief, on March 27, 1954. Five years later, Stanley Donen would film it as *Indiscreet,* with Cary Grant and Ingrid Bergman.

39

Superficially Superficial

New Yorker correspondent Janet Flanner described Louise de Vilmorin as a "writer, beauty, poet, musician, wit and eccentric, and one of the few gifted *précieuses* of the Paris *haut monde*."[1] Companion of Charles de Gaulle's adviser André Malraux and former lover of both Orson Welles and Antoine de Saint Exupéry, de Vilmorin often based her tales on the doings of her famous friends. But the anonymous title character in *Madame de . . .* could have lived in any era. No epoch had a monopoly on vanity, desire, and betrayal.

The wife of a wealthy and powerful man, Madame has overspent her clothing allowance, so she secretly sells some diamond earrings, a wedding gift from her husband, and tells him she lost them at the theater. But the jeweler to whom she sold them invites her husband to buy them back, and he impulsively presents them as a parting gift to the mistress he is discarding. She, in turn, sells the earrings, which are purchased by a foreign ambassador who, on his return to Paris, coincidentally begins an affair with Madame. He, of course, presents her with her own earrings, which continue to circulate, each exchange revealing some new aspect of duplicity in this superficial society.

With Marcel Achard, Max Ophuls dismantled de Vilmorin's story and used the basics to construct something more complex. Building on the hint that the husband reads military histories, they make him a general. Monsieur and Madame become Count (General) André and Countess Louise, and her lover becomes Baron Fabrizio Donati. Ophuls also gives the story a time and a place: 1880 Paris, which has recently been transformed by the wide boulevards and stately apartment buildings created by Georges-Eugene Haussmann. The army, recovered from its 1871 defeat by the Prussians, has not yet become embroiled in the Dreyfus scandal, which would expose its endemic prejudice and anti-Semitism. Parades and maneuvers preoccupy its modishly uniformed marshals and generals. "Max loved officers of the *belle* epoque," said Peter Ustinov, who appeared in Ophuls's last film, *Lola Montes.* He admired "their utter uselessness; their obligations towards virility; their statutory quick temper over imagined slights; their generous ability to make room for younger men by eliminating each other on the field of honor."[2]

The film required an actress of substance in the role of Louise, and few were more well suited than Danielle Darrieux. The Rizzoli family, as the price of investing in the film, demanded an Italian in a starring role, so Ophuls offered the part of Donati to director and actor Vittorio DeSica. Like Ophuls, DeSica was a womanizer, maintaining families in both Rome and Paris. His appetite for women was rivaled only by his love of roulette, which kept him permanently broke. When Ophuls approached him, he was bankrupt and had just spent two weeks in Hollywood trying, in vain, to interest Howard Hughes in producing a film. Even if he had not recognized something of himself in Donati, it was a role he could not afford to turn down.

Boyer, in contrast, could and did refuse to play General André. The salary was, he told Ophuls, an insult—petty cash by Hollywood standards. He finally consented, but with conditions. If he was not going to be paid like a star, he would at least be treated like one. A large car and chauffeur must be at his disposal throughout the production, and he would live in the city's most prestigious hotel, the Crillon. His behavior was a strategy, but an effective one, suggesting that he was still an international star who had made time in his busy schedule to work with Ophuls out of friendship.

All Paris regarded Boyer's return as a triumph, without a hint of the bitterness he had experienced in 1946. *Le Monde* reported breathlessly on a reception at Maxim's restaurant:

His eyes showed no concern; those beautiful dark eyes which
exerted so much charm on the beauties of Bernstein's plays in his
heyday. The face was still hairless, the hair thinner. Boyer
responded through the crackling halo of flashes to the testimonies
of sympathy lavished on him by his French friends. Kisses,
effusions, handshakes, requests for autographs and dates: he was
affectionately harassed. But his velvet gaze was wet and his smile
full of seduction when he recognized Françoise Rosay, Pierre
Blanchar, Jacques Becker and Anne Vernon, Maurice Chevalier,
Gaby Morlay, Marcel Achard, Danielle Darrieux finally, who was
his Marie Vetsera and will be, with Vittorio de Sica, his partner in
Max Ophüls's film, *Madame de. . . .* Twenty times he will offer his

left cheek to meet the requirements of photographers and those of his "good profile."[3]

Once shooting began, Ophuls was equally careful to shoot only that "good profile." He even put a mark on the inferior cheek of every actor to remind himself. His method was everything Boyer could have wished for. He never gave specific directions but let a performance grow out of the actors' natural reactions, planning his sinuous tracking and dolly shots only when the entire cast was comfortable with the action.

De Vilmorin disliked the specificity of Ophuls's version of her story. She felt that naming the characters and locating them in time and place weakened its universality. Ophuls, however, sees André and Louise as creatures of their society. He literally holds up a mirror to a world that assesses people according to what they own, as cinematographer Christian Matras repeatedly frames the couple in a mirror or a window. They seem trapped in the crowded interiors of their great houses, laced into uniforms and evening gowns, always attended by valets and maids, coachmen and tradesmen, musicians and flunkies who watch their every move.

The general is skilled at surviving in this social minefield. He does favors for people but never accepts them from others. In any situation, this gives him the upper hand. This is ingeniously illustrated in a scene where André is searching his carriage for the apparently lost earrings.

"Looking for something?" a passing friend asks.

"Yes," André says, continuing to rummage. "Those fifteen thousand francs you returned to me. You *did* return them, didn't you?"

Flustered, the friend mutters, "Well, things have been a bit tight," and retreats apologetically, muttering, "I'll be seeing you."

Again, without looking at him, the general says drily, "So you tell me."

Flanner acknowledged the contrast between de Vilmorin's essentially French sensibility and the more Germanic Ophuls. "His restless camera technique results in an incredible but fatiguing beauty and virtuosity. With his own marked European talent, he has succeeded in changing the Gallic *Madame de . . .* into Viennese baroque."[4] In line with this conception, Ophuls brings the story to a more cinematic conclusion. Impatient with the carousel of intrigue to which the earrings have bound him, André makes a characteristically military decision and kills Donati in a duel. We never see Louise again. In a final image, her earrings lie on the altar of the church she visited periodically to pray for intercession in her schemes.

At his best playing men of intelligence, Boyer pulls off the difficult task of showing the importance of games and rituals to this society without making his character seem trivial. "I'll tell you a secret," André warns his wife. "Our conjugal bliss is a reflection of ourselves. It's only superficially superficial." Louise is too much in thrall to her self-indulgent fantasies to realize that the earrings are not simply jewels but rather, in the phrase of British critic Peter Bradshaw, "a symbol of taboo, transgression and disloyalty."[5] Her failure to grasp this proves fatal. The general can shrug off sex, even love, but dignity is a matter of life and death. When Ophuls died in 1957 at age fifty-four, critics had begun to consider *Madame de . . .* a masterpiece.

Boyer, meanwhile, was enjoying life in France, which was tranquil compared with Hollywood. Back in California, something new or untoward always seemed to be happening to an old friend or former collaborator. Charlie Feldman and Jean had divorced but continued to live together. Walter Wanger went to jail for shooting agent Jennings Lang, lover of his then-wife Joan Bennett, in the testicles. Ever the gambler, Boyer decided to play what looked like a winning hand and stay in France. And he agreed to make another period film.

Costume pictures were the backbone of the French cinema, and director Christian-Jaque was an old hand at creating them. His loose adaptation of Emile Zola's *Nana* featured the fourth of his six wives, Martine Carol. Red-headed, crimson lipped, and seldom fully dressed, Carol was a pulp magazine heroine whose sex appeal made up for her lack of acting ability. Putting on and removing elaborate gowns in equally overdressed settings was her stock in trade. But Boyer dominates the film as Count Muffat, the protector Nana ends up destroying. Little remains of Zola's political subtext, intended to point up the deficiencies and corruption of Napoleon III's rule. We are left with the story of a courtesan's rise at the expense of a succession of lovers and her comeuppance at the hands of one of them.

The plot of *Nana* dovetails with that of *Madame de. . . .* Zola concludes his novel with Nana expiring from smallpox while the crowd in the street outside shouts, "To Berlin!" signaling the start of the Franco-Prussian War. General André would have been an officer in that conflict, which ended in France's defeat at Sedan, followed by the siege of Paris, the emperor's abdication, and the fall of the Second Empire. The ability to rise to command rank after such a disaster suggests a man of cunning and resources, and this knowledge illuminates Boyer's character in Ophuls's film. Christian-Jaque, however, is not concerned with politics. His Nana comes to an operatic end, strangled by the most wronged of her victims, her body sprawled on the marble staircase of the vulgar and overfurnished mansion he bought for her.

The color cinematography of Christian Matras expertly alternates studio interiors with the streets of Paris, little changed since the 1870s. When Carol is not hogging the screen, Robert Gys, Christian-Jaque's regular production designer, evokes a society in which everyone, including the emperor himself, appears in costume, the more gilded and embroidered the better.

Despite such tawdry material, Boyer appears at ease in both the milieu and his performance. For the first time in many years, he was playing a character his own age and acting in his own language. It amused him that he was once again in the world of *All This and Heaven Too,* but richer and gaudier than anything Warner Brothers could have devised.

One episode of *Nana* takes place in Laperouse, the former brothel overlooking the Seine that became the city's most select restaurant. In its private rooms, men of means can dine—and more—with their *poules de luxe,* knowing they will not be disturbed. The mirrors in its *salles privés* offer only blurred reflections, having been scratched by the women satisfying themselves, before satisfying their companions, that they are truly being offered diamonds and not glass. For all the trashiness of *Nana,* it was the diamond of this world, and *All This and Heaven Too* was the blurred reflection.

40

Great Body, Lovely Soul

B oyer was in no hurry to return to Los Angeles. As his search for a château continued, he took occasional film roles, some of which were little more than walk-ons. For the 1953 *Boum sur Paris* (*boum* is slang for "party"), Boyer is glimpsed as part of a show presented by the radio program *La Kermesse aux Étoiles* (The Carnival of Stars). Other celebrity participants included Gary Cooper and Gregory Peck, while Edith Piaf and Juliette Greco had larger roles in a framing story about a perfume called *Boum*.

Cooper, twelve years older than Boyer, still had a thriving Hollywood career, while Boyer was relegated to cameos in films such as Mike Todd's *Around the World in Eighty Days*. It took all the good nature he could muster not to resent that David Niven, only ten years his junior, had the starring role as Phileas Fogg in this lavish production. Boyer appears briefly as the Paris representative of the Thomas Cook travel agency. True to his image as a "great lover," he tries to interest Fogg's valet Passepartout in a world tour during which the traveler samples the women of every country he visits. After being turned down, he resourcefully sells Fogg the balloon that carries him to Spain on the next leg of his journey.

In the United States, television was now thoroughly ascendant. A week seldom went by without an invitation for Boyer to appear as a guest on radio or TV. His excursions into TV drama included the CBS series *Climax*. In 1956 he joined Jean-Pierre Aumont, Gracie Allen, and Jack Benny in *The Gay Illiterate: The Louella Parsons Story*. In 1957 he starred opposite Broadway legend Katherine Cornell in a TV adaptation of the Pulitzer Prize–winning *There Shall Be No Night* by Robert E. Sherwood for NBC's *Hallmark Hall of Fame*.

Occasionally, to promote a play, Boyer made a token appearance on the panel show *What's My Line?* He even stooged for Lucille Ball on *I Love Lucy*, once again as the great lover. Although the notoriously tightfisted Desilu production company required guests to supply their own clothing, even if it might be damaged during the show, it met its match in Boyer. The sketch ended with Lucy squirting ink on Boyer's shirt and tearing his raincoat. Fortunately, the trick ink obtained from a magic shop washed out, but Desi Arnaz had to provide a coat from his own wardrobe when Boyer refused to sacrifice his own.

Boyer was coaxed back to Hollywood in 1955 for a film that, for once, did not make a point of his nationality. Studios were tempted to use Cinema-Scope, which promised to stem the popularity of television, even for films that did not deserve such lavish treatment. Fritz Lang joked that the format was suitable only for films about snakes and funerals, and *The Cobweb* has a little of both. Based on a modest novel by William Gibson about the tensions within a private psychiatric clinic, *The Cobweb* mirrors *Private Worlds* in suggesting that those who treat the mentally ill are often as troubled as their patients. Therapy in this clinic takes a backseat to internal intrigues and rivalries, as its management is plunged into chaos by the question of replacing some curtains. Boyer saw it as a chance to revive his reputation as a screen lover, but MGM's eagerness to exploit the dimensions of wide screen forced him to compete with an all-star cast led by Richard Widmark, Gloria Grahame, Lauren Bacall, and Lillian Gish. Producer John Houseman did not want Boyer to play the clinic's philandering director, but Vincente Minnelli insisted. Pushed to the sidelines, Boyer responded by overplaying his character's lechery, nuzzling and groping where he once would have murmured a few words and lit a cigarette. Deservedly a disaster, *The Cobweb* lost $1.1 million on its first release, and a disconsolate Boyer returned to Paris.

He spent part of the summer of 1956 at Cinecittà in Rome filming *La Fortuna de Essere Donna* (What a Woman!) with Sophia Loren as a celebrity beauty and Marcello Mastroianni as a paparazzo. Boyer plays a lubricious count recruited to transform Loren into a potential movie queen. In his biggest scene, his wife confronts him and Loren in a restaurant and upends a messy salad on his head. Boyer did not look back on this film with affection. The same could be said of *Paris, Palace Hotel*, in which Boyer plays a retired businessman who intervenes to help manicurist Françoise Arnoul enjoy Christmas as a guest in the four-star hotel where she works.

Hollywood liked its stars to reveal their domestic sides—sharing their favorite recipes, being photographed working in the garden, or demonstrating their skill with watercolors. Boyer's preferred recreational activity—gambling— did not fit this cozy pattern, nor could the press find much to publicize in his other favorite activity—traveling. Extensive reading made him an armchair tourist with the power, conferred by his wealth, to visit the places he read about.

He and Pat often took long railway journeys together, exploring remote corners of the United States. He was also intrigued by the prospect of living on an island, the ultimate extension of his taste for seclusion. Lafcadio Hearn's novel *Chita: A Memory of Last Island* drew him to some tiny specks of land off the Louisiana coast, where he fantasized about building a holiday home. But the islands proved to be mostly uninhabited and regularly overwhelmed by hurricanes. He had better luck in the Mediterranean. Following *La Fortuna de Essere Donna*, Pat joined him in Rome for a holiday. Shunning congested Capri, they felt instantly at home on its nearest neighbor, the less intensively developed Ischia. It satisfied Boyer's need for a haven, and he leased a villa there, which became another stop on the peripatetic family's itinerary.

Michel Boisrond's *La Parisienne* was Brigitte Bardot's first film since her breakout appearance in *Et Dieu créa la Femme* (And God Created Woman) and existed solely to showcase her uninhibited sexuality. The opening—with Bardot in a red convertible speeding through Paris on a sunny morning to the wailing jazz vocals of Mimi Perrin and the Double Six de Paris—sold both Bardot and the pleasures of the French capital more effectively than any travel poster.

Bardot's character, the daughter of the French Prime Minister, is determined to marry his womanizing Chief of Staff (Henri Vidal), and she takes advantage of the state visit of Queen Greta (Nadia Gray) and Prince Charles (Boyer), a couple based on the recently crowned Elizabeth II and her consort Philip. Hired to add class to the film, Boyer as the prince receives an entrance appropriate to his eminence, and he tops it with a skilled piece of scene stealing. The royals arrive by train and proceed at a stately pace along the platform until the prince, apparently spontaneously, breaks away to shake hands with the grimy engine driver and his fireman. The gesture completed, he rejoins the royal progress. Then, in a touch that cynically undercuts our perceptions, he expressionlessly peels off one soiled white glove and, without looking, hands it to an aide, who silently provides a replacement.

Boyer insisted, as usual, that his name appear first in the credits, but it was a concession Bardot could afford to make, since this is indisputably her film. Plot takes a backseat to those essential *ooh-la-la* moments of her dressing, undressing, and bending down in a low-cut evening gown. Boyer is left to carry whatever narrative there is, particularly in the film's last third, where a stolen afternoon with Bardot at the beach in Nice, à la *Roman Holiday,* has him mistaken for a gang boss and subsequently involved in a brawl—a first in the career of a man who shunned physical violence.

Following *La Parisienne,* veteran director Henri Verneuil offered Boyer *Maxime,* a film that looks back to the start of the century, with echoes, not coincidentally, of *Madame de.* . . . To Verneuil, Boyer belonged to the belle epoque more than to the present day. Comparing him to one of the great dandies of that era, he said, "He had the charm, the elegance, the casualness and the good humor of Boni de Castellane."[1]

A five-minute introduction reminds audiences that the tour by the new Queen Elizabeth and her consort, parodied in *La Parisienne,* was preceded by similar state visits in 1938 and 1914 by her parents and grandparents, respectively, the earlier of which provides the setting for *Maxime.* Such patronizing attempts to sugarcoat an old-fashioned film for a young audience signify the long-overdue housecleaning that was about to be inflicted by the nouvelle vague.

Boyer's character, Maxime Cherpray, a famous boulevardier in his day, is just scraping by as fixer and adviser to the wealthy, brash young Hubert de Truffujean. When Hubert sets his sights on wealthy widow Jacqueline Monneron, Maxime pulls every trick to try to bring them together, only to fall in love with her himself. After a humiliating failure to capture her heart by the antiquated gesture of a duel, Maxime accepts the advice of Gazelle, an old friend and former lover, who tells him that love, like the marching troops in the street below his apartment, always passes. Across town, Hubert and Jacqueline plan an idyllic honeymoon, oblivious to the newspaper pushed under the door announcing the outbreak of war.

Boyer felt comfortable with cinematographer Christian Matras, who had shot both *Madame de* . . . and *Nana.* Michèle Morgan is Jacqueline, and Gazelle is played by the legendary Arletty, finally rehabilitated following her misbehavior during the occupation. (Asked to justify her German lovers, she dismissed them with a famous bon mot: "My heart is French but my ass is international.") But the film belongs entirely to Boyer, who brings his effortless wit and timing to the part.

Writer Henri Jeanson has fun parodying the louche society of Maxim's restaurant and its aging clientele who sample and assess the latest crop of *poules de luxe* with the same weary discrimination they bring to a vintage Bordeaux or a Cuban cigar. This is a low-budget version of the world Lerner and Loewe would popularize with *Gigi* and Maurice Chevalier would celebrate in the song "Ah Yes, I Remember It Well." Sharing a sherry at Maxim's bar with Gazelle and her husband, the General, Maxime identifies a man who glares at him as "my last duel."

"Brigitte?" inquires the General.

"Martine," says Maxime.

"Great body," the General reminisces.

"Lovely soul," he responds.

Offhand references to characters from Proust, poodles named for vaudeville and movie stars of the day, and the to-and-fro of witty conversation make the film a continuing delight to those who relish such things. It failed at the box office, however, in part because its producer, Ignace Mongenstern, was also the father-in-law of François Truffaut. He would help finance Truffaut's debut feature *Les Quatre Cent Coups* a year later. Truffaut's success spelled the end of films like *Maxime,* dismissed by Truffaut and others as— literally, in this case—*le cinema de papa* (daddy's movies).

41

Sins of the Father

Despite failing health, seventy-seven-year-old Cecil B. DeMille started work on what would be his last production, *The Buccaneer*, a remake of his 1938 film about pirate Jean Lafitte and his role in the War of 1812. Eventually, DeMille handed the film over to his then son-in-law, actor Anthony Quinn, to complete. The cast was a ragtag collection of old hands and newcomers, with Yul Brynner as Lafitte and Charlton Heston as Andrew Jackson. Boyer has a few scenes as Dominique You, Lafitte's second in command. Despite looking incongruous in a cocked hat and bits and pieces of several military uniforms, he has the best of the film's few good lines, appropriate to a former French military officer who joins the pirates after becoming disillusioned with the revolution of 1789.

Boyer was based at the Pierre in New York City, where he was appearing in Leslie Stephens's sex comedy *The Marriage-Go-Round*. The play opened on October 29, 1958, and ran for 431 performances until February 13, 1960, with a recess from June 1 to September 1, 1959. Boyer played his cameo in *The Buccaneer* during the summer break and also completed the exhausting task of dubbing his role in *Madame de . . .* into English.

A gold-plated crowd-pleaser, *The Marriage-Go-Round* cast Boyer opposite Claudette Colbert and the statuesque Julie Newmar, a substitute for first choice Anita Ekberg. Newmar arrives at the home of academic Boyer and announces her intention to bear a child possessing her body and his brain. Dancer Isadora Duncan made a similar offer to George Bernard Shaw, who discouraged her by raising the specter of such a child having his body and her brain. Newmar's scheme likewise fails, but not before the predictable domestic complications.

The stress of the long run added to the chronic health problems of both Boyer and Colbert. He suffered from persistent neuralgia and pain in his shoulder and right leg, not to mention the onset of prostatitis and incontinence. Colbert's repeated absences strained their relationship, until Boyer finally ordered the producer to keep her away from him. The play had just reopened in April 1959 after Colbert's latest five-day absence, blamed on bronchitis, when seventy-nine-year-old Louise Boyer entered the Clinique Font Redonde in Figeac for surgery. Unable to be with her, Boyer badgered her doctors with long-distance phone calls and telegrams, but he kept her spirits up with news of his various successes. In Los Angeles, Pat rallied the spiritual forces. "Pat tells me," he wrote to Louise, "that everywhere in Beverly Hills and Los Angeles, in all the religious schools, masses, prayers and novenas are joined with our wishes for your recovery. We are with you every hour of the day." Whether from divine intervention or effective medical care, she recovered fully.

In some of his letters, Boyer mentioned that Warner Brothers wanted him for a film of the musical *Fanny,* to be shot in southern France. Even though it would have allowed him to be with his mother during her convalescence, he initially refused, unwilling to work with director Joshua Logan. He still had vivid memories of Logan's hysterics during *Kind Sir,* but colleagues assured him that treatment with lithium had transformed the director's behavior. On that basis, and with the knowledge that he would be working with Maurice Chevalier, Boyer agreed to do the film once *The Marriage-Go-Round* closed. Rather than flying to France, the Boyers took the slower and more relaxing ocean voyage on the SS *United States,* one of the few liners still plying the transatlantic route.

Marcel Pagnol's *Marius, Fanny,* and *César* had been filmed individually, but for the musical version, Logan and writer Sam Behrman combined them. The film explores that most fundamental of French institutions—the family—through the lives of some colorful characters living in dockside Marseilles during the 1920s. When Marius (Horst Buchholz) abandons the bar of his father, César (Boyer), to fulfill his dream of going to sea, César disowns him. Marius's lover, Fanny (Leslie Caron), discovers she is pregnant, and César persuades her to marry his best friend, the elderly but prosperous Honoré Panisse (Chevalier). Panisse never reveals to the boy, Acolyte, the true identity of his father, but he too grows up longing to become a sailor and follows Marius to sea. Father and son return to fulfill Panisse's dying wish that the family be reunited.

Logan believed the film could repeat *Fanny*'s Broadway success and was not discouraged when Jack Warner decreed (notwithstanding *West Side Story*) that "musicals are finished" and removed all of Harold Rome's songs. A leisurely shoot on location around Marseilles and Cassis promised to erase Logan's memories of his last two films: a troubled screen version of *South Pacific* with an uncooperative Rossano Brazzi and the comedy *Tall Story,* during which both he and Jane Fonda fell in love with her costar Tony Perkins. Feeling a proprietary interest in the project, he tried to change the title to *Joshua Logan's Fanny,* until publicists pointed out the potential for bad jokes at his expense.

Boyer welcomed a role that allowed him to act in shirtsleeves and suspenders and that didn't require him to stand on a box or wear a corset, although his hairpiece remained a fixture. At night, while the other cast members partied in Marseilles, he and Chevalier, both millionaires, ate together at the hotel and billed their meals to the production. Frugality was a lifelong habit for Chevalier. At the end of each meal, he reserved the unused portion of their wine bottle by marking the level on the label and adding his initials with the expensive fountain pen and pencil set he always carried in his vest pocket. Boyer noticed that they were made of platinum. "I have a set in gold as well," Chevalier said contentedly. "Each morning, I choose which I'll carry that day." He had been both rich and poor, and rich was indisputably better.

Boyer also worked with another old friend, Marc Allégret, on the 1961 film *Les Demons de Minuit* (Demons at Midnight). A producer hoping to cash in on the vogue for Italian horror movies invented the catchpenny title, but the film has no demons or supernatural elements of any sort. The Demons is the name of the rock band of Claude (Charles Belmont), son of civil servant Pierre Guérande (Boyer). Just as he is about to leave the country on an important mission, Pierre is alerted that Catherine, his son's jilted mistress, has threatened to kill both Claude and herself. One of Claude's friends, Danielle (Pascale Petit), knows where the band is playing and leads Pierre on a tour of what the film's publicity calls "the surprising diversity of the nocturnal leisure activities of today's youth." Pierre even participates in a game of strip poker and, literally, loses his shirt. The murder and suicide are averted, and the night ends with the affectionate parting of Pierre and Danielle. The film was never released in the States and quickly disappeared, to Boyer's relief.

In 1961 *Fanny* was nominated for several Academy Awards, including for best film and best musical score, and both Boyer and Chevalier were nominated as best supporting actors. They won nothing, but Boyer's recognition by the Academy gave his late career a boost and led to MGM's offer to appear in its remake of *The Four Horsemen of the Apocalypse,* again directed by Vincente Minnelli. Given the success of *Ben Hur,* the studio reasoned that there was gold in its past successes, so it dusted off the Rex Ingram melodrama that had made a star of Rudolph Valentino in 1921. It is based on the novel by Vicente Blasco Ibáñez, which follows the fortunes of an Argentinian clan whose members intermarry with the German von Hartrotts, creating two hostile factions. While Otto, a von Hartrott grandson, becomes a militaristic Junker, Julio Desnoyers, his opposite number, idles away his time in Paris until the First World War and its baleful avatars War, Conquest, Pestilence, and Death introduce him to reality.

Repeated humiliations at the hands of MGM had not reduced Boyer's respect for the studio. Even its flops had a kind of majesty, a readiness to go down with every creative gun blazing. Similar to *Conquest,* though, everything went wrong with this film from the start. Over Minnelli's objections, the story was updated to World War II, and a new plot was added in which Julio redeems his wasted life by helping to target a Nazi stronghold for a bombing raid. Except for early scenes of the family patriarch (Lee J. Cobb) drinking and dancing himself to death in Argentina, the film takes place entirely in Europe, although, because of de Gaulle's objection to Nazi regalia in the streets of Paris, many exteriors had to be shot in Hollywood.

Marlon Brando declined to play Julio, citing his inability to tango (although Minnelli does not repeat the sensual dance number that made Valentino a star). Dirk Bogarde also refused. Alain Delon was rejected as not famous enough and foreign besides—objections that apparently did not apply to Swedish Ingrid Thulin, who plays Julio's married lover Marguerite. For the role of Julio, the eventual choice was Glenn Ford—a familiar face but, at forty-six, a puzzlingly mature one to play a contemporary of the boyish Karlheinz Bohm, his Nazi counterpart. But ages in this film are hopelessly muddled. Boyer, for example, was twelve years *older* than Cobb, cast as his father. Wearing a distinguished silver hairpiece, Boyer sensitively plays Marcel Desnoyers, a well-meaning humanist unable to endure the reality of war. However, his best speeches, such as when he confesses to Julio that he settled in Argentina to avoid military service, only distract from the Julio-Marguerite romance that MGM hoped would sell the film.

Minnelli's trademark richness of color and detail appears only fitfully, such as in a sequence, atmospherically lit, in which Julio and Marguerite wander through the bare wintry gardens of Versailles. He also invests considerable effort in re-creating occupied Paris, with German troops clustered around Napoleon's tomb and thronging the cafés of Place de l'Opéra. Unfortunately, these scenes only prolong the tedium. MGM tried several fixes, including replacing Alex North's musical score with a bombastic one by André Previn and having Angela Lansbury revoice Thulin's entire role. Nothing helped, and the film lost $3.6 million.

42

Men of Distinction

Some years after promising Boyer a Broadway play, Sam Behrman completed *Lord Pengo,* based on the life of art dealer Lord Duveen. Observing that Europe had a great deal of art and America had a great deal of money, Duveen employed everything from flattery to blackmail to sell art to millionaires and earned a baronetcy in the process. Boyer turned down a number of plays after *Red Hands,* but *Lord Pengo* caught his attention. Paul Gregory, who had produced *Don Juan in Hell,* was involved in the project, and Agnes Moorhead was cast as Boyer's long-suffering secretary. She considered the role sufficiently important to rate equal billing. "She can have any billing she likes," Boyer said with equanimity, "so long as it's below mine."[1]

Lord Pengo was a difficult play to present at a time when realism was in vogue. Preview audiences found it creaky, a characteristic that also applied to some of the cast. In the middle of one performance, aging actor Henry Daniell absentmindedly wandered onstage, blinked at the audience, muttered "My mistake," and walked off. The play opened on Broadway on November 19, 1962, and closed on April 20, 1963, after 175 performances. The run coincided with a newspaper strike that crippled Broadway, as there was nowhere to advertise. Without the advance sales attracted by Boyer, *Lord Pengo* would not have lasted as long as it did. His performance earned him a Tony Award nomination.

After *Lord Pengo* closed, Boyer went on to *A Very Special Favor,* a film for Universal with Leslie Caron and Rock Hudson. Producer-writer Stanley Shapiro and director Michael Gordon specialized in the style of sex comedy that made Hudson Hollywood's hottest romantic leading man. Boyer plays a Paris lawyer who loses a case because Hudson seduces the female judge. Hudson, whose character memorably defines the bedroom as "the perfumed battlefield," later apologizes for his tactics and offers to do Boyer a favor in return. Boyer's bossy psychoanalyst daughter (Caron) is about to marry a man she has effectively made into her slave, so he asks Hudson to introduce her to real passion. Hudson becomes Caron's patient, claiming to be irresistible to women and desperate to be cured. He then insists that her treatment has been so successful that he is now homosexual. Caron decides to reverse the process by becoming his lover. Boyer and Hudson shared a dislike of the film's humor. "The boundaries have been extended almost to the limit," Hudson told a reporter, "with producers trying to see how dirty it can get. [*A Very Special Favor*] was filthy."[2]

After the film, Boyer flew to London to open in *Man and Boy,* a new play by veteran British author Terrance Rattigan. Unlike the charming character in *Lord Pengo,* protagonist Gregor Antonescu is a ruthless tycoon who is unable to show love, even for his wife and son. He steadily alienates his family until, when his fortunes fail, there is no one he can turn to for solace. At a time when playwrights John Osborne and Harold Pinter were filling theaters, Rattigan hoped *Man and Boy* would restore confidence in the well-made play with which he had built his reputation. Boyer, who had been denied a West End debut in *Don Juan in Hell,* read *Man and Boy* at the home of producer Binkie Beaumont and agreed to play Antonescu. Rattigan had meant the part for waspish, dissolute Rex Harrison, but once Harrison and then Laurence Olivier turned it down, Beaumont convinced Rattigan of the advantages of casting a Hollywood star.

During the negotiations, director Jean-Pierre Melville offered Boyer an opportunity to appear with France's newest action hero, Jean-Paul Belmondo, in a film of Georges Simenon's novel *L'Aîné des Ferchaux* (The Eldest of the Ferchaux). When Melville's first choice, Spencer Tracy, pulled out because of ill health, Boyer seemed to be an ideal replacement to play a rich but corrupt banker for whom Belmondo, a down-on-his-luck boxer, becomes a bodyguard. Melville was among the most respected directors from the generation before the nouvelle vague, and Boyer was tempted, but the chance to make his much-delayed London stage debut won out. He clinched the deal with Beaumont, agreeing to appear in *Man and Boy* in both London and New York, which simplified its transfer to Broadway. Rattigan agreed.

Rehearsals in the seaside town of Brighton—a traditional try-out venue for London plays, just as New Haven, Connecticut, was for Broadway—went badly. Diagnosed with leukemia and fearing that this would be his last play, Rattigan badgered Boyer to emphasize Antonescu's unexpressed love for his son and the son's evolution into the voice of his father's conscience. As the real-life father of an often rebellious teenager, Boyer felt he understood father-son relations, but Rattigan feared that Boyer was giving a glib movie performance rather than a nuanced character study. He even contemplated writing to every theater critic in London to explain the play's intentions, but a horrified Beaumont talked him out of it.

The day before the London opening in September 1963, Boyer wrote to Rattigan, "Whatever happens tomorrow night I want you to know how thrilled and proud I am to portray your Gregor in your magnificent play." The playwright read this as an admission of defeat. As the curtain rose, he went to the bar and downed three large whiskeys. Before it fell, most of his fears had been realized. Lukewarm reviews ensured that *Man and Boy* ran for only sixty-nine performances. It opened on Broadway in November but managed a meager fifty-four outings. The *Village Voice* reviewer reflected the prevailing mood by accusing Rattigan of "writing not for the ages but for the middle class. His aim is not to change the world but to offer some brief diversion from it."[3] Boyer was consoled when his son, Michael, visited him in his dressing room on opening night, and they embraced—a poignant moment for a man who had barely known his own father.

Four-Star International continued to flourish under Dick Powell's management, extending its activities well beyond the original anthology series. Most of its income derived from TV programs such as *The Rifleman, Burke's Law,* and *Wanted: Dead or Alive* with Steve McQueen. The three partners had so little to do with these shows that when McQueen's first child was born and flowers arrived "From Dick, Charles, and David," his wife had to call the florist to find out who had sent them.

The popularity of television created a need for programming that Four-Star was well positioned to exploit. Official Films Inc. bought most of its series, including the *Playhouse* programs, for worldwide syndication. Over the years, these episodes appeared under different titles and were dubbed into a dozen languages, adding decades to the working lives of Boyer and Niven.

Four-Star Playhouse remained under the CBS umbrella until 1956, when the network substituted its own innovative *Playhouse 90.* The partners moved to rival network NBC, for which they created *The Rogues,* which debuted in September 1964. Set in London but shot in Hollywood, it featured a family of confidence men, the St. Clairs, who use their skills to do good deeds or target crooks who are more villainous than themselves. Boyer and Niven made token appearances but left most of the action to Gig Young, as a younger and more romantic family member. Other continuing characters included John

Williams as the perennial Scotland Yard detective, with Gladys Cooper and Robert Coote in reserve.

The Rogues ran for thirty fifty-minute episodes in the 1964–1965 season but was not renewed. It might have been, but for Young's alcoholism—Larry Hagman had to spell him for two shows in midseason—and Powell's death in January 1963. He left Four-Star in good shape, however, with assets of $25 million and an annual income of $50 million. Rather than continue without him and risk a decline in the company's fortunes, Boyer and Niven took Four-Star public and retired from active participation. Boyer retained an interest in the company. Among the assets listed in his will were 11,222 shares in Four-Star International, valued at $14,028.

Before he died, Powell had been developing a new series, *The Roads*, an ambitious joint venture with Barney Rosset's Grove Press. Believing that American television audiences were ready for more intellectually challenging material, Rosset commissioned European authors to write original stories that could be adapted for television by Four-Star. Each writer was paid $30,000, and their stories would subsequently be published in Grove's magazine *Evergreen Review*. Samuel Beckett, Eugene Ionesco, Harold Pinter, Alain Robbe-Grillet, and Marguerite Duras were among those who accepted, but the project died with Powell.

43

Calm before the Storm

After filming his final episodes for *The Rogues,* Boyer planned to spend the spring and summer of 1964 in Europe. Feldman obliged by finding him roles in two productions being filmed in Paris, including *Venus Rising,* a William Wyler comedy with Audrey Hepburn.

In May, Boyer served on the jury of the Cannes Film Festival, under the chairmanship of Fritz Lang. He also hosted the NBC documentary *The Louvre: A Golden Prison.* For the first time, cameras were admitted to the former royal palace that had become one of the world's great art galleries. As much about the building as the art, the documentary explored its evolution over 700 years. Boyer owned a few paintings, including a Dufy, a Cézanne, a Renoir, and a Vlaminck, but he was no expert. The producer glossed over his ignorance by invoking the "great lover" image. A press release announced Boyer's one condition for accepting the hosting job: "That you have the script written as if I was a French lover making love to a beautiful mistress who is Le Louvre." Sidney Carroll's narration smoothly disguised the gaps in his knowledge.

Hollywood in the mid-1960s was preoccupied with the phenomenon of "runaway" productions. Soaring union rates at home made Europe's cheap labor irresistible. Foreign governments welcomed American crews. They offered large empty studios and regiments of extras who were happy to work for a box lunch or even a sandwich. Producers also learned that the cheapest films became more commercial when they were shot in Rome or on the Côte d'Azur, and the addition of some local stars increased their attraction to the European market.

Love Is a Ball was that kind of film. Color, a wide-screen format, and Riviera locations transformed a story that wouldn't have sustained an episode of *The Love Boat.* As in *Maxime,* Boyer plays a fixer who arranges a marriage between class and money, represented in this case by Ricardo Montalban's penurious duke and an American heiress played by Inger Stevens. To get around the guardian of the heiress's millions (Telly Savalas), Boyer plants a former race-car driver (Glenn Ford) as her chauffeur, with predictable results. Fitted out with a beard and some good summer suits, Boyer ambles through a role that leaves the heavy lifting to an aging Ford and to Montalban, who is surprisingly convincing as a cultivated man embarrassed by the subterfuge. The *New York Times* praised the film's "sun-kissed scenery" but lamented that "its worldliness magnifies the cardboard capering front and center [so that] even Mr. Boyer's Gallic suavity seems strained."[1]

Boyer then went on to the charmless Austrian production *Julia, du bist Zauberhaft* (Julie, You Are Magic). Without the benefit of color or glamorous locations, it updates Guy Bolton's stage version of Somerset Maugham's 1937 novel *Theatre,* which mocked the vanities of actresses. Matinee idol Lilli Palmer keeps herself feeling young through a succession of affairs with younger men while her entrepreneur husband (Boyer) looks on with resignation, confident she will return to him in the end. Retitled *Adorable Julia* (or sometimes *The Seduction of Julia*) and shot in both English and German, partly on location in a drab London, it views Palmer's shenanigans with a camp bitchiness. "Because I was not much affected by the glamor of the brilliant creatures I had known in the flesh," Maugham wrote, "I drew the creature of my fancy, I dare say, with a certain coolness."[2] German reviewers liked the movie, but the direction was flat, and filming it in black and white made it an anachronism. While on location in London, Boyer bonded with young actor Jean Sorel, who played one of the lovers. A straight-faced Boyer told Sorel that his contract called for two young women each night. When they met for breakfast each morning, Sorel would raise an eyebrow in inquiry about the previous night's imaginary companion, to which Boyer responded with a moue or a wink, indicating disappointment or satisfaction.

Boyer was next offered a role in René Clément's film of the Larry Collins and Dominique Lapierre documentary novel *Is Paris Burning?* about the battle to save the city from being dynamited in the last days of the war. Boyer was philosophical about accepting the minor part of a doctor working for the resistance, consoling himself that there could be no stars in a film cast almost entirely with cameos. He arrived in Paris to find Clément close to tears at the complexity of the three-hour production and the need to juggle the schedules and idiosyncrasies of Jean-Paul Belmondo, Alain Delon, Kirk Douglas, Anthony Perkins, Leslie Caron, and a dozen others. Orson Welles was so affronted by the relatively lightweight Clément being handed such an assignment that he communicated with him only through an assistant, Yves Boisset.

The worst thorn in Clément's side was President de Gaulle, who controlled the film from his office in the Elysée palace as surely as if he stood beside the camera. Because of him, it had to be shot in black and white; he had sworn that the red and black Nazi flag would never again fly in France—not even for a movie. Repeated interference in the script ensured that the communists, the best organized and most effective of the resistance groups (and still a force in French politics), would seldom be mentioned. As Bosley Crowther noted in the *New York Times,* "the drama that might be derived from a forthright and forceful definition of the Resistance factions is lost through the clearly deliberate fuzzing of the political lines."[3]

By the time Boyer reported to William Wyler in Paris, *Venus Rising* had become *How to Steal a Million and Live Happily Ever After,* then simply *How to Steal a Million.* Audrey Hepburn, who lived in Switzerland, was happy to be working in France and was widely quoted as saying, "Paris is always a good idea." She had been assured ahead of time that she would be the star, and Harry Kurnitz tailored his script to her personality. Boyer no longer rated his name above the title but was credited separately for his "special guest appearance" in a handful of scenes as an art dealer involved in the theft of an apparently valuable (but actually fake) statue from the Louvre. As always, Boyer appreciated the leisurely pace of French filmmaking. Instead of the actors having to report before dawn for costumes and makeup, shooting began at noon. This schedule, however, was strictly observed, as George C. Scott discovered when he arrived on his first day at 5:00 p.m. and was promptly fired. Wyler replaced him with Eli Wallach.

Boyer finished work on the film on Friday, September 24. Retakes were scheduled the following week, after which Pat was planning to join him for a holiday. He returned to his hotel to find a crowd of journalists surrounding the door. Unaware of their reason for being there, he waved and then went up to his suite, where the film's publicist was waiting to break the worst news any father could receive: his son was dead.

44

Man and Boy

Among the credits for *The Rogues* was one for Michael Boyer as dialogue director. Boyer had arranged the ill-defined job in an attempt to create a career for his son, who had not yet found his feet. Education in private boarding schools and frequent visits to France had made Michael fluent in French, but he possessed no particular intellectual ability. Nor, aside from dabbling in painting, did he show an interest in any of the arts, least of all acting, given his stammer.

Though in some ways enviable, Michael's childhood left him ill equipped for adult life. Between films, his parents played tennis by day and bridge or rummy in the evening, if they were not hosting a dinner party or attending one. Traditionally, Sundays were reserved as family time, but in practice, this generally meant sharing breakfast, after which Charles retreated to his den, where he was not to be disturbed. To Michael, his father was a remote figure. When not commuting between Paris, Ischia, Los Angeles, and New York, Pat and Charles skied in Aspen or went on long railway holidays. This busy and nomadic life made it difficult for Michael to put down roots, form friendships, or take an interest in anything except for girls and fast cars. A later police report revealed that he also owned firearms and had a history of doing "funny things" with guns. As an only child himself, Boyer understood the psychological issues that could result from that situation and overcompensated by spoiling Michael. At the same time, he and Pat did not change their way of life to accommodate their child. The price of having every luxury and being forgiven every bad behavior was to be seen but not heard.

Michael inherited his father's good looks. Mia Farrow described the adult Michael as "darkly handsome, with a beautiful mouth and pensive shining eyes." Both families encouraged a romance between them, but without success. "Michael and I had been paired from infancy," writes Farrow. "I was crazy about Michael, who felt nothing at all for me."[1] Instead, he dated older and more sophisticated women of whom his parents disapproved—which may have been the point.

When the time came to enroll in college, Michael announced that he hoped for a career in television and believed he could receive the best grounding by working for Four-Star rather than getting a degree. But his attraction to television palled, and after *The Rogues* he expressed an interest in the music business. Turning once again to his father for help, he suggested that Boyer make his recording debut, with Michael producing. He sidestepped the fact that Boyer couldn't sing by suggesting that he recite song lyrics to music. Four-Star owned a small recording company, Valiant Records, and Michael became its promotion director. Through Valiant, Boyer recorded a single, "Where Does Love Go?" The record sold well, and *Billboard*, under the headline "Boyer's New Career A-OK," announced that he would record an album of the same name.

Michael and his arranger spent three weeks in Paris, recording Boyer during his downtime from *How to Steal a Million*. "I've never worked so hard in all my life," Boyer told a reporter. "In fact I could say I've just started a new career: a new career for my son. This is the least I can do for him." He described Michael as a very talented boy but without direction. "He's searching," he said. "I'm trying to help him find himself."[2]

Boyer spoke the lyrics to eight songs, with orchestral backing. In addition to the title track, there were seven standards: "What Now My Love," "When the World Was Young," "Autumn Leaves," "Gigi," "La Vie en Rose," "Once upon a Time," and "All the Things You Are." The last was also issued as a single, backed with a song that was not on the album, "I Believe." The album sold moderately well to the "easy listening" market and found some surprising admirers. One of them was Elvis Presley, who rated the album among his favorites and said that Boyer's "I Believe" inspired him to record the song himself. But Valiant shut down after Four-Star went public, leaving Michael adrift without a marketable talent and apparently doomed to live in his father's shadow.

For his twenty-first birthday, his parents bought him a two-bedroom apartment in upmarket Coldwater Canyon. But having all the trappings of success without the substance to back them up left a bitter taste. In September 1965 police were summoned to 1861 Heather Court by reports of a gunshot and the sound of shattering glass. They found a picture window blown out by a bullet. Michael claimed the gun had been fired by accident, and since he had a permit for the snub-nosed .38 revolver, they took no action.

Two days later, on the night of Thursday, September 23, neighbors called the police again. They found Michael dead in a pool of blood, with a bullet wound to the temple. Also in the apartment were his fiancée, Marilyn Campbell, and a young man named Jon Kirsch, described as Boyer's roommate. The investigating officer, Sergeant James Ryan, told the press: "The circumstances seem to indicate Russian Roulette. There was only one bullet in the six-shot revolver. The other five shells had been placed carefully on their bases, lined up in a row on the table."

Kirsch and Campbell confirmed that, earlier in the day and on several other occasions, Michael had played Russian roulette, but they had never participated. Kirsch said he was watching television in another room when he heard the shot. A moment later, Campbell ran in screaming. "She was so hysterical," said Kirsch, "I couldn't understand her." Police questioned this account, since Campbell had taken the time to remove the gun from Michael's hand and wipe the blood from his face with a towel. They also wondered why the two had not immediately called the police or an ambulance. Campbell told police that, earlier in the evening, she had told Michael she was breaking off their engagement of six weeks. He became morose and said, "I'm going to take care of something that has needed taking care of for some time. I'm a loser and have always been a loser, and I'm going to kill myself if I can't have you." Kirsch reassured Campbell that Michael was "just acting." Shortly thereafter, he fired the fatal shot. Campbell said she and Michael were alone in the den when he did so, but as her back was turned, she couldn't say whether he pulled the trigger intentionally or accidentally.

Investigators were still puzzling over these conflicting accounts when someone else came forward and gave the events a different spin. Sharon Heaslet, a divorcée with two children, explained that she had been Michael's lover before Campbell. They had hoped to marry, but the Boyers opposed it, and she ended the affair. Heaslet had visited Michael on the day of his death to collect some of her belongings. "As he wasn't alone," she said, "we met in the garage. With a smile, he told me he was trying to get over me with another woman. He seemed nervous, which worried me." Michael had also talked to her of suicide, but she believed he was "too much of a coward" to go through with it.[3] Heaslet's story put his actions in perspective. The end of one relationship, followed by the abrupt termination of another, might have caused a despairing Michael to end his life. His death was ruled a suicide.

An estimated 300 people attended the funeral. Each week for the remaining thirteen years of Boyer's life, a florist placed flowers on Michael's grave. Professional even in grief, Boyer flew back to Paris a week after the funeral to complete the few remaining shots of *How to Steal a Million*.

45

Fade to Black

Michael's death was catastrophic for the Boyers. "Charles adjusted better than Pat, I think," said an actress friend, "but you couldn't tell. He wasn't a happy person ever in outward appearance. Pat was devastated, though: Pat, who was always winking and beaming and laughing, and flashing those pretty teeth. Now years would pass and she wouldn't smile."[1] A distraught Boyer called Michael the greatest work of his life. To add to his burdens, his eighty-six-year-old mother died in June 1966.

Over the next year, the Boyers sold all their property and moved to Geneva, Switzerland. A spacious apartment in a distinguished older building at 8 Quai Gustave-Ador, with a view of the lake, became their European home. Two years later, Jean-Pierre Aumont worked on a film in Geneva and renewed his friendship with the Boyers. "I had the impression," he said, "that life for them had stopped at that moment [of Michael's death]. We dined together every day, and it was clear that Charles had become, almost overnight, an old man. He was still friendly, still generous and attentive, but I felt something was broken in him, and life had nothing more to offer."[2]

Rather than endure the European winters, the Boyers also bought a home in Arizona, at 58 Colonia Miramonte in the desert community of Paradise Valley. Low, thick-walled houses were sited along wide roads that wound through a landscape where the only vegetation was cacti and mesquite. Electric golf carts were the main means of getting around within the community. For longer journeys, one took an air-conditioned car, in the Boyers' case, driven by their one servant—a combination cook-houseboy-chauffeur.

They were sufficiently wealthy to live comfortably for the rest of their lives, but Charlie Feldman coaxed Boyer back to work. In the 1960s he acquired the rights to *Casino Royale,* the first of the James Bond novels, hoping to film it as a straight thriller with Sean Connery. When Connery demanded $1 million to participate, Feldman turned it into a spoof, with various actors playing alternative Bonds, including David Niven and Woody Allen. Boyer appears in a single scene as the head of the French secret service, opposite John Huston, William Holden, and Kurt Kasznar as other spymasters. It was a trivial role, but the urge to act transcended personal tragedy. "If I stopped working," Boyer acknowledged, "it would be death."

During breaks from this project, which was shot mainly in Britain and Ireland, Boyer had a small role in a Spanish action comedy variously called *The Hot Line, The Day the Hot Line Got Hot,* and *The Rouble Has Two Faces.* "Phone phreaks," who manipulated telephone lines to make free calls and eavesdrop on others, were a phenomenon at the time, and this feeble film imagines the results if one of them hacked into the line linking Washington and Moscow. Boyer's costar was a weary Robert Taylor as head of the KGB, belatedly attempting comedy at the end of his career. He would die the following year at age fifty-seven of lung cancer, brought on by a lifetime of smoking. Boyer, after a number of attempts, had finally kicked his own smoking habit.

Despite experiencing symptoms of prostatitis, Boyer refused treatment and insisted that he felt well enough to accept a physically demanding role in Gene Saks's film of the Neil Simon play *Barefoot in the Park,* which had just closed on Broadway after three years and 1,530 performances. Jane Fonda plays the lead opposite Robert Redford, repeating his Broadway role. Boyer replaced Kurt Kasznar as Victor Velasco, an eccentric neighbor who introduces some continental complexity into the lives of a young Manhattan lawyer and his new wife. That she is more accepting than her husband of novel experiences provides the film's fragile story. More animated than he had appeared in years, Boyer is charming as the raconteur, gastronome, linguist, and flirt who invites the newlyweds and the wife's mother up to his attic apartment for exotic appetizers, then lures them to Staten Island for dinner at an Albanian restaurant run by old friend Fritz Feld. Mildred Natwick, playing Fonda's frazzled middle-class mother, earned an Academy Award nomination for best supporting actress.

Boyer's next film, *The April Fools,* was tailored to the self-effacing comic talent of Jack Lemmon, whose company had bought the script. The intention had been to repeat his pairing with Shirley MacLaine in *The Apartment* and *Irma la Douce,* but MacLaine was too busy campaigning for Bobby Kennedy. In her place, Lemmon and director Stuart Rosenberg hired French actress Catherine Deneuve, an art-house darling following her work in

The Umbrellas of Cherbourg and *Belle de Jour* but unknown to the larger American public.

In common with *The Graduate* and Blake Edwards's *The Party,* made the previous year, *The April Fools* is a fish-out-of-water comedy in which an innocent is thrown into the deep end of the high life and extricates himself with the help of another lost soul. Lemmon is once again a sweaty struggler on the corporate greasy pole. Invited to the apartment of his boss (Peter Lawford), he finds himself at a rowdy cocktail party where beautiful people compete in gaudiness with a collection of avant-garde art. The one congenial soul is Deneuve, with whom Lemmon flees, unaware that she is his boss's alienated wife. For the rest of the night, they wander through a city competing with itself to invent new and eccentric diversions. At the Safari Club, where wild animals prowl the edges of the dance floor, they meet Myrna Loy, who takes them home to her husband (Boyer), identified, accurately, as "a displaced Parisian." While he and Lemmon duel with foils, Loy reads Deneuve's future with tarot cards and predicts that she and Lemmon will find happiness in Paris. Their affectionate good nature and impeccable manners make Boyer and Loy the film's sole representatives of rationality. They are the true April fools, even more out of sync with their culture than Deneuve and Lemmon.

In increasingly poor health, Boyer felt less inclined to work, particularly after the death of Charles Feldman in 1968, which severed one of his last links with Hollywood. As Paris became increasingly inhospitable following the 1968 student revolution, he and Pat spent more time in Arizona, returning to Geneva only when the desert summer became uncomfortable.

During one such return to Europe in the spring of 1969, he took a small role in *The Madwoman of Chaillot,* shot at Victorine. When Jean Giraudoux wrote the play in 1948, Paris's older districts were crumbling after centuries of neglect. Architect Le Corbusier even suggested leveling the ancient Marais quarter and erecting high-rises in its place. Giraudoux's satiric response was to imagine a consortium of bankers and military men plotting to drill for oil within sight of the Eiffel Tower. They are opposed by a handful of eccentrics, among them Countess Aurelia (Katharine Hepburn), who still lives in an imaginary belle epoque and dresses accordingly. She rallies the outcasts of Paris and puts the developers on trial. The play's imaginary Paris, which exists largely in the minds of Aurelia and her supporters, suggested a similarly insubstantial film treatment. Instead, production designer Ray Simm built a facsimile Paris as solid as the city itself, inconsistent with Hepburn and her tattered group.

Director John Huston resigned seventeen days before the start date. British director Bryan Forbes took over but lacked the authority to handle the miscellany of fading international stars and character actors, including Danny Kaye, Oskar Homolka, Yul Brynner, Giulietta Masina, and Boyer in a cameo role. Forbes's authority was further undermined by the presence of Federico Fellini, who arrived, uninvited, and stood in silence at the edge of the set during every scene in which his wife, Masina, appeared.

Paris under threat reflected the process taking place in Hollywood as the American film industry presided over its own demise. In 1970 MGM, assuming that the dwindling and overwhelmingly young cinema audience would prefer intimate personal films shot in natural light on location with handheld cameras, auctioned off all the props, costumes, and furniture it had accumulated over half a century. Twentieth Century–Fox sold its former back lot as real estate and watched Century City rise from the ruins. Universal put itself on exhibit, turning the filmmaking process into a carnival and inviting the public to witness it—for a price. All the studios closed their special-effects departments, as the escapism of science fiction and fantasy clearly had no place in the new Hollywood. David Niven's forecast that cinema was a thing of the past appeared to be coming true.

It took courage, not to mention a sense of humor, for septuagenarian Boyer to play a character who was even older—by three centuries. He never explained his reasons for agreeing to take the role of the High Lama in the ill-fated musical version of James Hilton's visionary novel *Lost Horizon*. John Gielgud, who pleaded a particularly large tax bill, confessed that the film contained "not a moment that gives one the slightest opportunity to act and I feel a bit ashamed of the bribery that makes me accept it."[3] Money could not have been Boyer's motive. Nor did the role demand even a fraction of his acting skills. He has only one scene, with Peter Finch, for which he endured three hours of makeup each morning. (A joke circulated that the cosmeticians' task was to make Boyer look younger, not older.) A mane of silver hair and skillful lighting by veteran Robert Surtees allows Boyer's still-resonant voice to carry the scene, one of the more dignified in a film that was almost universally reviled.

As a bibliophile, Boyer was amused to see that the library of Shangri-La, supposedly containing the essence of everything great in human thought, relied heavily on Reader's Digest Condensed Books. In 1970 Boyer had cut one of his last ties with the past when he donated his book collection, numbering about 3,000 volumes, to UCLA. The university had already accepted the library of the French Research Foundation, bringing Boyer's total contribution to about 10,000 volumes. According to the UCLA catalog, this included "a 1771 edition of Diderot's *Encyclopedie* and complete or long runs of several major French literary and satiric journals as well as carefully assembled ephemera: posters, press clippings, and other materials."

It was also with a sense of finality that, in June 1971, Boyer wrote a new will, leaving his entire estate, worth $1.8 million (about $5 million in 2020 dollars) to Pat. His principal asset was the Arizona house, along with shares in Four-Star International and quantities of cash in various accounts. In 1974 he made some changes to the will that suggested suspicions of Pat's declining health. If she died before him, everything would go to her brothers. He added an additional bequest of £10,000 to Pat's mother, Hannah Paterson. As executor he appointed Marjorie L. Everett, described as his personal representative. Everett was the Boyers' neighbor in Arizona; it was in her house that Pat would pass her last months and where both Boyers would die.

Lost Horizon closed the book on Boyer's Hollywood career. He never fulfilled Walter Wanger's ambition to make him the new Rudolph Valentino, in part because the female audience no longer yearned for a lover who threw women over his saddle and carried them off to his tent. Women might occasionally succumb to the sort of brute represented by Stanley Kowalski in *A Streetcar Named Desire,* but most expected to be wooed, not kidnapped. They wanted a man they could introduce to their friends and who came complete with an engagement ring and a solid job. The urge once satisfied by Valentino was now gratified by Rock Hudson.

Boyer survived as the perennial displaced person, a Graham Greene character in a James Bond world. The American cinema had little use for him, but in Europe, his reputation remained high. Since directing the enigmatic and, for many, impenetrable *Last Year in Marienbad,* Alain Resnais had made his peace with the mainstream cinema. He even filmed some theater successes from the 1930s, including Henry Bernstein's *Mélo,* which had once been a hit for Boyer. Resnais had long wanted to work with Boyer. According to scriptwriter Jorge Semprun, "All Resnais wants to do is make a film starring [Jean Paul] Belmondo and Boyer, with music by Stephen Sondheim. He couldn't care less what the subject is, so long as he has those three men."

Resnais realized his dream in *Stavisky . . .,* written by Semprun and scored (unmemorably) by Sondheim. It is an account of the 1934 fall of the financier whose empire, supported by bribery on an epic scale, would be exposed as an accumulation of smoke reflected in a multiplicity of mirrors.

Resnais never intended the film, originally called *Biarritz-Bonheur* (a slang term for French high life), to be a Stavisky biopic; rather, it was supposed to be a panorama of the period that had allowed his swindles to flourish. But as the distributors pressured him, Resnais compromised with the title *Stavisky . . .,* the ellipsis suggesting there is much more to tell.

With his beautiful wife, former Chanel model Arlette Simon, on his arm and bodyguard Jo Jo le Terreur at his back, Serge Stavisky was the uncrowned king of Paris until his violent and suspicious death revealed the extent of his swindles, not to mention his disreputable early life as a con man and a pimp. At times, Resnais's film, sumptuously designed by Jacques Saulnier, resembles a *concours d'elegance;* such an automobile fashion parade provides one of the film's most stylish set pieces (rigged, of course, to ensure that Arlette's car wins).

Modishly dressed in Yves St. Laurent's pastiches of 1920s tailoring, Belmondo brings Stavisky to life. Boyer's character, Baron Jean Raoul, lost his own fortune many years ago and now survives on charm, style, and impeccable manners. The embodiment of noblesse oblige, he represents all those members of the French aristocracy and high society bewitched by Stavisky's charm and blinded by their own greed. Raoul confesses that he understands nothing of business. "There is no need," smiles Stavisky. "You just need to have confidence in *me.*" The Baron is so completely taken in by the charming Stavisky that, right up to the end, he cannot believe the man is a fake. In his rueful realization of how far he has been misled by the object of his affection and admiration, the Baron may reflect Boyer's disappointment at the loss of his own charming but wayward son.

With silver hair, mustache, and beard and wearing a succession of perfectly cut suits, Boyer has seldom appeared so dignified or in such complete control of his performance. For the character of Raoul, he had no problem finding motivation—the model was Boyer himself. Resnais reminds us of Boyer's stage triumphs when the Baron helps a young actress audition for a role at Stavisky's theater, reading the male part in a scene from a Guitry play. Intrigued, Stavisky steps up to read for the next candidate, except that the play is Giraudoux's *Intermezzo* and his character is a phantom—the best performance of his life, decrees the Baron over the ruins of Stavisky's empire.

Against the advice of Belmondo, who also coproduced, the film debuted at the 1974 Cannes Film Festival, where it was almost universally dismissed. "A massacre!" Belmondo recalled. "Critics have never prevented me from sleeping—except on *Stavisky. . . .*" But the jury, chaired by René Clair, had the good sense to exempt Boyer from the film's general condemnation and awarded him the Palme d'Or as best actor, shared with Jack Nicholson for *The Last Detail*. Equally agreeably, *Stavisky . . .* went on to be a major international success.

A Matter of Time, also known as *Nina*, was Boyer's last film, and it might have been planned with that in mind. Vincente Minnelli was among the last representatives of the Hollywood polish that Boyer so admired in MGM productions. His character, an aged Italian count who philosophically accepts the passing of the years, might have been tailored to his dwindling skills.

The film was almost not made. Despite having Ingrid Bergman and his daughter Liza as stars, the seventy-three-year-old Minnelli was turned down by every major studio owing to fears about his health. He found an improbable backer in Samuel Z. Arkoff, whose American International Pictures specialized in horror, science fiction, and beach-party movies. His success in these disreputable genres made Arkoff anxious to leave a more lasting legacy than *Attack of the Crab Monsters* and *How to Stuff a Wild Bikini,* and he agreed to back *A Matter of Time* in collaboration with producers in Rome, where it would be shot.

Maurice Druoun's source novel was inspired by the last days of Italian eccentric Marchesa Luisa Casati, whose sensational life as the lover of poet Gabriele D'Annunzio ended in poverty and delusion. The Contessa Lucretia Sanziani lives in Rome's once grand but now shabby Imperial Hotel. Nina (Liza Minnelli) arrives from the country to work there as a maid and is dazzled by the flamboyant dowager (Ingrid Bergman) who still lives in the imaginary world of her past fame and beauty. She encourages the starstruck girl to exploit her singing talent—an excuse for some grossly overproduced musical numbers in which Liza, in a succession of lavish gowns, storms through opulent Roman interiors singing at the top of her lungs.

Boyer plays the Contessa's husband, Count Carlos Sanziani, from whom she has been estranged for forty years. It was the first time since *Arch of Triumph* that he and Bergman acted together. In his single scene, he calls on her at the hotel and is surprised but not particularly distressed by her poverty; he has long since relinquished responsibility for her welfare. Still imagining herself young, the Contessa believes he has come to persuade her not to run off with a long-dead lover. In a performance with more than a few echoes of Gloria Swanson in *Sunset Boulevard,* Bergman prowls the mean little room, boasting that her new lover satisfies her as the Count never did. Not realizing that his delusional wife is living in the past, he expresses distaste at her indulging in sex at her age, as well as surprise that this particular admirer is still alive. "Age has taught you nothing," he says wearily. He leaves her to her fantasies, but not before instructing the hotel manager, "If anything happens, I *don't* want to be informed."

As the shoot stretched from fourteen weeks to twenty, Boyer was anxious to return to the calm of Geneva and to Pat. Acts of terrorism were a daily feature of life in Rome. Prime Minister Aldo Moro would be kidnapped and murdered not far from the studio, and director Pier Paolo Pasolini would be killed nearby. The film's producer and Liza's husband at the time, Jack Haley Jr., savagely cut the film, resulting in no improvement to its commercial fortunes. The truncated version had a brief European run in 1977, a melancholy coda to the distinguished careers of Boyer and Bergman.

46

The Role of a Lifetime

In February 1978 the Boyers closed the Geneva apartment and relocated to Arizona for the winter. It was their forty-fourth wedding anniversary, and friends had arranged a small gathering in Los Angeles. Boyer, in increasing pain from arthritis and other chronic complaints, took the opportunity to enter the hospital for a checkup, and he persuaded Pat to have her own health assessed. The tests revealed that although Boyer's conditions were not life-threatening, Pat had advanced colon and liver cancer. Doctors gave her less than a year to live.

So began the last act of Boyer's life and marriage and the beginning of what one newspaper called "the most intense role of his acting career."[1] Once he had absorbed the news, he had one paramount response: *she must not know.* He explained her condition to their few remaining friends and insisted that they maintain the fiction of her good health. A doctor was persuaded to write a medical certificate attributing Pat's growing debility to hepatitis.

In May they returned to Geneva to terminate their lease on the apartment and remove their remaining belongings. Back in Arizona, Boyer assured a puzzled Pat that her lack of energy and weight loss would be reversed by rest and a change in diet. They hired a servant, and Pat—always a dog lover—acquired a terrier. When she became too tired to go out, she rested most of the day with Boyer at her side. He refused to hire nurses to share the burden of her care. "He protected her, remained with her, comforted her," wrote the local newspaper, "made plans for the Christmas he knew she would never see."

To maintain the pretense that they would leave Arizona and spend the summer somewhere cooler, Boyer sent their servant on holiday and closed the house. They moved into the home of longtime friend and neighbor Marjorie T. Everett, a retired widow who lived at 6802 Desert Fairways Drive. As her houseguest, Boyer was free to devote himself to Pat. They played gin rummy, and he read to her, mostly from the English literary classics she had known since childhood. Sometimes he would read a play, taking all the roles and changing his accent and intonation.

In August, Boyer set out to read aloud Charles Dickens's *Martin Chuzzlewit*. He never finished it. On the twenty-third, Pat spent a quiet day in bed. They played gin and then fell asleep together, hand in hand. At dawn, the coldness of her touch woke him. She had peacefully slipped away at about three in the morning. She was sixty-seven years old.

They had few friends in Arizona, so the funeral took place in Los Angeles. Boyer did not attend, pleading his own ill health. The day after, he found Pat's dog scrabbling frantically at the door to her bedroom. After persuading someone to look after the dog, he phoned a friend. He was racked with pain, he said—the worst pain he had ever felt. He kept repeating, "If only it could have been me." Shortly thereafter, he swallowed three times the recommended dose of Seconal. He was found unconscious and, despite twenty minutes' effort by paramedics, could not be revived. At a small private ceremony at Holy Cross Cemetery in Los Angeles, he was buried under a single gravestone with Pat, next to Michael.

47

Envoi

Events have conspired to make Charles Boyer less well known to modern filmgoers than he should be. He was an only child whose one child died childless, ending his line as definitively as the snuffing of a candle flame. His few friends spoke frequently of his reticence. He left no diary and no extensive correspondence, and during his life he refused all requests to be interviewed at any length. He predated the era of film studies and cinematheques, but had they existed, he would have evaded their attentions as well. "He is innately suspicious," observed a 1937 profile, "and distrusts anything with which he is not thoroughly familiar."[1] Had he wished, he could have remade himself, as did many other stars such as Cesar Romero, Fred MacMurray, Lucille Ball, and John Forsythe, some of them his friends. He could have clowned in comic-book TV, parodied himself in sitcoms, appeared in feuilletons such as *Dynasty* or *Dallas,* or joined other wizened veterans in horror films. He flirted with this idea once or twice but quickly shut the door on it—seeing this path as a tightening spiral into conformity during which his true achievements would have been fatally marred.

"Although his screen image was often frivolous and lightweight," wrote critic David Thomson, "Boyer's career speaks for the durability of a dedicated professional. But he did more than survive; he kept intact that very 'continental' flirtatious waywardness that made him a Hollywood exotic. It is no small accomplishment to have maintained his rather vacant intimations of gallic romance in the face of constant parody and imitation. Even at the height of his comic notoriety in America as the French lover, sighing with thoughts of 'the casbah,' he was a terrific and generous actor."[2] It is an evenhanded eulogy of which Boyer would have approved.

Filmography

Only feature film appearances are included. The film title is followed by the director and Boyer's character (in parentheses).

1976. *Nina.* Vincente Minnelli. (Count Sanziani)

1974. *Stavisky. . . .* Alain Resnais. (Baron Jean Raoul)

1973. *Lost Horizon.* Charles Jarrott. (High Lama)

1969. *The Madwoman of Chaillot.* Bryan Forbes. (Broker)

1969. *The April Fools.* Stuart Rosenberg. (André Greenlaw)

1968. *The Day the Hot Line Got Hot.* Etienne Périer. (Vostov)

1967. *Barefoot in the Park.* Gene Saks. (Victor Velasco)

1967. *Casino Royale.* Val Guest and others. (Legrand)

1966. *Is Paris Burning?* René Clément. (Doctor Monod)

1966. *How to Steal a Million.* William Wyler. (DeSolnay)

1965. *A Very Special Favor.* Michael Gordon. (Michel Boullard)

1963. *Love Is a Ball.* David Swift. (Etienne Pimm)

1962. *Adorable Julia.* Alfred Weidenman. (Michael Grosselyn)

1962. *The Four Horsemen of the Apocalypse.* Vincente Minnelli. (Marcel Desnoyers)

1961. *Demons at Midnight.* Marc Allégret. (Pierre Guérande)

1961. *Fanny.* Joshua Logan. (César)

1958. *The Buccaneer.* Anthony Quinn. (Dominique You)

1958. *Maxime.* Henri Verneuil (Maxime Cherpray)

1957. *La Parisienne.* Michel Boisrond. (Prince Charles)

1956. *Paris, Palace Hotel.* Henri Verneuil. (Henri Delormel)

1956. *Around the World in Eighty Days*. Michael Anderson. (Monsieur Gasse)

1956. *La Fortuna de Essere Donna/What a Woman!* Alessandro Blasetti. (Count Gregorio Sennetti)

1955. *Nana*. Christian-Jaque. (Count Muffat)

1955. *The Cobweb*. Vincente Minnelli. (Dr. Devanal)

1953. *Boum sur Paris*. Maurice de Canonge. (Himself)

1953. *Madame de. . . .* Max Ophuls. (General André de . . .)

1952. *The Happy Time*. Richard Fleischer. (Jacques Bonnard)

1952. *Thunder in the East*. Charles Vidor. (Prime Minister Singh)

1952. *The First Legion*. Douglas Sirk. (Father Arnoux)

1951. *The 13th Letter*. Otto Preminger. (Dr. Paul Laurent)

1948. *Arch of Triumph*. Lewis Milestone. (Dr. Ravic)

1948. *A Woman's Vengeance*. Zoltan Korda. (Henry Maurier)

1946. *Cluny Brown*. Ernst Lubitsch. (Adam Belinski)

1945. *Confidential Agent*. Herman Shumlin. (Luis Denard)

1944. *Together Again*. Charles Vidor. (George Corday)

1944. *Gaslight*. George Cukor. (Gregory Anton)

1943. *Flesh and Fantasy*. Julien Duvivier. (Paul Gaspar)

1943. *The Constant Nymph*. Edmund Goulding. (Lewis Dodd)

1942. *Tales of Manhattan*. Julien Duvivier. (Paul Orman)

1941. *Appointment for Love*. William A. Seiter. (André Cassil)

1941. *Hold Back the Dawn*. Mitchell Leisen. (Georges Iscovescu)

1941. *Back Street*. Robert Stevenson. (Walter Saxel)

1940. *All This and Heaven Too*. Anatole Litvak. (Duc de Praslin)

1939. *Le Corsaire*. Marc Allégret. (Kid Jackson)

1939. *When Tomorrow Comes*. John M. Stahl. (Philip Chagal)

1939. *Love Affair*. Leo McCarey. (Michel Marnay)

1938. *Algiers*. John Cromwell. (Pépé le Moko)

1938. *Orage*. Marc Allégret. (André Pascaud)

1937. *Tovarich*. Anatole Litvak. (Prince Mikail Ouratieff)

1937. *Conquest*. Clarence Brown. (Napoleon Bonaparte)

1937. *History Is Made at Night*. Frank Borzage. (Paul Dumond)

1936. *The Garden of Allah*. Richard Boleslavski. (Boris Androvsky)

1936. *Mayerling*. Anatole Litvak. (Archduke Rudolf)

1935. *Shanghai*. James Flood. (Dmitri Koslov)

1935. *Break of Hearts*. Philip Moeller. (Franz Roberti)

1935. *Private Worlds*. Gregory La Cava. (Dr. Charles Monet)

1934. *Caravan/Caravane*. Erik Charell. (Latzi)

1934. *Le Bonheur*. Marcel L'Herbier. (Philippe Lutcher)

1934. *Liliom*. Fritz Lang. (Liliom Zadowski)

1934. *Thunder in the East/La Bataille*. Victor Tourjansky. (Yorisaka)

1933. *Ich und Die Kaiserin*. Paul Martin. (Duke)

1933. *Les Amoureux*. Marcel L'Herbier. (Comte Georges de Dasetta)

1933. *I.F. 1 Ne Répond Plus*. Karl Hartl. (Ellisen)

1932. *Red-Headed Woman*. Jack Conway. (Albert)

1932. *The Man from Yesterday*. Berthold Viertel. (René Gaudin)

1932. *Tumultes*. Robert Siodmak. (Ralph Schwarz)

1931. *Le Procès de Mary Dugan* (Prosecutor)

1931. *The Magnificent Lie*. Berthold Viertel. (Jacques)

1931. *Big House*. Pál Fejös. (Fred Morgan)

1930. *War Nurse*. Edgar Selwyn. (French Surgeon)

1930. *Barcarolle d'amour. Brand in der Oper*. Henry Roussell. (André le Kerdec)

1929. *Le Capitaine Fracasse*. Alberto Cavalcanti. (Duc de Vallombreuse)

1928. *La Ronde Infernale*. Maurice Radiguet as Luitz Morat. (René)

1922. *Le Grillon du Foyer*. Jean Manoussi. (Edouard Caleb)

1921. *Chantelouve*. Etienne Rey. (Roger de Thièvres)

1920. *L'Homme du Large*. Marcel L'Herbier. (Guenn la Taupe)

Notes

Preface

1. *Los Angeles Times,* October 11, 2018.

I. The Eyes of a Stranger

1. Guy Chassagnard, "Birth and Affirmation of an Actor: Charles Boyer at the Theater," talk at Figeac, October 24, 2019.
2. Swindell, *Reluctant Lover.*
3. Swindell, *Reluctant Lover.*
4. "Charles Boyer's True Life Story," *Modern Screen,* February 1937.

2. All Quiet on the Western Front

1. "Charles Boyer's True Life Story," *Modern Screen,* February 1937.
2. Guégan, *Cité Champagne.*
3. "Charles Boyer's True Life Story."

3. Paris

1. Du Bois, *Raphaël Duflos.*
2. Guy Chassagnard, "Birth and Affirmation of an Actor: Charles Boyer at the Theater," talk at Figeac, October 24, 2019.
3. Chassagnard, "Birth and Affirmation of an Actor."
4. Chassagnard, "Birth and Affirmation of an Actor."

4. On the Road

1. "Portrait with a French Accent," *Photoplay,* July 1938.
2. Guy Chassagnard, "Birth and Affirmation of an Actor: Charles Boyer at the Theater," talk at Figeac, October 24, 2019.
3. Chassagnard, "Birth and Affirmation of an Actor."

5. To Be Famous and to Be Loved

1. "Portrait with a French Accent," *Photoplay,* July 1938.

2. Guy Chassagnard, "Birth and Affirmation of an Actor: Charles Boyer at the Theater," talk at Figeac, October 24, 2019.

3. Capua, *Anatole Litvak.*

6. Movies

1. Robert A. Monsees, "Charles Boyer," *Films in Review,* May 1971.

2. Howard Sharpe, "The Strange Past of Charles Boyer," *Liberty,* November 1939.

3. Faivre-Zellner, *Firmin Gémier, Heralt du Thetre Populaire.*

7. Bernstein

1. Goding, *Henry Bernstein.*

2. François Mauriac, *Nouvelle Revue Francaise,* January 1923.

3. Aumont, *Sun and Shadow.*

4. Chevalier, *Man in the Straw Hat.*

8. On Trial

1. Hart-Davis, *Hugh Walpole.*

2. Amy Fine Collins, "A Perfect Star," *Vanity Fair,* April 2000.

9. Ufa and After

1. Buñuel, *My Last Breath.*

2. Baxter, *Hollywood Exiles.*

3. Dumont, *Robert Siodmak.*

10. Mid-Atlantic

1. *Time,* June 13, 1932.

2. Baxter, *Hollywood Exiles.*

3. "Jean Murat et les histoires de l'Ile d'Oie," in *Charles Boyer. Sa Vie. Ses Films* (Paris: n.p., March 10, 1937).

4. Viertel, *Kindness of Strangers.*

5. Zuckmayer, *Part of Myself.*

11. A Ride on the Carousel

1. McGilligan, *Nature of the Beast.*

12. The Boyer Type

1. *Ciné-Miroir,* August 4, 1933.

13. The Love of His Life

1. "Charles Boyer's True Life Story," *Modern Screen,* February 1937.
2. *New York Times,* March 23, 1934.
3. Robert Lord, American Film Institute Oral History.
4. "Charles Boyer's True Life Story."
5. *New York Times,* September 28, 1934.
6. Swindell, *Reluctant Lover.*

14. Japanese Sandman

1. Dan Thomas, "Girls' Hearts Throb at New French Screen Idol," *San Bernardino County (CA) Sun,* June 2, 1935.
2. Bernstein, *Walter Wanger.*
3. Amy Fine Collins, "A Perfect Star," *Vanity Fair,* April 2000.

15. Think American

1. Swindell, *Reluctant Lover.*
2. *New York Times,* July 20, 1935.
3. *New York Times,* July 20, 1935.

16. Discord

1. *New York Times,* July 20, 1935.
2. Greene, *Graham Greene Film Reader.*
3. Swindell, *Reluctant Lover.*
4. *New York Times,* July 23, 1936.

17. The Sleeping Prince

1. Capua, *Anatole Litvak.*
2. *New York Times Book Review and Magazine,* March 26, 1922.
3. Greene, *Graham Greene Film Reader.*
4. Greene, *Graham Greene Film Reader.*
5. Capua, *Anatole Litvak.*

18. "Only God and I Know What Is in My Heart"

1. *New York Times,* April 3, 1936.
2. American Film Institute Catalog.

3. Selznick, *Memo from David O. Selznick.*
4. Selznick, *Memo from David O. Selznick.*
5. *New York Times,* November 20, 1936.
6. *Daily Variety,* October 31, 1936
7. *New York Times,* November 20, 1936.

19. The Best Headwaiter in Europe

1. Selznick, *Memo from David O. Selznick.*
2. Bernstein, *Walter Wanger.*
3. Bernstein, *Walter Wanger.*
4. Bernstein, *Walter Wanger.*
5. Oller, *Jean Arthur.*
6. Thomson, *New Biographical Dictionary of Cinema.*
7. *Daily Variety,* March 31, 1937.

20. Immortal Longings

1. Viertel, *Kindness of Strangers.*
2. Rifkin, *Sun and Her Stars.*
3. Rifkin, *Sun and Her Stars.*
4. Young, *Clarence Brown.*
5. Young, *Clarence Brown.*
6. Greene, *Graham Greene Film Reader.*
7. *Variety,* October 27, 1937.

21. Exiles

1. Letter from Robert Florey to the author, January 17, 1974.
2. Robert Lord, American Film Institute Oral History, May 6, 1972.
3. Lord Oral History.
4. https://www.derekwinnert.com/all-this-and-heaven-too-1940-bette-davis-charles-boyer-jeffrey-lynn-classic-movie-review-2741/.
5. Lord Oral History.

22. Lazy and Hot and Happy

1. Frank Nugent, *New York Times,* December 25, 1937.
2. L. Massar, "Michèle Morgan, ou le Roman d'une Jeune Fille Pauvre," *Lecture Pour Tous,* May 7, 1946.
3. Greene, *Graham Greene Film Reader.*

23. "Come with Me to the Casbah"

1. Barton, *Hedy Lamarr.*

2. Shearer, *Beautiful.*
3. Barton, *Hedy Lamarr.*
4. Barton, *Hedy Lamarr.*
5. Barton, *Hedy Lamarr.*
6. Selznick, *Memo from David O. Selznick.*
7. *Cinématographie Française,* September 1938.

24. Sex on the High Seas

1. Lombardi, *Allan Dwan.*
2. Baxter, *Hollywood Exiles.*
3. Jewell and Harben, *RKO Story.*
4. Chassagnard, *Charles Boyer.*

26. Blood, Toil, Sweat, and Tears

1. *New York Times,* August 17, 1939.
2. Catalog, Bonham's Auction House, London, November 22, 2018. The letter was sold at auction to a private buyer and has not been published.
3. Wood Soames, "Charles Boyer Tries Propaganda. French Star Freed from Army to Deliver Lecture Tour for La Belle France," *Oakland (CA) Tribune,* November 29, 1939.

27. The World's Best-Dressed Governess

1. Capua, *Anatole Litvak.*
2. Capua, *Anatole Litvak.*

28. The War at Home

1. Cull, *Selling War.*
2. Lieder, *Myrna Loy.*
3. André David, *Revue des Deux Mondes,* October 1978.
4. Henri Diamant-Berger, "One Free Frenchman among 61,375" (oral history).
5. Annabella Charpentier, "Mon Ami Charles Boyer," *Elle,* July 22, 1948.
6. Aumont, *Sun and Shadow.*
7. Dalio, *Mes Années Folles.*
8. Aumont, *Sun and Shadow.*
9. Aumont, *Sun and Shadow.*

29. A Voice Singing in the Snow

1. *Variety,* June 12, 1940.
2. *New York Times,* July 5, 1940.
3. Capua, *Anatole Litvak.*

30. The Golden Door

1. Brackett, *It's the Pictures that Got Small.*
2. Brackett, *It's the Pictures that Got Small.*

31. The Most Popular Frenchman in America

1. Chevalier, *Man in the Straw Hat.*
2. Rinilla, *Margaret Sullavan.*
3. Leaming, *If This Was Happiness.*
4. Duberman, *Paul Robeson.*
5. Antoine de Saint Exupéry, letter in the author's collection.
6. André David, *Revue des Deux Mondes,* October 1978.

32. Love and Death

1. Lejeune, *Chestnuts in Her Lap.*
2. *New York Times,* July 24, 1943.
3. Capra, *Name above the Title.*
4. Capra, *Name above the Title.*

33. Not What It Looks Like

1. Selznick, *Memo from David O. Selznick.*
2. Selznick, *Memo from David O. Selznick.*
3. Selznick, *Memo from David O. Selznick.*
4. Smit, *Ingrid Bergman.*
5. Smit, *Ingrid Bergman.*

34. Love in a Cold Climate

1. "A Gentleman Who Held in His Arms the Biggest Stars of the Screen," *Cinemonde,* November 1959.
2. Greene, *Graham Greene Film Reader.*
3. Agee, *Agee on Film.*
4. *New York Times,* November 3, 1945.
5. Bacall, *Lauren Bacall.*

35. Stranger in a Strange Land

1. *London Sunday Express,* {date}.
2. *La Depeche,* March 4, 2012.
3. Conversation with the author, London, 1978.
4. *New Yorker,* January 24, 1959.

5. Remarque, *Arch of Triumph.*
6. *New Yorker,* May 22, 1948.
7. Bedford, *Aldous Huxley.*

36. "Why, This Is Hell, nor Am I out of It"

1. Florey, *Hollywood d'Hier et d'Aujourd'hui.*
2. *New York Times,* April 21, 1948.
3. *New Yorker,* April 24, 1948.
4. Farrow, *What Falls Away.*
5. Smit, *Ingrid Bergman.*
6. John Simon, "Don Juan in Hell," *New York Magazine,* September 4, 2000.
7. "Charles Laughton: The Happy Ham," *Time,* March 31, 1952.
8. "Charles Laughton."
9. Morley, *John Gielgud.*

37. No Fixed Place of Abode

1. UCLA Catalog.
2. Farrow, *What Falls Away.*
3. Farrow, *What Falls Away.*
4. Minne, *Louis Jourdan.*
5. Halliday, *Sirk on Sirk.*
6. Halliday, *Sirk on Sirk.*
7. Halliday, *Sirk on Sirk.*
8. Smith, *Walter Hampden.*
9. *New York Times,* April 28, 1951.
10. *Variety,* January 24, 1951.

38. One Star Short

1. Morley, *Other Side of the Moon.*
2. Bacall, *Lauren Bacall.*
3. Morley, *Other Side of the Moon.*
4. Davis, *Mary Martin.*

39. Superficially Superficial

1. Flanner, *Paris Was Yesterday.*
2. Ustinov, *Dear Me.*
3. *Le Monde,* March 30, 1953.
4. Flanner, *Paris Was Yesterday.*
5. *Manchester Guardian,* February 14, 2013.

40. Great Body, Lovely Soul

1. Vignaud, *Henri Verneuil*.

42. Men of Distinction

1. Nissen, *Agnes Moorehead on Radio, Stage and Television*.
2. "Bed Scenes Aren't Fun Says Actor Rock Hudson," *Daily Record*, March 31, 1965.
3. Wansell, *Terrance Rattigan*.

43. Calm before the Storm

1. *New York Times*, April 25, 1963.
2. Maugham, introduction to *Theatre*.
3. *New York Times*, November 10, 1966.

44. Man and Boy

1. Farrow, *What Falls Away*.
2. *Desert Sun*, September 23, 1965; *New York Times*, September 24, 1965.
3. *Los Angeles Times*, September 24, 1965.

45. Fade to Black

1. *Arizona Republic*, September 3, 1978.
2. Aumont, *Sun and Shadow*.
3. Morley, *John Gielgud*.

46. The Role of a Lifetime

1. *Arizona Republic*, September 3, 1978.

47. Envoi

1. "Charles Boyer's True Life Story," *Modern Screen*, February 1937.
2. Thomson, *New Biographical Dictionary of Cinema*.

Bibliography

Agee, James. *Agee on Film*. New York: McDowell Obolensky, 1958.

Aumont, Jean-Pierre. *Sun and Shadow: An Autobiography*. New York: Norton, 1976.

Bacall, Lauren. *Lauren Bacall: By Myself*. New York: Doubleday, 1978.

Barton, Ruth. *Hedy Lamarr: The Most Beautiful Woman in Film*. Lexington: University Press of Kentucky, 2010.

Baxter, John. *The Hollywood Exiles*. New York: Doubleday, 1976.

———. *Hollywood in the Thirties*. London: Tantivy, 1971.

Bedford, Sybille. *Aldous Huxley: A Biography*. London: Chatto & Windus/Collins London, 1974.

Bernstein, Matthew. *Walter Wanger: Hollywood Independent*. Minneapolis: University of Minnesota Press, 2000.

Brackett, Charles. *It's the Pictures that Got Small*. New York: Columbia University Press, 2014.

Buñuel, Luis. *My Last Breath*. London: Jonathan Cape, 1984.

Capra, Frank. *The Name above the Title: An Autobiography*. London: W. H. Allen, 1972.

Capua, Michelangelo. *Anatole Litvak: The Life and Films*. Jefferson, NC: McFarland, 2015.

Chassagnard, Guy. *Charles Boyer: Profession—Acteur*. Paris: Segnat, 2018.

Chevalier, Maurice. *I Remember It Well*. New York: Macmillan, 1970.

———. *The Man in the Straw Hat: My Story*. London: Odhams, 1950.

Cull, Nicholas John. *Selling War: The British Propaganda Campaign against American "Neutrality" in World War II*. London: Oxford University Press, 1996.

Dalio, Marcel. *Mes Années Folles*. Paris: Ramsay, 1993.

Davis, Ronald L. *Mary Martin, Broadway Legend*. Norman: University of Oklahoma Press, 2008.

Duberman, Martin. *Paul Robeson: A Biography*. New York: Open Road, 1995.

Du Bois, Albert. *Raphaël Duflos*. Paris: Sansot, 1923.

Dumont, Hervé. *Robert Siodmak: Le Maitre du Film Noir*. Paris: L'Age d'Homme, 1996.

Faivre-Zellner, Catherine. *Firmin Gémier, Heralt du Thetre Populaire*. Rennes, France: Presses Universitaires de Rennes, 2006.

Farrow, Mia. *What Falls Away: A Memoir*. New York: Doubleday, 1997.

Flanner, Janet. *Paris Was Yesterday 1925–1939*. London: Penguin, 1981.

Florey, Robert. *Hollywood d'Hier et d'Aujourd'hui*. Paris: Prisma, 1948.

Bibliography

Frings, Ketti. *Hold Back the Dawn.* New York: Triangle Books, 1942.

Goding, Stowell C. *Henry Bernstein: The Evolution of a Playwright.* Madison: University of Wisconsin, 1942.

Greene, Graham. *The Graham Greene Film Reader.* Manchester, UK: Carcanet, 1993.

Guégan, Gerald. *Cité Champagne, esc. i, appt. 289, 95—Argenteuil.* Paris: Grasset, 2006.

Halliday, Jon. *Sirk on Sirk.* London: Secker & Warburg/British Film Institute, 1971.

Hart-Davis, Rupert. *Hugh Walpole: A Biography.* New York: Harcourt Brace, 1962.

Higham, Charles, and Joel Greenberg. *Hollywood in the Forties.* London: Tantivy, 1970.

Higham, Charles, and Roy Moseley. *Princess Merle.* New York: Coward McCann, 1984.

Jewell, Richard B., and Vernon Harben. *The RKO Story.* New York: Arlington House, 1982.

Leaming, Barbara. *If This Was Happiness: A Biography of Rita Hayworth.* New York: Random House, 1990.

Lejeune, C. A. *Chestnuts in Her Lap 1936–1946.* London: Phoenix House, 1947.

Lieder, Emily W. *Myrna Loy: The Only Good Girl in Hollywood.* Berkeley: University of California Press, 2011.

Lombardi, Frederick. *Allan Dwan and the Rise and Decline of the Hollywood Studios.* Jefferson, NC: McFarland, 2013.

Maugham, Somerset. *Theatre.* 1937. Reprint, London: Vintage, 2001.

McCann, Ben. *Julien Duvivier.* Manchester, UK: Manchester University Press, 2017.

McGilligan, Patrick. *The Nature of the Beast: Fritz Lang.* Minneapolis: University of Minnesota Press, 2018.

Minne, Olivier. *Louis Jourdan: Le Dernier French Lover d'Hollywood.* Paris: Seguier, 2017.

Morley, Sheridan. *John Gielgud: The Authorized Biography.* New York: Simon & Schuster, 2002.

———. *The Other Side of the Moon: The Life of David Niven.* London: Weidenfeld & Nicolson, 1985.

———. *Tales from the Hollywood Raj: The British Film Colony on Screen and Off.* London: Weidenfeld & Nicolson, 1988.

Nissen, Axel. *Agnes Moorehead on Radio, Stage and Television.* Jefferson, NC: McFarland, 2017.

Oller, J. *Jean Arthur: The Actress Nobody Knows.* New York: Limelight Editions, 1997.

Remarque, Erich Maria. *Arch of Triumph.* Translated by Walter Sorell and Denver Lindley. New York: D. Appleton-Century, 1945.

Rifkin, Donna. *The Sun and Her Stars. Salka Viertel and Hitler's Exiles in the Golden Age of Hollywood.* New York: Other Press, 2020.

Rinilla, Michael D. *Margaret Sullavan: The Life and Career of a Reluctant Star.* Jefferson, NC: McFarland, 2019.

Selznick, David O. *Memo from David O. Selznick.* New York: Viking, 1972.

Shearer, Stephen Michael. *Beautiful: The Life of Hedy Lamarr.* New York: Thomas Dunne, 2010.

Smit, David. *Ingrid Bergman: The Life, Career and Public Image.* London: McFarland, 2012.

Bibliography

Smith, Geddeth. *Walter Hampden, Dean of the American Theatre.* Madison, WI: Fairleigh Dickinson, 2008.

Swindell, Larry. *The Reluctant Lover: Charles Boyer.* New York: Doubleday, 1983.

Thomson, David. *The New Biographical Dictionary of Cinema.* New York: Knopf, 2004.

Ustinov, Peter. *Dear Me.* London: William Heinemann, 1977.

Viertel, Salka. *The Kindness of Strangers.* New York: Holt, Rinehart, and Winston, 1969.

Vignaud, Roger. *Henri Verneuil: The Greatest Successes of Cinema.* Ann Arbor: University of Michigan, 2020.

Wansell, Geoffrey. *Terrance Rattigan: A Biography.* London: Oberon, 2000.

Young, Gwenda. *Clarence Brown: Hollywood's Forgotten Master.* Lexington: University Press of Kentucky, 2018.

Zuckmayer, Karl. *A Part of Myself.* New York: Harcourt Brace, 1970.

Index

Abel, Walter, 133
Academy Awards: nominations for *Algiers*,
  102; nominations for *All This and
  Heaven Too*, 128; nominations for
  Fanny, 196; nominations for *Gaslight*,
  152; nominations for *Hold Back the
  Dawn*, 135; nominations for *Love
  Affair*, 106; nominations for *The
  Constant Nymph*, 145; special award
  to Boyer in 1943, 143
Achard, Marcel, 97, 98, 113, 184
"Adios, Muchachos" (song), 151
Adorable (film), 42
Adorable Julia (film), 203
Agee, James, 153
Aherne, Brian, 144
Akins, Zöe, 87
Albers, Hans, 43, 46
album recordings, 154, 206
Aldrich, Robert, 180, 181
Alfa, Michele, 113
Algiers (film), 99–102. See also *Pépé le
  Moko*
Allégret, Marc, 96, 97, 113, 139, 196
Allen, Gracie, 179, 189
Allen, Woody, 210
Allgood, Sara, 158
All Quiet on the Western Front (film), 161
All Quiet on the Western Front
  (Remarque), 5
All This and Heaven Too (film), 94, 108,
  116–18, 120, 128, 149, 188
America First movement, 123
American International Pictures, 215
Amos and Andy (radio program), 126
Andy Hardy films, 143

Angel Street (film), 147
Annabella. *See* Charpentier, Suzanne
Anna Christie (film), 40
Anslinger, Harry J., 135
anti-communist movement, 169, 178
anti-Semitism: French response to *Liliom*
  and, 48–49; Germany detainment of
  Austrian Jews in 1938, 103; Nazi rise to
  power and dismissal of Jewish film
  artists, 46; Vichy France and, 122
Appointment for Love (film), 136–37
Arc de Triomphe, 10, 163
Arch of Triumph (film), 95, 160–64,
  166–67, 168
Ariane (film), 108–9
Arizona, 209, 211, 217–18
Arkoff, Samuel Z., 215
Arletty, 192
Arnaz, Desi, 179
Arnoul, Françoise, 190
Around the World in Eighty Days (film),
  189
art-house cinemas, 173
Arthur, Jean, 82, 83
Astaire, Fred, 59
Asther, Nils, 58, 66
Astoria studios, 33
Aumont, Jean-Pierre, 26, 122, 124, 125,
  189, 209
Austrian cinema, 203
Autant-Lara, Claude, 35
Aux Jardins de Murcie (play), 16, 17, 18
Ayres, Lew, 28

Baarová, Lida, 46–47, 106
Bacall, Lauren, 152–53, 154, 169, 180, 190

237

Back Street (film), 129–30, 131, 136
Bagni, John and Gwen, 181
Baker, Graham, 66, 82–83
Balanchine, George, 79
Ball, Lucille, 179, 189
Balzac, Honoré de, 22
Barcarole (film), 47
Bardot, Brigitte, 191, 192
Barefoot in the Park (film), 210
Baroncelli, Jacques de, 22
Barrymore, John, 68
Baur, Harry, 19, 54
Beatty, Warren, 182
Beaumont, Binkie, 199
Beery, Wallace, 36
Behrman, Sam, 86, 87, 89, 164, 195, 198
Bellamy, Ralph, 37
Belmondo, Jean-Paul, 199, 203, 214
Belmont, Charles, 196
Benchley, Robert, 142
Bennett, Joan, 187
Benny, Jack, 189
Bergeron, René, 72
Bergman, Ingrid: *Arch of Triumph,* 161,
    162, 163, 167; on Boyer in *Red Gloves,*
    170; *Gaslight,* 148–49, 152; *Indiscreet,*
    183; *Intermezzo,* 81; *A Matter of Time,*
    215–16
Bergner, Elizabeth, 46, 108
Berkeley, Busby, 59
Berley, André, 36
Berman, Pandro, 68
Bern, Paul, 28, 36, 41, 42, 62
Bernstein, Henry: *Le Bonheur,* 51–52, 60;
    boulevard theater in Paris and, 4;
    Boyer's theater career with, 25–27, 28;
    Mélo, 28, 213; restrictive contracts with
    actors, 26, 66; *La Venin,* 97; World War
    II and, 125
Bernstein, Matthew, 82–83
Big House, The (film), 35–36, 41
Big Parade, The (film), 37
Big Sleep, The (film), 152, 154
Big Two, The (Bus-Fekete), 164
Bing, Herman, 122
Biro, Lajos, 58
blacklists, 126
Blanc, Mel, 154–55

Blanchar, Pierre, 119; on Boyer's
    background in Figeac, 2; Boyer's
    relationship with Alice Fille and, 50;
    Boyer's reunion with in 1946, 159;
    Captain Fracasse, 27; *Cette Vielle
    Canaille,* 54; at the Conservatoire with
    Boyer, 12–13; *La Prière aux Étoiles,*
    115; as a lifelong friend of Boyer, 14
Blue Angel, The (film), 31, 38, 44
Boehm, David, 87
Bogarde, Dirk, 197
Bogart, Humphrey, 140, 152, 169
Boissy, Gabriel, 24
Boleslavski, Richard, 78, 79, 80
Bolton, Guy, 203
Bonaparte, Napoleon, 85, 86
book collection: of Boyer, 21, 212–13
Borzage, Frank, 83
Bottome, Phyllis, 63
Bottoms Up (film), 55, 58
boulevard theater, 4
Boum sur Paris (film), 189
Bourdet, Edouard, 20
Boyer, Charles: Academy Awards and,
    102, 143; acting intensity when
    impersonating a lover, 18, 19–20; aid
    to French expatriates in America
    during World War II, 121–27; album
    recordings, 154, 206; American
    anti-communist hysteria and, 169; Lida
    Baarová and, 46–47, 106; birth and
    childhood, 1–4; book collection of, 21,
    212–13; Cannes Film Festival and, 202;
    car accident of, 166; career assessment,
    219; caricatured in Looney Tunes,
    154–55; Suzanne Charpentier and, 34,
    110; Maurice Chevalier and, 4, 29, 33,
    84, 159, 196; chronic health problems,
    194, 210; cigarette smoking and, 22, 36,
    131, 210; Claudette Colbert and, 32, 40,
    63, 64, 195; André Daven and, 22, 23,
    97; death of, 218; development as an
    actor, 10, 12, 15; donations to the
    French Red Cross, 123; Raphael Duflos
    and, 9–10, 11; Irene Dunne and, 106;
    emergence as a leading man, 24; Mia
    Farrow and, 173; Charles Feldman and
    (*see* Feldman, Charles K.); Figeac and

(*see* Figeac); Alice Fille and, 50; film persona as a displaced person, 94–95; film persona as a romantic leading man, 62, 80, 84; film production and, 128, 130, 139–40; films of (*see* French cinema; Hollywood film industry; Universum Film A.G.); final will of, 213; Free World Association and, 126; French army service and, 15, 114, 115; French Research Foundation and, 121, 122–23, 126–27, 143, 160, 166, 173, 213; gambling and, 14–15, 21, 32, 44, 66, 77–78, 107; Firmin Gémier and, 18–19; Grauman's Chinese Theater imprints, 141; home and domestic life in Hollywood, 77–78; home in Arizona, 209, 211, 217; home in Geneva, Switzerland, 209, 211, 2127; homes and domestic life in Beverly Hills, 66, 84, 156, 157, 160; Gregory La Cava and, 65; Légion d'Honneur and, 167; Joshua Logan and, 81–82; marriage to and married life with Pat Paterson, 55–56, 107, 146, 217–18 (*see also* Boyer, Pat); memory of, 16, 17–18; monuments to in France, 1; as the most popular Frenchman in America, 140–41; naturalized as an American citizen, 140; Irving Newton and, 84; nostalgia for country life, 2; Nathalie Paley and, 51; Palme d'Or award, 215; physical appearance at age fifty, 156; propaganda activities and aid to French expatriates during World War II, 121–27, 140–41, 143, 150, 154; radio and, 110–11, 126, 169, 170; reading habits of, 21; Erich Maria Remarque and, 44; response to the fall of France in 1940, 118–19, 120; Eleanor Roosevelt and, 140, 170; Franklin Roosevelt and, 152; son Michael Charles and, 149, 150, 204, 205, 206, 207, 208; television and, 179–82, 189–90, 200, 202; theater and (*see* theater); Tony Award, 172; views of and attitude toward women, 5–6, 19, 20, 50, 51, 62, 69; visit to France following the release of *Arch of Triumph*, 167–68;

visit to France in 1939 and the beginning of World War II, 112–13, 114, 115; visit to France in 1946, 159
Boyer, Louise (née Durand): birth and childhood of Charles, 1, 2, 3, 4; with Charles and Pat in America during World War II, 123, 124; Charles's entry into theater and, 7, 19; Charles's friendship with Raphael Duflos and, 10; death of, 209; hospitalization in 1959, 195; marriage to Maurice Boyer, 1; remarriage of, 19; visit to France in 1946, 159
Boyer, Maurice, 1, 2
Boyer, Michael Charles: birth of, 149, 150; childhood of, 159, 160, 205; death of, 204, 207–8; Mia Farrow and, 205–6; firearms and, 205, 206–7; stammering and, 167, 173; Valiant Records and, 206
Boyer, Pat (née Paterson): aid to French expatriates during World War II, 124; Louise Boyer and, 159, 195; career with Fox Films, 55, 58, 59, 68, 69; with Charles in Italy, 191; Charles's appearance in *Private Worlds* and, 64; Charles's car accident and, 166; Charles's final will and, 213; depression and conversion to Catholicism, 173; Charles Feldman and, 69, 109; final film and retirement of, 106–7; final illness and death of, 217–18; home and domestic life in Hollywood, 77, 78; homes and domestic life in Beverly Hills, 66, 84, 156, 157, 160; marriage to Charles, 55–56, 61, 64; naturalized as an American citizen, 140; outbreak of World War II and, 114; return to England in 1940, 118; role in *Vogues of 1938* declined, 84; son Michael Charles and, 146, 149, 150, 167, 173, 208; *Spendthrift*, 70; visit to France following the release of *Arch of Triumph*, 167, 168
Brackett, Charles, 131, 132, 133, 134, 135
Bradshaw, Peter, 187
Brand in der Oper (film), 34–35
Brando, Marlon, 197
Brasseur, Pierre, 9, 14, 20, 54

Brazzi, Rossano, 196
Break of Hearts (film), 68–69
Brecht, Bertolt, 164, 169
Breen, Joseph L., 76–77, 87, 104, 135, 143, 144, 162
Bridge of San Luis Rey, The (film), 36
Broadway. *See* theater
Brook, Clive, 40
Brooks, Louise, 129
Brown, Clarence, 87–88, 90, 106
Brown, Harry, 164
Brown Houses, 121
Brush, Katherine, 41
Brynner, Yul, 194, 212
Buccaneer, The (film), 194
Buchholz, Horst, 195
Buckner, Robert, 153
Buñuel, Luis, 35, 36–37
Burgère, André, 32, 36
Burns and Allen Show, The (radio program), 126
Bus-Fekete, Ladislao, 136, 164
Buster Ste. Marie (film), 29, 35

Cain, James M., 99, 109, 110
Calhern, Louis, 167
California Studios, 160–61
Calling All Aliens! (film), 123
Call It Luck (film), 58
Call of the Wild (film), 67
Calmon, Philippe, 159
Campbell, Marilyn, 207
Camus, Albert, 168
Cannes Festival of Free Nations, 112
Cannes Film Festival, 112, 113, 114, 159, 202, 214–15
Canutt, Yakima, 88
Capra, Frank, 126, 146, 160
Captain Fracasse (film), 27–28
Caravan (film), 54–55, 56–58, 61, 63
Carné, Marcel, 160
Carnet de Bal (film), 137
Carol, Martine, 187
Caron, Leslie, 195, 198–99, 203
Carousel (film), 48
Carr, Richard, 181
Carrillo, Leo, 83
Carroll, Leo G., 175

Carroll, Madeleine, 62, 66, 74
Carroll, Sidney, 202
Casablanca (film), 44, 122, 162
Casino Royale (film), 209–10
Catelain, Jaque, 61
Cauvin, André, 150
Cavalcanti, Alberto, 27
CBS, 189, 200
Cerdan, Simone, 34
Cette Vielle Canaille (film), 54
Champollion, Jean-François, 1
Chaney, Lon, 35–36
Chantelouve (film), 22
Charell, Erik, 44, 53, 54, 56, 57
Charlie Chan in Egypt (film), 68, 69
Charly (play), 19
Charpentier, Suzanne (Annabella): *La Bataille,* 52, 53; *Brand in der Oper,* 34; *Caravan,* 54; on French expatriates in America during World War II, 123–24; Jean Murat and, 43; Tyrone Power and, 53, 110, 112; relationship with Boyer, 34, 110
Chatterton, Ruth, 37, 38
Chautard, Émile, 125
Chekhov, Michael, 163
Chevalier, Maurice: on Boyer's marriage to Pat Paterson, 55; departure from Hollywood in 1934, 58; *Fanny,* 195, 196; film career, 4, 28; on music-hall artists versus theater actors in France, 136; relationship with Boyer, 4, 29, 33, 84, 159, 196; return to America in 1947, 169
Children, The (film), 128–29
Children of Tragedy (film), 154
Chita (Hearn), 191
Choiseul-Praslin, Duchess de, 117
Christian-Jaque, 187–88
cigarette smoking: Boyer and, 22, 36, 131, 210
Cinecittà, 190
CinemaScope, 190
Cirque d'Hiver, 16
Clair, René, 123, 124, 174, 214–15
Claudel, Paul, 103
Clément, René, 150
Climax (television series), 189

Climax, The (film), 145–46, 147
Clive, Colin, 82
Clouzot, Henri-Georges, 176
Cluny Brown (film), 157–59
Cluny Brown (Sharp), 157
Cobb, Lee J., 197
Coburn, Charles, 151, 152
Cobweb, The (film), 190
Cocteau, Jean, 4
Cohen, Octavus Roy, 181
Cohn, Harry, 74, 151, 178
Colbert, Claudette: Boyer and, 32, 40, 63, 64, 195; in films produced by Walter Wanger, 63, 66; *The Marriage-Go-Round,* 194–95; marriage to Joel Pressman, 63–64; *Tovarich,* 93, 94
Collége Champollion, 1, 3
Collins, Larry, 203
Colman, Ronald, 81
Columbia Pictures, 74, 147, 151–52, 178
Comédie-Française, 8, 9, 10–11, 19, 60
Comédie-Montaigne, 23
Comer, Sam, 135
Committee for the First Amendment, 169
Concordia company, 71, 74
Confessions of a Nazi Spy (film), 108, 109
Confidential Agent, The (film), 152–54, 156, 159, 161
Confidential Agent, The (Greene), 152, 153
Congo (film), 150
Connery, Sean, 209
Conquest (film), 85–89, 90
Conservatoire National Superieur de Musique et de Déclamation, 3, 8, 9, 10, 11, 12–13
Constant Nymph, The (film), 143–45
Cooper, Gladys, 201
Coote, Robert, 201
Cornell, Katherine, 189
Cossart, Ernest, 158
Cotten, Joseph, 148, 176
Coulouris, George, 154
Coward, Noel, 143
Cram, Mildred, 104, 106
Cromwell, John, 100, 101, 157
Crosby, John, 170
Crowther, Bosley, 153, 167, 204
Cukor, George, 87, 148, 149

Cummings, Robert, 142
Curtis, Alan, 142
Czinner, Paul, 46

Dali, Salvador, 35
Dalio, Marcel, 14, 122, 124, 177
Dall, John, 169
Dalrymple, Jean, 168, 182
Damita, Lili, 36, 48
Daniell, Henry, 198
Dark Angel, The (film), 52
Darnell, Linda, 176
Darrieux, Danielle, 73, 74, 185
Daven, André: on Boyer and reading, 21; Boyer's first film appearances and, 22, 23; on Boyer's marriage to Pat Paterson, 56; *Caravan,* 54; *Le Corsaire,* 108, 109, 113–14; departure from Nazi Germany, 45, 46; friendship with Boyer and Marc Allégret, 97; *La Venin,* 96, 97–98; *Liliom,* 47; marriage to Daniele Parola, 43; parallel film productions with Ufa, 38, 44; RKO Pictures and, 108; *Tales of Manhattan,* 138–39; World War II and, 120, 124
Daves, Delmer, 104
David, André, 121, 140–41
David Harum (film), 54
Davies, Marion, 41, 93
Davis, Bette, 94, 116–17, 118, 120, 128
Daybreak (film), 37
Day the Hot Line Got Hot, The (film), 210
de Bergy, Simone, 15, 20
Decoin, Henri, 27
de Gaulle, Charles, 115, 118, 119, 120, 126, 150–51, 204
de Havilland, Olivia, 133, 134–35
Delannoy, Jean, 159, 160
Delon, Alain, 197, 203
Deluzy-Desportes, Henriette, 117
Demarest, William, 175
DeMille, Cecil B., 32, 142, 194
Deneuve, Catherine, 210–11
Der Kongress Tanzt (film), 44
de Sano, Marcel, 31, 40
DeSica, Vittorio, 185
Desilu Productions, 179, 189–90
Destiny (film), 142

DeSylva, Buddy, 105
Deval, Jacques, 91, 123
Devil Is a Woman, The (film), 103–4
Deyers, Line, 27, 28
Diamant-Berger, Henri, 123, 126
Dieterle, William, 122
Dietrich, Marlene: *Confessions of a Nazi Spy,* 109; excellence as an actress, 129; Jean Gabin and, 124; *The Garden of Allah,* 76, 78–79; *I Loved a Soldier,* 58–59; Erich Maria Remarque and, 161
Disney, Walt, 126
Dmytryk, Edward, 106
Dolivet, Louis, 126
Donat, Robert, 143
Donen, Stanley, 183
Don Juan in Hell (Shaw), 171–72
Douglas, Melvyn, 148
Dreier, Hans, 135
Dreyer, Carl, 19
Driscoll, Bobby, 178
Druoun, Maurice, 215
Ducos, Yvonne, 18
Duflos, Hughuette, 32
Duflos, Raphael, 9–10, 11
du Maurier, Gerald, 148
Dunkirk, 119
Dunne, Irene: Boyer and, 106; *Gaslight,* 147, 148; *Love Affair,* 104, 105–6; marriage to Francis Griffin, 64; *Together Again,* 151, 152; *When Tomorrow Comes,* 108, 109, 110
Durbin, Deanna, 113, 116
Duvivier, Julien: *Flesh and Fantasy,* 142; Hollywood French community during World War II and, 123; *Pépé le Moko,* 97, 99, 101, 102; production contract with Universal, 142; revival of postwar European cinema and, 174; *Tales of Manhattan,* 137, 138; *Untel Pere et Fils,* 115, 119–20, 143

Ecstasy (film), 100
Edwards, Blake, 180
Edward VIII, 91
Einfeld, Charles, 160
England. *See* Great Britain

Enterprise: Boyer and *Arch of Triumph,* 160–64, 166–67, 168; founding members, 160
Escande, Maurice, 10
European Film Fund, 122
Everett, Marjorie, 213, 217

Falaise de Coudraye, Henri de la, 23
Falconetti, Renée, 17, 18, 135
Famous Artists agency, 56
Fanny (film), 195–96
Farkas, Nicolas, 52
Farrère, Claude, 23
Farrow, John, 156
Farrow, Mia, 156, 167, 173, 205–6
Fejös, Pál, 35
Feld, Fritz, 110, 122
Feldman, Charles K.: agent representing Boyer, 56, 61, 63, 66, 69, 77, 85, 86, 129; Lauren Bacall and, 152–53; Ingrid Bergman and, 162; Pat Boyer and, 69, 106; Boyer's appearance in *Arch of Triumph* and, 161; Boyer's appearance in *Hold Back the Dawn* and, 132; Boyer's appearance in *How to Steal a Million* and, 202; Boyer's appearance in *The Confidential Agent* and, 152–53; Boyer's appearance in *The Constant Nymph* and, 144; Boyer's appearance in *Tovarich* and, 92–93; Boyer's entry into film production and, 128, 130; Maurice Chevalier and, 169; death of, 211; gambling and, 66, 77; Jean Howard, 85, 187; interest in and entry into film production, 56, 174; Anatole Litvak and, 74, 91, 92; production of *Casino Royale,* 209–10
Feldman, Jean, 157
Feyder, Jacques, 29, 35, 36, 37, 40, 115, 160
Field, Alice. *See* Fille, Alice
Field, Betty, 142
Field, Rachel, 108, 116, 117
Fields, W. C., 138
Figeac: Boyer and World War I, 5–7; Boyer's birth and childhood in, 1–4; Boyer's donations to, 115, 159; Louise Boyer's hospitalization in 1959, 195; Boyer's relationship with Raphael

Duflos and, 9–10; the Boyers' visit to following release of *Arch of Triumph*, 167–68; the Boyers' visit to in 1939, 112, 114; the Boyers' visit to in 1946, 159; lasting significance to and influence on Boyer, 2

Fighting Lady, The (film), 126, 152

Fille, Alice (Alice Field), 50, 54

film noir, 39

Finch, Peter, 212

firearms: Michael Boyer and, 205, 206–7

First Legion, The (film), 174–76

First Love (film), 113

Fitzgerald, F. Scott, 41

Flanner, Janet, 62, 184, 186

Fleischer, Richard, 178

Fleming, Victor, 149

Flesh and Fantasy (film), 142, 143, 145, 150

Flood, James, 67

Florelle. *See* Rousseau, Odette

Florey, Robert, 90, 166, 180, 181

Flying Down to Rio (film), 59

Flynn, Errol, 116, 144, 158

Folies Bergère de Paris (film), 58

Fonda, Henry, 62, 66, 138

Fonda, Jane, 196, 210

Fontaine, Joan, 144–45

Fontanne, Lynn, 62

Forbes, Bryan, 212

Ford, Glenn, 197, 203

Foreign Correspondent (film), 116

Foster, Susanna, 146

Four Horsemen of the Apocalypse, The (film), 196–97

Four-Star International, 180, 182, 200–201, 206

Four-Star Playhouse (television series), 179–82, 200

Fox, William, 53

Fox-Europe studio, 47–49, 91

Fox Film Corporation: Boyer in *Caravan*, 54–55, 56–58; émigré talent of the early 1930s and, 53–54; Pat Paterson (Boyer) and, 55, 58, 59, 68, 69. *See also* Twentieth Century–Fox

F.P. 1 Antwortet Nicht (film), 43–44, 53

France: Boyer and army service, 15, 114, 115; Boyer appointed a chevalier of the Légion d'Honneur, 167; Boyer's popularity in the mid-1930s, 96; the Boyers' visit to following release of *Arch of Triumph*, 167–68; the Boyers' visit to in 1939 and the beginning of World War II, 112–13, 114, 115; the Boyers' visit to in 1946, 159; fall to Germany in 1940, 118–20; monuments to Boyer, 1; music-hall artists versus theater actors in, 136; political disorder in the early 1930s, 60; protests about Hollywood's film representations of, 103; response to *Liliom*, 48–49; response to *Mayerling*, 74; rise of the Popular Front, 71. *See also* Figeac; French cinema; Paris

France Forever, 126

Francen, Victor, 11, 96, 122, 133, 153

Francis, Kay, 93

Freeman, Mona, 151

Free World (magazine), 126

Free World Association, 126

Fréhel, 29, 101

French cinema: Boyer and the *Le Corsaire* film project, 108, 109, 112, 113–14; Boyer in *Boum sur Paris*, 189; Boyer in *Is Paris Burning?*, 203–4; Boyer in *La Bataille*, 52, 53; Boyer in *La Parisienne*, 191–92; Boyer in *Le Bonheur*, 60–61; Boyer in *Les Amoureux*, 50–51; Boyer in *Les Demons de Minuit*, 196; Boyer in *Madame de . . .* , 182, 184–87, 194; Boyer in *Maxime*, 192–93; Boyer in *Mayerling*, 71–74; Boyer in *Nana*, 187–88; Boyer in *Orage*, 96, 97–98; Boyer in *Paris, Palace Hotel*, 190; Boyer in *Stavisky . . .* , 213–15; Boyer's aid to expatriates in America during World War II, 121–27; Boyer's early film appearances, 21–23, 27–28; French artists in Hollywood, 90; major films of the mid-1930s, 96–97; parallel film productions, 42; revival of postwar European cinema and, 174; *Untel Pere et Fils*, 115, 119–20, 143

French Red Cross, 123

French Research Foundation (FRF), 121, 122–23, 126–27, 143, 160, 166, 173, 213

Fresnay, Pierre. *See* Laudenbach, Pierre Jules Louis
FRF. *See* French Research Foundation
Frings, Ketti, 131–32, 134
Frings, Kurt, 131–32, 135
Frohlich, Gustav, 46, 47
Frondaie, Pierre, 23
Frye, William, 180
futuristic films, 43–44

Gabin, Jean, 96, 97, 100, 102, 115, 119, 124
Gable, Clark, 67, 106, 116
gambling, 14–15, 21, 32, 44, 66, 77–78, 107
Gambon, Philippe, 6, 167
Garand, Yves, 6
Garat, Henri, 42, 44, 48
Garbo, Greta: *Anna Christie,* 40; Boyer and, 29–30; *Conquest,* 85, 87, 88, 89, 90; Graham Greene on, 98; *The Kiss,* 28, 29–30; Salka Viertel and, 37
Garden of Alla, 80, 90
Garden of Allah, The (film), 74, 75–77, 78–80
Garden of Allah, The (Hichens), 74
Gardiner, Reginald, 101
Garfield, John, 160
Garland, Judy, 89
Garnett, Tay, 66
Garson, Greer, 159
Gaslight (film), 147–49, 152
Gaudio, Tony, 138
Gautier, Théophile, 27
Gay Illiterate, The (television program), 189
Gaynor, Janet, 42
Gémier, Firmin, 18–19, 23, 26
General Services Studios, 65
Geneva, 209, 211, 217
German cinema, 42–43, 46. *See also* Universum Film A.G.
Germany: annexation of Austria and detainment of Austrian Jews, 103; invasion of Poland, 113; Anatole Litvak's *Confessions of a Nazi Spy* and, 108, 109; Nazi Brown Houses, 121; Nazi infiltration of the German film industry, 42–43; Nazi rise to power and dismissal of Jewish film artists, 45, 46;

occupation of and retreat from Paris, 150–51; offensive into Europe in 1940 and the fall of France, 118–20; social conditions in 1932, 44–45
Gibson, William, 190
Gide, André, 97, 159, 160
Gielgud, John, 172, 212
"Gioconda Smile, The" (Huxley), 164
Giraud, Henri, 120
Giraudoux, Jean, 115, 119, 211
Gish, Lillian, 190
Goddard, Paulette, 133, 161
Goebbels, Joseph, 38, 42–43, 46, 47, 52, 106, 119
Goldstuck, Henri, 17
Goldwyn, Samuel, 39, 52, 175–76
Goldwyn Girls, 56, 85
Gone with the Wind (film), 108, 116
Gordon, Michael, 198
Goulding, Edmund, 143, 144, 145, 152
Grahame, Gloria, 190
Grant, Cary, 140, 183
Grauman's Chinese Theater, 141
Gravet, Fernand, 100
Gray, Nadia, 191
Great Britain: Pat Boyer and, 113, 114, 118, 167; Boyer in *Man and Superman,* 172; response to *Cluny Brown,* 158–59; World War II and, 118, 119
Great Waltz, The (film), 137
Greene, Graham, 69, 73, 88–89, 98, 152, 153
Gregory, Paul, 171, 172, 198
Greig, Robert, 138
Griffin, Francis, 64
Grove Press, 201
Grué, Louis, 160
Guégan, Gerald, 6
Guerlain, Jacques, 52
Guitry, Lucien, 4, 12
Guitry, Sacha, 11
Gypsy Melody (film), 54
Gys, Robert, 188

Hagman, Larry, 201
Haley, Jack, Jr., 216
Hallmark Hall of Fame (television program), 189

Hampden, Walter, 118, 175
Happy Time, The (film), 177–78
Hara Kiri (film), 139
Hardwicke, Sir Cedric, 54, 165, 171–72
Harlow, Jean, 41, 42
Harrison, Rex, 199
Hartley, Katherine. *See* Frings, Ketti
Hartmann, Paul, 43
Harvey, Lilian, 44, 46, 68
Hathaway, Henry, 58
Hawks, Howard, 152
Haydn, Richard, 158
Hays, Will, 103
Hayward, Leland, 56, 129
Hayworth, Rita, 138
Hearn, Lafcadio, 191
Hearst, William Randolph, 41
Heartbreak (film), 136
Heart of a Nation (film), 143
Heart Song (film), 68
Heaslet, Sharon, 207
Hecht, Ben, 81, 115, 138
Heflin, Van, 169
Hemingway, Ernest, 153
Hendrix, Wanda, 153
Hepburn, Audrey, 202, 204
Hepburn, Katherine, 68, 69, 211
Herbert, F. Hugh, 151, 179
Hériat, Philippe, 9, 12, 14, 16, 22, 71
Herman, Al, 106
Heston, Charlton, 194
Hichens, Robert, 74, 75, 76
Hill, George, 35
Hilton, James, 157, 212
History Is Made at Night (film), 82–84, 105, 151
Hitchcock, Alfred, 65, 149
Hitler, Adolf, 38, 58–59, 103, 106, 113, 150
Hoffenstein, Samuel, 87, 157
Hoffman, David, 142
Hold Back the Dawn (film), 131–35, 161
Hold Back the Dawn (Frings), 132
Holden, William, 210
Hollander, Friedrich, 44, 46
Hollywood Fights Back (radio documentary), 169
Hollywood film industry: anti-communist movement and, 169, 178; blacklists and,

126; Boyer and film production, 128, 130, 139–40; Boyer in *A Matter of Time*, 215–16; Boyer in *Arch of Triumph*, 160–64, 166–67, 168; Boyer in *Around the World in Eighty Days*, 189; Boyer in *Barefoot in the Park*, 210; Boyer in *Casino Royale*, 209–10; Boyer in films produced by Walter Wanger (*see* Wanger, Walter); Boyer in *How to Steal a Million*, 202, 204, 208; Boyer in *Is Paris Burning?*, 203–4; Boyer in *Lost Horizon*, 212, 213; Boyer in *Love Is a Ball*, 202–3; Boyer in *The April Fools*, 210–11; Boyer in *The Buccaneer*, 194; Boyer in *The Cobweb*, 190; Boyer in *The First Legion*, 174–76; Boyer in *The Garden of Allah*, 75–77, 78–80; Boyer in *The Happy Time*, 177–78; Boyer in *The Madwoman of Chaillot*, 211–12; Boyer's aid to French expatriates in America during World War II, 121–27; Boyer's film persona as a displaced person, 94–95; Boyer's film persona as a romantic leading man, 62, 80, 84; Boyer's final film, 215–16; Boyer's first years in, 28–30, 31–32, 35–38; decline of in the 1970s, 212; émigré talent of the early 1930s and, 53–54, 57; European films compared to, 72; European protests about cultural appropriations and insensitivities of, 103–4; foreign language parallel productions, 28–30, 31–32, 35–37; French artists in, 90; plagiarism and, 110; postwar independent producers and, 160; Production Code Administration and, 76–77, 87; "runaway" productions in Europe, 202–3, 204; stock market crash of 1929 and, 53; Technicolor and, 75–76. *See also individual film studios*
Hollywood Playhouse (radio program), 111, 116
Hollywood Ten, 106
Hollywood Victory Caravan, 140
Hollywood Victory Committee, 123
Holmes, Phillips, 55, 57
Holmes, Taylor, 175

Hopkins, Miriam, 91, 92, 117
Hornblow, Arthur, Jr., 126, 132, 134, 135, 148, 149
Hotel Imperial (Biro), 58
Hotel Pierre, 170
Hot Line, The (film), 210
Houseman, John, 190
House Un-American Activities Committee, 169
Houston, John, 210, 212
Howard, Jean, 56, 85, 187
Howard, Leslie, 81, 143–44
Howe, James Wong, 102
How to Steal a Million (or *Venus Rising*; film), 202, 204, 208
Hudson, Rock, 198, 199
Hughes, Howard, 185
Hull, E. Mayne, 62
Hurst, Fannie, 129, 130
Huxley, Aldous, 164, 165
Hyman, Bernie, 87

Ibáñez, Vicente Blasco, 196–97
"I Believe" (album), 206
Ich und die Kaiserin (film), 44, 46
Idiot's Delight (film), 106–7
I.F. 1 Ne Répond Plus (film), 43–44, 46, 54
"I Get Ideas" (song), 151
Ile de France (ocean liner), 54, 63, 104
I Loved a Soldier (unfinished film), 58–59
I Love Lucy (television series), 189–90
Immortal France (film), 143
Indiscreet (film), 183
Ingram, Rex, 75
Intermezzo (film), 81
international style, 72
In Which We Serve (film), 143
Ischia, 191
Is Paris Burning? (film), 203–4
Italian cinema, 190
Italy, 190, 191
It Happened One Night (film), 66
It's a Date (film), 116

Jannings, Emil, 38, 46
Jeanson, Henri, 192
Jennings, Talbot, 87
Jerome, Helen, 87

Jewish film artists: dismissal from Nazi Germany, 46
Jezebel (film), 116
Jones, Chuck, 154–55
Jones, Jennifer, 157, 158
Joseph, Rudi, 174
Joubé, Romauld, 16
Jourdan, Louis, 113, 115, 119, 174, 177
Jouvet, Louis, 113, 115, 119, 125
Julia, du bist Zauberhaft (film), 203

Kane, Robert, 72
Kasznar, Kurt, 178, 210
Kaufman, Willy, 162
Keaton, Buster, 29, 35, 138
Keisler, Hedwig. *See* Lamarr, Hedy
Kellino, Roy, 180
Kelly, Gene, 89
Kempson, Rachel, 165
Kennedy, Joseph P., 109
Kennedy, Margaret, 143
Kerr, Philip (Lord Lothian), 121
Kessel, Joseph, 39, 71, 74
Kettelhut, Erich, 38–39
Kind Sir (Krasna), 182, 183
King, Andrea, 180
Kirsch, Jon, 207
Kisling, Moise, 123, 124
Kiss, The (film), 28, 29, 30
Koch, Howard, 176
Korda, Alexander, 52, 53, 164–65
Kraly, Hans, 54
Kramer, Stanley, 177
Krasna, Norman, 182
Kurnitz, Harry, 204

La Bataille (Farrère), 23
La Bataille (film), 52, 53, 62, 139
La Bataille (play), 23–24
La Bataille du Rail (film), 150
La Captive (Méré), 19
La Cava, Gregory, 65
Ladd, Alan, 177
Lafitte, Jean, 194
La Fortuna de Essere Donna (film), 190
La Galerie des Glaces (Bernstein), 25–26
L'Age d'Or (film), 35
La Grand Illusion (film), 96–97

Index

La Grand Jeu (film), 160

L'Aiglon (play), 6

L'Aîné des Ferchaux (film), 199

La Jeune Fille avec Joues des Roses (play), 15, 20

Lamarr, Hedy, 100–101, 102, 124, 147, 148

Lanchester, Elsa, 172

Lang, Charles, 94

Lang, Fritz, 45, 46, 47–48, 49, 190, 202

Lang, Jennings, 187

Lansbury, Angela, 148, 152, 197

La Parisienne (film), 191–92

Lapierre, Dominique, 203

La Prière aux Étoiles (unfinished film), 115

L'Arlésienne (play), 15

La Ronde Infernale (film), 27

Last Class, The (film), 140

La Symphonie Pastorale (film), 159, 160

Laudenbach, Pierre Jules Louis (Pierre Fresnay), 11, 14, 60, 71, 96–97

Laughton, Charles: *Arch of Triumph*, 163, 164, 167; *The Life of Galileo*, 164, 169; *Man and Superman*, 170, 171, 172; Mayflower Films and, 91; *Tales of Manhattan*, 138; *This Land Is Mine*, 129

Lavery, Emmet, 174

Lawford, Peter, 158, 211

Lawson, John Howard, 99

Lebeau, Madeleine, 122

Le Bonheur (Bernstein), 51–52, 60

Le Bonheur (film), 60–61

Le Corbeau (Clouzot), 176

Le Corsaire (unfinished film), 108, 109, 112, 113–14

Lederer, Francis, 68

Ledoux, Fernand, 13

Le Flibustier (Richepin), 17–18

Legende de Gaillardet (Grué), 160

Légion d'Honneur, 167

Legion of Decency, 77

Le Grillon du Foyer (film), 22

Leisen, Mitchell, 132

Lejeune, C. A., 144

Lelong, Lucien, 51

Lemmon, Jack, 210

Le Monde, 185–86

Lengyel, Melchior, 54

Le Pére Goriot (Balzac), 22

L'Eprevier (play), 50

Le Procès de Mary Dugan (film), 31–32, 35, 40

L'Equipage (film), 91

Le Reléve (film), 115, 119–20

Le Route Imperiale (film), 61

Les Amoureux (film), 50–51

L'Esclave (film), 22

Les Demons de Minuit (film), 196

Leslie, Joan, 144

Les Mains Sales (Sartre), 168

Les Quatre Cent Coups (film), 193

Lesser, Sol, 173

Lester, Seeleg, 181

Les Visiteurs du Soir (Carné), 160

Lewis, David, 161, 162

L'Herbier, Marcel, 22, 51, 52, 61

L'Homme du Large (Balzac), 22

L'Homme Enchainé (Bourdet), 20

Liebmann, Robert, 46, 54

Life of Galileo, The (Brecht), 164, 169

Liliom (film), 47, 48–49, 62, 68

Lindbergh, Charles, 123

Little Lord Fauntleroy (film), 75

Litvak, Anatole: *All This and Heaven Too*, 116, 117, 118, 128; American anti-communist hysteria and, 169; arrival in Hollywood, 90–91; on Boyer's attitude toward women, 19; *Cette Vielle Canaille*, 54; *Confessions of a Nazi Spy*, 108, 109; Miriam Hopkins and, 91, 92; *Mayerling*, 71–74, 90–91; *Tovarich*, 91–95, 96

Lloyd, Norman, 164

Lockhart, Gene, 102

Loew, David, 160

Logan, Joshua, 81–82, 183, 195–96

Lola Montes (film), 185

London, 61, 199–200

London Films, 53

Looney Tunes, 154–55

Loos, Anita, 41

Lord, Robert, 56, 91–92, 94

Lord Pengo (Behrman), 164, 198

Loren, Sophia, 190

Lorre, Peter, 46, 153, 154

Los Angeles: Boyer's arrival in, 29; the Boyers' home and domestic life in Hollywood, 77–78; the Boyers' homes and domestic life in Beverly Hills, 66, 84, 156, 157, 160; gambling ships, 32

Losch, Tilly, 79

Losey, Joseph, 169

Lost Horizon (film), 212, 213

Lothian, Lord. *See* Kerr, Philip

Lottery Lover (film), 58

Lourié, Eugene, 165

Louvre, The (television documentary), 202

Love Affair (film), 104–6, 182

Love in the Afternoon (film), 109

Love Is a Ball (film), 202–3

Love Parade, The (film), 33

Love Time (film), 58

Loy, Myrna, 122, 211

Lubitsch, Ernst, 33, 58, 62, 69, 122, 126, 157–58

Luitz-Morat, 27

Lumina company, 22

Lunt, Alfred, 62

Lupino, Ida, 180, 181

Lustig, Jan, 97, 98

Lux Radio Theatre (radio program), 111, 142

Lys, Lya, 35

MacArthur, Charles, 81

Macbeth (Shakespeare), 7

Machaty, Gustav, 100

MacLaine, Shirley, 210

Madame de . . . (film), 182, 184–87, 194

Madame de . . . (Vilmorin), 182

Madame Sans Gene (film), 23, 85

Madwoman of Chaillot, The (film), 211–12

Magnificent Lie, The (film), 37–38

Maibaum, Richard, 115

Major and the Minor, The (film), 134

Malone, Dorothy, 181

Malraux, André, 184

Man and Boy (Rattigan), 199–200

Man and Superman (Shaw), 170–72

Man from Yesterday, The (film), 40–41, 42

Manning, Bruce, 129–30

March, Frederic, 92

Marchal, Arlette, 31

Maria del Carmen (play), 16

Marie Walewska (film), 85–86. See also *Conquest*

Marion, Frances, 35, 36

Marius (Pagnol), 112

Marriage-Go-Round, The (Stephens), 194

Marshall, Herbert, 116

Martin, Mary, 182, 183

Martin, Paul, 44, 46

Masaryk, Jan, 122

Mason, James, 177

Mastroianni, Marcello, 190

Matras, Christian, 186, 188, 192

Matter of Time, A (film), 215–16

Maugham, Somerset, 203

Mauriac, François, 26

Maxime (film), 192–93

Mayer, Louis B., 75, 85, 86, 100, 147, 148, 151

Mayer, Martin, 145

Mayerling (film), 71–74, 90–91

Mayflower Films, 91

McCarey, Leo, 104, 105, 106

McCarten, John, 167

McCrea, Joel, 63, 116, 179, 180

McQueen, Steve, 200

Mélo (Bernstein), 28, 213

Melville, Jean-Pierre, 199

memory: Boyer and, 16, 17–18

Menjou, Adolphe, 56, 66, 126, 169

Menzies, William Cameron, 160–61

Méré, Charles, 19

Method, the, 12

Metro-Goldwyn-Mayer (MGM): *The Big House,* 35–36, 41; *The Big Parade,* 37; Boyer and foreign language parallel productions, 28–30, 31–32, 35–37; Boyer in *Conquest,* 85–89, 90; Boyer in *Gaslight,* 147–49, 152; Boyer in *Red-Headed Woman,* 41–42; Boyer in *The Four Horsemen of the Apocalypse,* 196–97; decline of in the 1970s, 212; Irene Dunne and, 151; *The Great Waltz,* 137; Ernst Lubitsch and, 69; ParUfaMet agreement, 35; *Le Procès de Mary Dugan,* 31–32, 35, 40; David Selznick and, 75; Walter Wanger and, 62

Mexico, 131–32, 135

Milestone, Lewis, 161, 162, 164
military service: Boyer and, 15, 114, 115
Minnelli, Liza, 215
Minnelli, Vincente, 148, 190, 196, 197, 215
Mitchneck, Simon, 161
Mitsouko fragrance, 52
"Modern Cinderella, A" (Cain), 109
Moeller, Philip, 68
Molnar, Ferenc, 47, 125
Mongenstern Ignace, 193
Monsieur Beaucaire (film), 23
Montalban, Ricardo, 202, 203
Montgomery, Robert, 36
Moon Is Blue, The (Herbert), 179
Moorhead, Agnes, 171–72, 198
Moorhead, Alan, 177
Moreno, Marguerite, 27, 28
Morgan, Michèle: Marc Allégret and, 96; *The Children*, 128, 129; *La Symphonie Pastorale*, 159; *Maxime*, 192; *Orage*, 98; *Untel Pere et Fils*, 119, 143
Morlay, Gaby, 61
Morley, Robert, 85
Moro, Aldo, 216
Morris, Chester, 36
Morros, Boris, 137
Mortal Coils (film), 164–65
Moscow Art Theater, 12
Mostel, Zero, 178
Motion Picture Alliance for the Preservation of American Ideals, 126
Mrs. Miniver (film), 159
Mundin, Herbert, 58
Murat, Jean, 43, 54
Murder in Thornton Square, The (film), 147
Mussolini, Benito, 112
My Man Godfrey (film), 65

Nagel, Conrad, 28
Nana (film), 187–88
Natan, Bernard, 52, 53, 61, 91
Natwick, Mildred, 210
Nazimova, Alla, 80
NBC, 170, 181, 189, 200, 202
Nebenzal, Seymour, 72
Newton, Irving ("Fig"), 84
New York City, 170

New Yorker, 127
Nichols, Dudley, 126, 128
Nicholson, Jack, 215
Niven, David: *Around the World in Eighty Days,* 189; *Casino Royale,* 210; Four-Star International productions and, 200, 201; *Four-Star Playhouse,* 179, 180, 181, 182; World War II and, 121
Normandie (ocean liner), 96, 112
North, Alex, 197
Nugent, Frank, 70, 96

Oberon, Merle, 52, 76, 82, 123, 140
Oberon, Myron, 76
Objective Burma (film), 158
Odéon, 23
Odor-able Kitty (cartoon), 154–55
Official Films Inc., 200
O'Hara, Maureen, 129, 176
Oland, Warner, 66
Olivier, Laurence, 82, 199
On a Volé un Homme (film), 47–48
O'Neil, Barbara, 109, 117–18, 128
Only Girl, The (film), 46, 68
Ophuls, Max, 46, 47–48, 174, 182, 184–87
Orage (film), 96, 97–98, 139
O'Sullivan, Maureen, 156
Ouspenskaya, Maria, 105, 106

Pagnol, Marcel, 112, 115, 195
Paley, Princess Natalia Pavlovna (Nathalie Paley), 51
Pallette, Eugene, 57–58, 138
Palme d'Or award, 215
parallel film productions: Boyer and the German film industry, 32–33, 34–35, 38–39, 43–44; Boyer and the Hollywood film industry, 28–30, 31–32, 35–37
Paramount Pictures: Boyer in *Hold Back the Dawn,* 131–35; Boyer in *I Loved a Soldier* project, 58–59; Boyer in *The Magnificent Lie,* 37–38; Boyer in *The Man from Yesterday,* 40–41; Boyer in *Thunder in the East,* 177; émigré talent of the early 1930s and, 57; films produced by Walter Wanger, 63, 65, 69–70 (*see also* Wanger, Walter);

ParUfaMet agreement, 35; Spain's protest regarding *The Devil Is a Woman* and, 103–4

Paris: Boyer and gambling, 14–15, 21; Boyer's early acting experiences and theater education in, 8–9, 10–13, 14, 15, 16; Boyer's first successes in theater, 16, 17–19, 23–24; Boyer's introduction to theater and, 4; Boyer's reception in 1953, 185–86; the Boyers' visit to following release of *Arch of Triumph*, 167, 168; filming of *How to Steal a Million* in, 202, 204, 208; flight of German Jewish film artists to, 46–47; Fox-Europe studio, 47–49; World War I and, 5, 8; World War II and, 150–51

Paris, Palace Hotel (film), 190

Parker, Jean, 57

Parlor, Bedroom, and Bath (film), 29

Parola, Daniele, 43, 54

Parrish, Robert, 160

ParUfaMet agreement, 35

Pasolini, Pier Paolo, 216

Passion of Joan of Arc, The (film), 19, 135

Paterson, Hannah, 213

Paterson, Pat. *See* Boyer, Pat

Pathé/Natan films, 34, 47, 52, 53, 61, 91

Paxinou, Katina, 153–54

Penelope Pussycat, 155

penicillin, 115, 159

Pépé le Moko (film), 97, 99, 101, 102. See also *Algiers*

Pépé le Pew, 155

Périgord, Paul, 126

Perkins, Anthony, 196, 203

Perret, Léonce, 23

Perske, Betty Joan. *See* Bacall, Lauren

Personal History (Sheean), 114–15

Pétain, Philippe, 120, 122, 125

Petit, Pascale, 196

Pidgeon, Walter, 116

Pinza, Ezio, 182

Pirandello, Luigi, 26

Pirate, The (film), 89

plagiarism, 110

"Plaisir d'Amour" (song), 105

Players, the, 123

Playhouse 90 (television program), 200

Poland, 109, 113

Polglase, Van Nest, 106

Pommer, Erich, 38, 45, 46, 47–48, 53, 91

Porché, François, 15

Porter, Cole, 157

Portrait of a Defeatist (Bernstein), 125

Pouctal, Henri, 9

Powell, Dick, 179, 181, 182, 200, 201

Powell, William, 81

Power, Tyrone, 53, 109, 112

Preminger, Otto, 176, 177

Presenting Charles Boyer (radio program), 170

Presley, Elvis, 206

Pressman, Joel, 63–64

Previn, André, 197

Price, Vincent, 147

Prim, Suzy, 115, 119

Printemps, Yvonne, 60

Private Worlds (Bottome), 63

Private Worlds (film), 65, 66, 67

Production Code Administration, 76–77, 87, 104, 135, 143, 144, 163

Queen Christina (film), 98

Queen Mary (ocean liner), 168

Quinn, Anthony, 194

Radiguet, Maurice (Luitz-Morat), 27

radio: Boyer's initial involvement with, 110–11; Boyer's radio persona, 170; Boyer's war effort and, 126; *Hollywood Fights Back* documentary broadcast, 169; *Presenting Charles Boyer* program, 170

Rage of Paris, The (film), 74

Raimu, 96, 115, 119

Rambova, Natacha, 23

Rameau, Emil, 162

Rathbone, Basil, 75, 78, 92, 93, 117

Rattigan, Terrance, 199

Redford, Robert, 210

Red Gloves (Sartre), 168, 169–70

Red-Headed Woman (film), 41–42

Reinhardt, Max, 45

Reisch, Walter, 147

Remarque, Erich Maria, 5, 44, 161, 163, 164

Renaissance theater, 4, 12
Rennie, Michael, 176
Renoir, Jean, 96–97, 120, 123, 124, 125, 128–29
Resnais, Alain, 213–14
Reynaud, Paul, 115, 118, 119
Richepin, Jean, 17–18
Riggs, Lynn, 77
Ripley, Arthur, 66, 82
Rittau, Gunther, 39
RKO Pictures: Boyer in *Break of Hearts*, 68–69; Boyer in *Love Affair*, 104–6; André Daven and, 108; *This Land Is Mine*, 129; *The Woman I Love*, 91
Robeson, Paul, 138, 139
Robinson, Casey, 92, 117
Robinson, Edward G., 108, 112, 138, 142, 145
Robison, Arthur, 31
Roger-Marx, Claude, 19
Rogers, Ginger, 59, 138
Rogers, Will, 53, 54
Rogues, The (television series), 200–201
Roland, Gilbert, 76
Romanoff, Michael, 162
Rome, 190, 191, 215, 216
Rome, Harold, 195
Rooney, Mickey, 143
Roosevelt, Eleanor, 140, 170
Roosevelt, Franklin D., 152
Rosay, Françoise, 40, 115, 119; *The Big Parade,* 37; *Buster Ste. Marie,* 35; *Le Procès de Mary Dugan,* 31; relationship with Boyer, 29; *The 13th Letter,* 176
Rosenberg, Stuart, 210
Rosencrantz and Guildenstern Are Dead (Stoppard), 19
Rossellini, Roberto, 149
Rosset, Barney, 201
Rossignol-Boyer, Louise. *See* Boyer, Louise
Rouble Has Two Faces, The (film), 210
Rousseau, Odette (Florelle), 38, 39, 48
Roussell, Henry, 34
Rózsa, Miklós, 165
Rudolf, Crown Prince of Austria, 71–72
Ruehmann, Heinz, 44
Rush, Barbara, 175
Russell, Rosalind, 180

Rust, Henry, 94
Ryan, James, 207

Sahara (film), 74
Saint Exupéry, Antoine de, 120, 140, 184
Saks, Gene, 210
Salzburg Festival, 45
Samson (Bernstein), 4, 12
Sarris, Andrew, 83
Sartre, Jean-Paul, 162, 168
Saulnier, Jacques, 214
Savalas, Telly, 203
Schallert, Edwin, 164
Schenck, Joe, 107
Schmitz, Sybille, 43
Schnitzler, Arthur, 37
Schwegler, Edward S., 77, 79
Scott, George C., 204
Scotto, Vincent, 101
Screen Writers Guild, 178
Seconal, 218
Secrets of F.P. 1 (film), 43–44, 53
Seduction of Julia, The (film), 203
Seiter, William A., 136–37
Sellers, Peter, 210
Selwyn, Edgar, 37
Selznick, David O., 56; on *Algiers,* 102; *The Garden of Allah,* 74, 75–77, 78–80; *Gaslight,* 148, 149; *Gone with the Wind* and, 116; *Intermezzo,* 81; Jennifer Jones and, 157
Selznick, Myron, 56
Selznick International Pictures, 75
Selznick-Joyce agency, 56
Semprun, Jorge, 213
Serenade (Cain), 110
Seymour, Dan, 154
Shanghai (film), 66–67, 68
Shapiro, Stanley, 198
Sharp, Margery, 157
Shaw, George Bernard, 100, 170
Shaw, Irwin, 161, 163, 164
Shearer, Norma, 32, 85, 106, 112
Sheean, Vincent, 114–15, 116
Sheehan, Winfield, 54–55
Sheik, The (film), 62
Sherwood, Robert E., 87, 91, 106, 189
Shumlin, Herman, 153, 154

Sidney, Sylvia, 66, 81, 101
Siegel, "Bugsy," 77–78
Sign of the Cross, The (film), 32
Simenon, Georges, 199
Simili (Roger-Marx), 19
Simm, Ray, 211
Simon, John, 171
Simon, Neil, 210
Siodmak, Curt, 145–46
Siodmak, Robert, 38, 39
Sirk, Douglas, 174, 175
Slezak, Walter, 129
Smith, Alexis, 144
Smith, C. Aubrey, 158
Smith, Constance, 176
Sondheim, Stephen, 213
Sorbonne, 8, 19
Sorel, Jean, 203
South Pacific (film), 195–96
South Pacific (play), 182, 183
Spaak, Charles, 119
Spain, 103–4
Spanish cinema, 210
Spanish Earth (film), 153
Spellbound (film), 65
Spendthrift (film), 69–70
Spiegel, Sam, 137–38
Stage Door (film), 65
Stahl, John M., 110
Stanislavsky, Konstantin, 12
Stanwyck, Barbara, 124, 142, 145
Starling, Lynn, 63, 67, 146
Stavisky . . . (film), 213–15
Sten, Anna, 38, 39
Stephens, Leslie, 194
Sternberg, Josef von, 31
Stevens, Inger, 202
Stevenson, Robert, 130
Stewart, Donald Ogden, 87, 104, 106, 138
stock market crash of 1929, 53
Stokowski, Leopold, 68–89
Stone, Lewis, 32, 143
Stoppard, Tom, 19
Struss, Karl, 41
Sturges, Preston, 123
Sturm der Leidenschaft (film), 38
Sullavan, Margaret, 129–30, 131, 136–37

Surtees, Robert, 212
Swanson, Gloria, 23, 86

Tales of Manhattan (film), 137–39
Tall Story (film), 196
Tamiroff, Akim, 66
Tandy, Jessica, 165
Taradash, Daniel, 168
Taylor, Dwight, 110
Taylor, Robert, 126, 210
Technicolor, 75–76
television: Boyer and *Four-Star Playhouse*, 179–82, 200; Boyer and *The Louvre* documentary, 202; Boyer's appearances in the 1950s, 189–90; Four-Star International productions, 200–201
Terry, Alice, 75
Tetzel, Joan, 169
Thalberg, Irving: *The Big House*, 35; Boyer and *Conquest*, 85–86, 87; Boyer and *Red-Headed Woman*, 41; death of, 87; death of Paul Bern and, 42; producers of *Mayerling* and, 74; Walter Wanger and, 62
April Fools, The (film), 210–11
theater: Boyer and amateur theater productions during World War I, 6–7; Boyer in *Kind Sir,* 182, 183; Boyer in *Lord Pengo,* 198; Boyer in *Man and Boy,* 199–200; Boyer in *Man and Superman,* 170–72; Boyer in *Red Gloves,* 169–70; Boyer in *The Marriage-Go-Round,* 194; Boyer in touring companies, 14, 21; Boyer's acting intensity when impersonating a lover, 18, 19–20; Boyer's career with Henry Bernstein, 25–27, 28; Boyer's decision to pursue a career in, 7; Boyer's development as an actor, 10, 12, 15; Boyer's early acting experiences and theater education in Paris, 8–9, 10–13, 14, 15, 16; Boyer's early successes in the Parisian theater, 16, 17–19, 23–24; Boyer's emergence as a leading man, 24; Boyer's introduction to, 4
Theatre (Maugham), 203
Théâtre Antoine, 18, 19
Théâtre des Champs-Elysées, 16

Théâtre du Gymnase, 26
Theatre Guild, 164
Theodora Goes Wild (film), 151
There Shall Be No Night (Sherwood), 189
Thirard, Armand, 98
13th Letter, The (film), 176–77
This Land Is Mine (film), 129
Thompson, Walter, 169
Thomson, David, 219
Thulin, Ingrid, 197
Thunder in the East (film), 52, 68, 139, 177
Todd, Mike, 189
Together Again (film), 151–52
To Have and Have Not (film), 152, 154
Toland, Gregg, 83
Toluboff, Alexander, 66, 102
Tony Awards, 172, 198
Toscanini, Arturo, 68–89
touring companies, 14, 21
Tourjansky, Viktor, 52
Tourneur, Jacques, 125
Tovarich (film), 91–95, 96
Tover, Leo, 135
Towne, Gene, 66, 82–83
Tracy, Spencer, 55, 199
Trapnell, Coles, 181
Travail (film), 9
Trial of Mary Dugan, The (film), 30, 31–32, 41
Truffaut, François, 193
Tumultes (film), 38–39, 43
Twentieth Century–Fox: Boyer in *Cluny Brown,* 157–59; Boyer in *Tales of Manhattan,* 137–39; Boyer in *The 13th Letter,* 176–77; decline of in the 1970s, 212; World War II and, 126
Twenty-Seventh Colonial Artillery, 114

Ufa. *See* Universum Film A.G.
United Artists, 69, 167, 175
Universal Pictures: Boyer as producer/star with, 139–40, 145–46; Boyer in *Appointment for Love,* 136–37; Boyer in *A Very Special Favor,* 198–99; Boyer in *Back Street,* 129–30, 131; Boyer in *Flesh and Fantasy,* 142, 143, 145, 150; Boyer in *Mortal Coils,* 164–65; Boyer in *When Tomorrow Comes,* 108, 109–10, 112–13; decline of in the 1970s, 212; *It's a Date,* 116
University of California, Los Angeles, 212–13
Universum Film A.G. (Ufa), 32–33, 34–35, 38–39, 43–44, 46, 47
Untel Pere et Fils (film), 115, 119–20, 143
Usher, Robert, 135
Ustinov, Peter, 184–85
US Treasury Department, 135
utopischefilme, 43–44

Valentino, Rudolph, 23, 62
Valiant Records, 206
Vallée, Marcel, 43, 44, 54
van Druten, John, 148
Van Upp, Virginia, 151
Veidt, Conrad, 43, 44, 46
Veiller, Bayard, 31
Venice Film Festival, 112
Le Venin (Bernstein), 96, 97, 139
Venus Rising (or *How to Steal a Million;* film), 202, 204, 208
Verneuil, Henri, 192
Very Special Favor, A (film), 198–99
Vetsera, Baroness Marie, 71–72
Vichy France, 120, 122
Vidal, Henri, 191
Vidor, Charles, 151, 152
Viertel, Berthold, 37, 38, 40, 41, 44, 45, 65
Viertel, Salka, 37, 85, 86, 122
Vilmorin, Louise de, 182, 184, 186
Vinneuil, François, 49
visas, 122, 125
Vogues of 1938 (film), 84
Voice of America, 126
von Choltitz, Dietrich, 150
von Sternberg, Josef, 58, 59, 129
Vuillermoz, Emile, 98

Waggner, George, 146
Wagner, Fritz Arno, 35
Walbrook, Anton, 147
Walewska, Marie, 85
Wallach, Eli, 204
Walpole, Hugh, 32
Walsh, Raoul, 70

Index

Wanger, Walter: Boyer and the *Wuthering Heights* project, 81–82; Boyer in *Algiers*, 99–102; Boyer in *History Is Made at Night*, 82–84; Boyer in *Private Worlds*, 63, 64, 65, 66; Boyer in *Shanghai*, 66–67, 68; Boyer in *Spendthrift*, 69–70; Boyer's film persona as a romantic leading man and, 62, 80, 84; Free World Association and, 126; *Le Grand Jeu* and, 160; independent film production and, 62–63, 66; Gregory La Cava and, 65; *Pépé le Moko* and, 97; producers of *Mayerling* and, 74; Vincent Sheean's *Personal History* and, 114–15; shooting of Jennings Lang, 187; United Artists and, 69; *Vogues of 1938*, 84

Warner, H. B., 32

Warner, Jack: Lauren Bacall and, 152, 154; *The Constant Nymph*, 144; *Fanny*, 195; *Gone with the Wind* and, 116; *Tovarich*, 91–92, 93

Warner Brothers: Boyer caricatured in Looney Tunes, 154–55; Boyer in *All This and Heaven Too*, 94, 108, 116–18, 120, 128, 149, 188; Boyer in *Fanny*, 195–96; Boyer in *The Confidential Agent*, 152–54, 156, 159, 161; Boyer in *The Constant Nymph*, 143–45; Boyer in *Tovarich*, 91–95, 96; unfinished project on de Gaulle, 126

War Nurse (film), 37

Weill, Pierre, 35

Welles, Orson, 126, 138, 154, 184, 203

What's My Line? (television program), 189

When Tomorrow Comes (film), 108, 109–10, 112–13

"Where Does Love Go?" (song), 206

Why We Fight (film), 126

Widmark, Richard, 190

Wilder, Billy, 42, 109, 131–35, 138

Williams, Guinn, 65

Williams, John, 200–201

Willkie, Wendell, 123

Wing, Ward, 35

"Wishing" (song), 105–6

Woman I Love, The (film), 91

Woman's Privilege, A (Herbert), 151

Woman's Vengeance, A (film), 165

women: Boyer's acting intensity when impersonating a lover and, 18, 19–20; Boyer's views of and attitude toward, 5–6, 19, 20, 50, 51, 62, 69

Wood, Sam, 126

World War I, 5–7, 8

World War II: Boyer and the French army, 114, 115; Boyer's propaganda activities and aid to French expatriates during, 121–27, 140–41, 143, 150, 154; German occupation of and retreat from Paris, 150–51; German offensive and the fall of France, 118–20; Germany's invasion of Poland, 113

Wright, Leah Curran, 127

Wuthering Heights (film), 81–82

Wyler, William, 116, 160, 202, 204

Wynyard, Diana, 147

Ygerbuchen, Mohamed, 101

Young, Gig, 200

Young, Loretta, 54, 55, 67

Young, Victor, 135

Zanuck, Darryl, 107, 110, 138–39, 157, 176

Zinnemann, Fred, 38

Zola, Emile, 187

Zucco, George, 175

Zukor, Adolph, 104

Screen Classics

Screen Classics is a series of critical biographies, film histories, and analytical studies focusing on neglected filmmakers and important screen artists and subjects, from the era of silent cinema through the golden age of Hollywood to the international generation of today. Books in the Screen Classics series are intended for scholars and general readers alike. The contributing authors are established figures in their respective fields. This series also serves the purpose of advancing scholarship on film personalities and themes with ties to Kentucky.

Series Editor
Patrick McGilligan

Books in the Series

Olivia de Havilland: Lady Triumphant
   Victoria Amador
Mae Murray: The Girl with the Bee-Stung Lips
   Michael G. Ankerich
Harry Dean Stanton: Hollywood's Zen Rebel
   Joseph B. Atkins
Hedy Lamarr: The Most Beautiful Woman in Film
   Ruth Barton
Rex Ingram: Visionary Director of the Silent Screen
   Ruth Barton
Conversations with Classic Film Stars: Interviews from Hollywood's Golden Era
   James Bawden and Ron Miller
Conversations with Legendary Television Stars: Interviews from the First Fifty Years
   James Bawden and Ron Miller
You Ain't Heard Nothin' Yet: Interviews with Stars from Hollywood's Golden Era
   James Bawden and Ron Miller
Charles Boyer: The French Lover
   John Baxter
Von Sternberg
   John Baxter
Hitchcock's Partner in Suspense: The Life of Screenwriter Charles Bennett
   Charles Bennett, edited by John Charles Bennett
Hitchcock and the Censors
   John Billheimer
A Uniquely American Epic: Intimacy and Action, Tenderness and Violence in Sam Peckinpah's The Wild Bunch
   Edited by Michael Bliss
My Life in Focus: A Photographer's Journey with Elizabeth Taylor and the Hollywood Jet Set
   Gianni Bozzacchi with Joey Tayler

Hollywood Divided: The 1950 Screen Directors Guild Meeting and the Impact of the Blacklist
    Kevin Brianton
He's Got Rhythm: The Life and Career of Gene Kelly
    Cynthia Brideson and Sara Brideson
Ziegfeld and His Follies: A Biography of Broadway's Greatest Producer
    Cynthia Brideson and Sara Brideson
The Marxist and the Movies: A Biography of Paul Jarrico
    Larry Ceplair
Dalton Trumbo: Blacklisted Hollywood Radical
    Larry Ceplair and Christopher Trumbo
Warren Oates: A Wild Life
    Susan Compo
Improvising Out Loud: My Life Teaching Hollywood How to Act
    Jeff Corey with Emily Corey
Crane: Sex, Celebrity, and My Father's Unsolved Murder
    Robert Crane and Christopher Fryer
Jack Nicholson: The Early Years
    Robert Crane and Christopher Fryer
Anne Bancroft: A Life
    Douglass K. Daniel
Being Hal Ashby: Life of a Hollywood Rebel
    Nick Dawson
Bruce Dern: A Memoir
    Bruce Dern with Christopher Fryer and Robert Crane
Intrepid Laughter: Preston Sturges and the Movies
    Andrew Dickos
Miriam Hopkins: Life and Films of a Hollywood Rebel
    Allan R. Ellenberger
Vitagraph: America's First Great Motion Picture Studio
    Andrew A. Erish
Jayne Mansfield: The Girl Couldn't Help It
    Eve Golden
John Gilbert: The Last of the Silent Film Stars
    Eve Golden
Stuntwomen: The Untold Hollywood Story
    Mollie Gregory
Saul Bass: Anatomy of Film Design
    Jan-Christopher Horak
Otto Preminger: The Man Who Would Be King, updated edition
    Foster Hirsch
Hitchcock Lost and Found: The Forgotten Films
    Alain Kerzoncuf and Charles Barr
Pola Negri: Hollywood's First Femme Fatale
    Mariusz Kotowski
Sidney J. Furie: Life and Films
    Daniel Kremer
Albert Capellani: Pioneer of the Silent Screen
    Christine Leteux
Ridley Scott: A Biography
    Vincent LoBrutto
Mamoulian: Life on Stage and Screen
    David Luhrssen
Maureen O'Hara: The Biography
    Aubrey Malone

My Life as a Mankiewicz: An Insider's Journey through Hollywood
    Tom Mankiewicz and Robert Crane
Hawks on Hawks
    Joseph McBride
Showman of the Screen: Joseph E. Levine and His Revolutions in Film Promotion
    A. T. McKenna
William Wyler: The Life and Films of Hollywood's Most Celebrated Director
    Gabriel Miller
Raoul Walsh: The True Adventures of Hollywood's Legendary Director
    Marilyn Ann Moss
Veit Harlan: The Life and Work of a Nazi Filmmaker
    Frank Noack
Harry Langdon: King of Silent Comedy
    Gabriella Oldham and Mabel Langdon
Charles Walters: The Director Who Made Hollywood Dance
    Brent Phillips
Some Like It Wilder: The Life and Controversial Films of Billy Wilder
    Gene D. Phillips
Ann Dvorak: Hollywood's Forgotten Rebel
    Christina Rice
Mean . . . Moody . . . Magnificent! Jane Russell and the Marketing of a Hollywood Legend
    Christina Rice
Fay Wray and Robert Riskin: A Hollywood Memoir
    Victoria Riskin
Lewis Milestone: Life and Films
    Harlow Robinson
Michael Curtiz: A Life in Film
    Alan K. Rode
Arthur Penn: American Director
    Nat Segaloff
Film's First Family: The Untold Story of the Costellos
    Terry Chester Shulman
Claude Rains: An Actor's Voice
    David J. Skal with Jessica Rains
Barbara La Marr: The Girl Who Was Too Beautiful for Hollywood
    Sherri Snyder
Buzz: The Life and Art of Busby Berkeley
    Jeffrey Spivak
Victor Fleming: An American Movie Master
    Michael Sragow
Hollywood Presents Jules Verne: The Father of Science Fiction on Screen
    Brian Taves
Thomas Ince: Hollywood's Independent Pioneer
    Brian Taves
Picturing Peter Bogdanovich: My Conversations with the New Hollywood Director
    Peter Tonguette
Carl Theodor Dreyer and Ordet: My Summer with the Danish Filmmaker
    Jan Wahl
Wild Bill Wellman: Hollywood Rebel
    William Wellman Jr.
Clarence Brown: Hollywood's Forgotten Master
    Gwenda Young